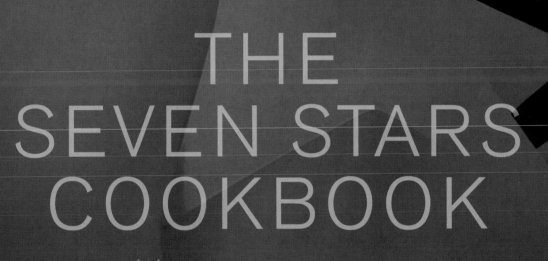

THE SEVEN STARS COOKBOOK

HARRAH'S ENTERTAINMENT

PRESENTS

✦

THE
SEVEN STARS
COOKBOOK

RECIPES FROM WORLD-CLASS CASINO RESTAURANTS

EDITED AND INTRODUCED BY JOHN SCHLIMM
FOREWORD BY PAULA DEEN
PREFACE BY GARY W. LOVEMAN
PHOTOGRAPHS BY FRANKIE FRANKENY

CHRONICLE BOOKS
SAN FRANCISCO

ISBN: 978-0-8118-7475-5

Manufactured in China.

Design by Public.

This book has been set in Akzidenz Grotesk and Vendetta.

10 9 8 7 6 5 4 3 2 1

Chronicle Books LLC
680 Second Street
San Francisco, California 94107

www.chroniclebooks.com

TO ALL THOSE WHO LOVE
TO EAT, LAUGH, AND LIVE LIFE TO THE FULLEST,
THIS BOOK IS FOR YOU.

1
APPETIZERS
✦

2
SALADS
✦✦

Seared Beef Tenderloin & Goat Cheese Salad   54
Augustus Café at Caesars Windsor / Executive Chef Patrick McClary

Tennessee Prosciutto & Warm Goat Cheese Salad with   57
Honey-Walnut Truffle Dressing
Magnolia, A Delta Grille at Horseshoe Tunica

Cucumber & Mint Salad   58
Harrah's Lake Tahoe & Harveys Lake Tahoe / Executive Chef Joe Wells

Fresh Market Potato Salad   58
Fresh Market Square Buffet at Harrah's Cherokee /
Executive Chef Keith Andreasen

Apple & Blood Orange Vinaigrette over Bibb   60
Lettuce & Watercress
Harrah's Joliet / Chef Peter Jeschke

Pecan Herbed Orzo Salad   62
Harrah's North Kansas City / Chef Roy Askren

Fennel, Endive & Arugula Salad   65
with a Citrus-Basil Vinaigrette & Parmesan Cheese Twists
Reflections Café at Harrah's Resort Atlantic City / Chef James Coombs

Garden Basket-Weave Salad   67
with Heirloom Tomatoes & Fresh Mozzarella
Harrah's Metropolis / Executive Chef Jon M. Kell

Fried Green Tomatoes   68
The Range Steakhouse & Bar at Tunica Roadhouse Casino & Hotel /
Executive Chef & Director of Food & Beverage Christopher J. Hencyk

Roasted Pepper Antipasto   72
Caesars Atlantic City / Chef de Cuisine John Mejlak

Fiore Tomato Caprese   74
Fiore at Harrah's Rincon Casino & Resort / Executive Chef Vesa Leppala

3
SOUPS
✦✦✦

Leek, Sun-Dried Tomato, Shiitake Mushroom   79
& Champagne Soup
K-Paul's Louisiana Kitchen / Chef Paul Prudhomme

Grilled Shrimp Gazpacho   80
Reserve at Harrah's Joliet / Chef de Cuisine Tye Nielsen

Harrah's Steak House Creamy Five-Onion Soup   82
Harrah's Steak House at Harrah's Reno / Executive Chef Klaus Feyersinger

Wild Mushroom Chowder   84
Caesars Windsor / Executive Chef Patrick McClary

Pickles' Famous Mushroom-Barley Soup   87
Pickles at Bally's Atlantic City / Chef Rolf Bechtold

Seven Stars Split Pea Soup   87
Fresh Market Buffet at Harrah's North Kansas City / Chef Jeff Craig

Classic Gumbo   88
Harrah's Louisiana Downs / Executive Chef J. Ryan Gillespie

Gumbo   89
The Range Steakhouse & Bar at Tunica Roadhouse Casino & Hotel /
Executive Chef & Director of Food & Beverage Christopher J. Hencyk

New Orleans Gumbo   90
The Buffet at Harrah's at Harrah's New Orleans / Chef Hoyce Oatis

Beef & Onion Soup with Short Rib Croutons &   92
Five-Onion Salad
The Steakhouse at Harrah's Resort Atlantic City / Chef Richard Leadbetter

Chicken & Shrimp Jambalaya   93
French Quarter Buffet at Showboat Atlantic City /
Chef Todd Bannan & Chef Armando Cortes

Roasted Eggplant Soup   94
Waterfront Buffet at Harrah's Resort Atlantic City / Chef David Suscavage

Selu Turkey & Roasted Corn Soup   96
Selu Garden Café at Harrah's Cherokee / Executive Chef Keith Andreasen

Italian Meatball & Sausage Chili   98
Breakaway Café at Bally's Atlantic City /
Food Service Director Rolf J. Weithofer

4
SIDE DISHES
✦✦✦✦

5
BEEF + PORK
✦✦✦✦✦

FOREWORD
by Paula Deen

I was delighted when my friends at Harrah's Entertainment asked me to write a foreword for *The Seven Stars Cookbook*. This is an area I know well. After all, between my husband, Michael, and me, we must have dined at nearly every restaurant they have.

I had the pleasure of partnering with this fine company when Harrah's approached me a couple years ago about opening a restaurant with them. I mean, we're talking about my two absolute favorite passions: food and casinos! Within a short time of working with the Harrah's team, I realized that these folks are the ultimate pros and the best in the industry. More importantly, they share my vision when it comes to our customers, and that's to provide people with entertainment and great food at a good value.

Together, in May 2008, we launched the Paula Deen Buffet at Harrah's Tunica. That was one of the proudest days of my life. After years of turning down offers to open more restaurants with other investors, I realized that I had waited for the perfect partner. These folks are the best of the best.

What impresses me most about Harrah's is their approach to business. Unlike most companies, they challenge their people to think outside the box. Take my restaurant, for instance. The inspired result of our collaboration, the Paula Deen Buffet Tunica, is a series of rooms that are exact replicas of my home in Savannah. Not only can folks taste my delicious Southern Fried Chicken and Biscuits, they can experience what it's like to visit my home. The setting is so real I have to stop myself from reaching into the cupboards to search for my things!

I love the Harrah's folks, and I know you will, too. It doesn't matter which location you visit, you can be sure that you will have the best in dining and entertainment. Whether you're looking for a casual quick bite or the ultimate in fine dining, Harrah's will bring it to the table.

That's where *The Seven Stars Cookbook* comes in. This is a beautiful collection of recipes created by Harrah's many talented chefs. This compilation not only allows you to bring your Seven Stars dining experience home, but it is also full of great entertaining ideas and tips from the pros. Y'all, take it from me—you will hit the jackpot with this book!

I know you will enjoy every delicious recipe. In the meantime, I hope I bump into you the next time I drop by a Harrah's.

Best dishes,

—Paula Deen

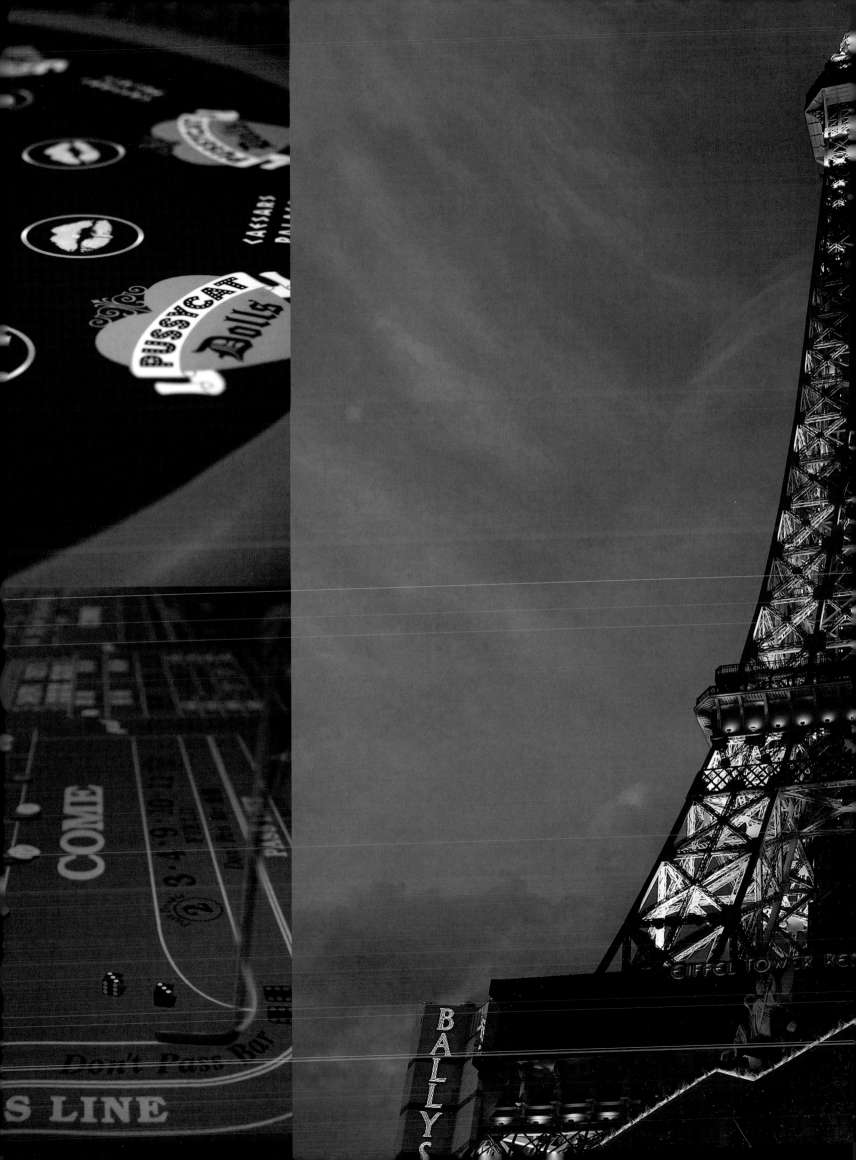

PREFACE

by Gary W. Loveman
CEO, Harrah's Entertainment, Inc.

Great food and first-class service have been hallmarks and sources of pride at Harrah's Entertainment for more than seventy-one years. Our founder, William F. Harrah, was a firm believer in rolling out the red carpet and offering wonderful amenities to augment the excitement of gaming and enhance the customer experience. It was his way of saying, "We're delighted to have you as our guest."

From a humble beginning in 1937 in Reno, Nevada, Harrah's has grown into the world's largest gaming-entertainment company, with fifty-three locations in seven countries. Our owned or managed facilities include thirty-six properties in the United States operating primarily under the Harrah's, Caesars, and Horseshoe brand names, as well as casinos in Canada, Uruguay, the United Kingdom, Egypt, and South Africa and a world-class golf course in Macau. Yet we still approach our business one guest at a time, offering personal touches to our loyal customers in a spirit Bill Harrah would admire.

One of Mr. Harrah's earliest efforts in the culinary realm was The Summit, a restaurant offering spectacular views of Lake Tahoe and its surrounding snow-capped mountains from atop Harrah's Tahoe, Nevada's first five-star resort. From the table settings to the menus to the quality of the food served, The Summit epitomized Bill Harrah's commitment to offering guests the best experience possible. That's still what we strive to do every day.

In 1992, a time when casino food service generally centered on all-you-can-eat buffets for $1.99, Caesars Palace invited celebrity chef Wolfgang Puck to open a branch of his famed Los Angeles restaurant, Spago, in The Forum Shops in Las Vegas. The guests loved his fresh, bold flavors. That was followed by the opening of Napa at the Rio Las Vegas, with vaunted French chef Jean-Louis Palladin at the helm. It, too, was a smash hit.

The larger result was an industry trend at casinos worldwide. Celebrity chefs became the next best thing since foie gras. Closer to home, for Harrah's customers, food took on a meaning greater than its traditional role as fuel for gaming. For all levels of Harrah's customers, dining blossomed into a source of pleasure all its own, one more way that friends and family could gather at our casinos and resorts to relax in the spirit of celebration.

That's what *The Seven Stars Cookbook* is all about. More than a memento of great times at Harrah's, it is a book to take home and use in your own kitchen. The recipes have been scaled for the home cook, and make it easy to bring the touch of Harrah's style to any gathering.

Glitz and glamour have always been part of the fun at Harrah's. Our guests have been thrilled by the vast array of celebrity entertainers who've performed in years past at our supper clubs and now in our concert venues. Frank Sinatra, Bill Cosby, Sammy Davis Jr., Cher, Elton John, Bette Midler, and Celine Dion are among the headliners who have and do grace our stages.

The corollary in the culinary world is our partnership with celebrity chefs who bring bold entertainment to the dining table. Among them are American icons Paula Deen, Bobby Flay, and Bradley Ogden, along with renowned French chef Guy Savoy and pastry chef François Payard. They've weighed in here with delicious dishes served in their establishments.

Among the recipes, you'll find treats from their acclaimed venues at Caesars Palace in Las Vegas, including Blue Corn–Crusted Red Snapper with Warm Tomato Relish from Bobby Flay's Mesa Grill, Colors of Caviar from Restaurant Guy Savoy, Blue Corn Muffins from Bradley Ogden, and a decadent Chocolate-Coconut Cake from Payard Pâtisserie & Bistro.

Southern cooking maven and Food Network star Paula Deen is represented by her down-home Cheese Biscuits, Gooey Butter Cake, and Hoecakes as served at Harrah's Tunica. And there are crowd-pleasing offerings from Sammy Hagar's The Cabo Wabo Cantina at Harveys Lake Tahoe, Toby Keith's I Love This Bar & Grill at Harrah's Las Vegas and Harrah's North Kansas City, and more.

But the heart and soul of restaurant experiences at our properties reside in the many chefs who have worked their way up through the ranks of our own kitchens. Growing such talent from within and making sure they have the support and inspiration required to do their best work is essential to the Harrah's Code of Commitment.

The Harrah's Code governs how we do business. It expresses our respect for Harrah's employees and our pledge to provide them with opportunities to build satisfying careers. It speaks to our commitment to our guests to promote responsible gaming. And it details our desire to help make every community in which we do business a vibrant place to live and work. In that spirit, across the Harrah's brand, our kitchens are manned by men and women who hold Bill Harrah's core principle of pleasing customers close to heart. They take their work very seriously. And, as you might expect, these folks play to win.

A great example is Michael D'Angelo, executive pastry chef at Bally's Atlantic City. He was awarded Pastry Chef of the Year 2009 by the Professional Chefs Association of South Jersey. In this cookbook, you'll find his recipe for Passion Fruit Crème Brûlée. Another is Tammy Williams-Hansen, executive sous-chef at Harrah's Tunica, who was awarded Chef of the Year 2008 by the American Culinary Federation, Greater Memphis Chapter. Her recipes in collaboration with Paula Deen from the Paula Deen Buffet throughout this book include Paula Deen's Hoecakes, Paula Deen's Cheese Biscuits, and Paula Deen's Gooey Butter Cake.

William Becker, vice president of food & beverage at Rio All-Suite Hotel & Casino, was the team captain for Team Las Vegas at the 2004 Culinary Olympics in Erfurt, Germany, where he won three silver medals. Be sure to check out his Top 10 List for the pots and pans every kitchen should have. And Carnaval Court at Harrah's Las Vegas employs more champion entertainment flair bartenders than any other place on the Las Vegas Strip.

Many of the recipes in *The Seven Stars Cookbook* are for the dishes our guests love best. Peel & Eat Shrimp from Jimmy Buffett's Margaritaville, Crab Cakes from Jack Binion's Steak House at Horseshoe Council Bluffs, Wild Mushroom Chowder from Caesars Windsor, and Pecan Praline Cheescake from Fresh Market Buffet at Harrah's North Kansas City give you a glimpse of the pleasures that await you at every Harrah's property.

You'll also find a chapter on cocktails, with exemplars drawn from our casinos across the United States. Any one of them is sure to liven up your next party. From haute cuisine to down-home cooking, Harrah's has something for everyone.

We're very proud of this cookbook. It is a wonderful testament to the talent and dedication of our culinary professionals. A sincere thank-you is due every member of Harrah's kitchen brigades around the world and all who contributed to the book. It is a great pleasure to work with you every day.

To our guests, we're happy to share the secrets of our kitchens with you and to help you bring the fun of Harrah's home with you. Enjoy! Even more, we look forward to seeing you on your next visit with us. Now, if you'll excuse me, I'm off to whip up a batch of P.E.I. Mussels in Magners Cider from Trinity Pub & Carvery at The Pier Shops at Caesars Atlantic City. Care to join me?

—Gary W. Loveman

INTRODUCTION

by John Schlimm

The first time I saw a casino was at age twelve, when my mother and grandparents took me to Atlantic City. I remember chewing taffy amidst the salty breeze and crashing waves of the ocean as the iconic wind-battered boardwalk ran off ahead of me. I was flanked on one side by the hot sand and waving grass, while flashy, towering edifices touched the blue sky on the other side of me. It was like a surreal landscape straight out of some fantastic fairy tale.

Although I wasn't allowed on the casino floor, my mother and I walked into the grand lobby of one casino to wait there for my grandparents, great aunts, and cousins, who were inside trying their hand at courting Lady Luck. I can still see the plush staircase rising up in front of me while my mother and I sat on a nearby bench. We were surrounded by a kaleidoscope of rich reds, purples, silvers, and golds. There were ornate chandeliers and shards of mirrors that sparkled like a million captured stars, all igniting my wide-eyed imagination. I can still hear the jovial *ching-ching-ching-clang-clang-clang-ding-ding-ding-ding* followed by laughter and cheers that echoed from inside the cavernous casino floor, heralding the latest jackpot winner.

As a little kid from a small rural town, I had, indeed, just walked into a bona fide fantasyland. And what I walked away with that day so long ago was something I've always carried in my heart. It was a taste of the authentic glamour and excitement that only a casino can induce; an indoctrination into true fabulousness that dates back to the era of the Rat Pack and other Old Hollywood types, and even a few swanky gangsters, who interjected their imitable sophistication and star power up and down the Vegas Strip.

Every casino, whether on the two coasts or tucked away in the heartland and desert, is an allusion to all those legendary luminaries. Their colorful sense of style and zest for life provide the true, underlying prologue to our story herein, reminding us what it really means to possess elegance and to live life to the absolute fullest with laughter and adventure. Little did I know back then that my first visit to that casino was a mere prologue to my life and this book as well.

The next time I found myself inside a casino, it was on a warm spring evening, and I was standing alone quietly in a back hallway just off the large commercial kitchen at Harrah's North Kansas City. Chefs and waiters buzzed around me, carrying trays of Blue Cheese Dip and crackers, Blazing Hot Chicken Wings, Onion Rings, and Beach Party Punch. A thin head mike hugged my head and cheek, coming to rest comfortably near my mouth. It was connected to a sound crew I'd never see.

When I peeked out through a crack in the door, I could watch the large banquet hall on the other side without being seen myself. At the front was an enormous stage, erected just for the occasion and filled with lush greenery as a backdrop and a well-prepped stainless-steel table. On either side were cinema-size movie screens. At the back of the room on a dais, there was a film crew with a large camera, and another camera was suspended above the main stage for aerial closeup shots. The cameras would record what was about to happen and project the images onto the screens so the guests in the back could see it all, larger than life.

The middle of the room was filled with hundreds of people, talking, laughing, and eating. Long buffet tables, set with shiny platters and elaborate chafing dishes, ran alongside the walls, framing the room.

After several minutes, I heard my name introduced from onstage by the emcee. The door was opened, and I strode through, smiling and waving, and hoping I wouldn't stumble up the five or so steps onto the stage. Applause thundered from the guests, now shadowed as the bright lights exploded in front of me, bathing both me and the stage. For a moment in time, I got to play rock star. I was once more walking into that fairy tale I had glimpsed many years earlier, only this time it was the culmination of many years of hard work and dreaming combined with the pure adrenaline rush that only Harrah's Entertainment can provide.

Almost three decades after I sat in awe with my mother on a bench in that Atlantic City casino, I was now launching the national Harrah's Entertainment tour for my latest book at the time, *The Ultimate Beer Lover's Cookbook*. From that stage in North Kansas City, I would go on to crisscross the country, visiting Harrah's Entertainment properties on what seemed akin to a magic carpet ride. And the best part is, I was able to take everyone with me.

Along the way, I met thousands of my fellow food (and beer) lovers, and I got to feast on some of the best dishes prepared by some of the world's top chefs, all in residence at the Harrah's Entertainment properties. In North Kansas City, I savored the award-winning Best Steak in Kansas City and Toby Keith's Who's Your Daddy? Chicken Wings. At Harrah's Tunica near Memphis, I enjoyed Jumbo Lump Crab Cakes from '37, and Veal Chops Portobello from Murano's, and I went absolutely crazy for Paula Deen Buffet, which is a replica of Paula's home in Savannah. One night I ate in her pantry, another night in her dining room, and I devoured her Gooey Butter Cake (which can even do its own Elvis impersonation—see page 269) on her screened-in porch on my third night at the property. In Lake Tahoe, the chefs at Harrah's and Harveys introduced me to their delicious Cucumber & Mint Salad and the Forest Buffet's Applewood-Smoked Molasses & Five Peppercorn–Crusted Pork Loin.

At Harrah's Joliet outside Chicago, I dined on Grilled Shrimp Gazpacho at Reserve. My stop at Harrah's Rincon Casino & Resort, north of San Diego, gave me the chance to dive into the decadence of Fiore Tomato Caprese and many other outstanding dishes. Finally, at Bally's in Atlantic City, where my journey had begun as a child, I had Pickles' Famous Mushroom-Barley Soup and Braised Short Rib Sliders with Goat Cheese, Ricotta & Horseradish Gremolata. And this was all just for starters.

At each Harrah's Entertainment property I visited, I made a point of exploring every restaurant on-site, from the wonderful cafés, delis, and endless signature buffets just off the casino floors to the higher-end restaurants that have become regular hangouts among Seven Stars guests, celebrities, and other discerning foodies. After doing a show and visiting with the hundreds of new friends who were in the audience, I would often saunter alone through the rows of slot machines and game tables and then dine, savoring every moment and slowly digesting the marvelous spectacle going on around me.

My private tour of all these culinary gems from coast to coast quickly sparked the inspiration for *The Seven Stars Cookbook*. With each bite, I realized more and more that I had discovered an untapped gold mine of talent unparalleled anywhere else on the planet. While Harrah's Entertainment is the largest gaming company in the world, I soon came to appreciate what others had known for years, that it has now also become a mecca for food connoisseurs, who are as interested in hitting a jackpot on their plates as they are striking it rich at the slots. Indeed, today, this company started by the visionary William F. Harrah in 1937 is the ultimate purveyor of entertainment and luxury in all its many forms, not least of which is fine dining. I became determined to give the many new friends I had met on my *Ultimate Beer Lover's* book tour as well as the millions of other Harrah's Entertainment guests and food lovers everywhere the opportunity to bring this same eloquence and artful dining into their own homes and parties.

During the two years I compiled and edited this cookbook, I had the honor of working with the executive chefs at each Harrah's Entertainment property across the United States and in Canada, and the dozens of other chefs and staff members who make sure every bite their guests take is a memorable experience. Consummate professionals and artisans, these men and women know full well how to rock the kitchen!

What has emerged from this unprecedented partnership between an author and a dream team of chefs is a collection of recipes that not only promises to satisfy your hunger for the good life, but that also encapsulates the vibe and culinary heritage of who we are as a people. These recipes are pure poetry for the palate and the spirit.

On the following pages, you will find food and drinks that celebrate and unite our regional diversity in one glowing tapestry. You'll revel in the classic gumbos from Harrah's Louisiana Downs and Harrah's New Orleans; Fried Green Tomatoes from Tunica Roadhouse Casino & Hotel; Sweet Iowa Creamed Corn from Harrah's Council Bluffs; Peanut-Crusted Trout from Harrah's Cherokee; Clam Bake for Two from Phillips Seafood at The Pier Shops at Caesars Atlantic City; Red Grouper with Stewed Tomatoes, Okra & Crawfish from Horseshoe Tunica; and cocktails such as Sex in the Biggest Little City from Harrah's Reno, Mint Julep from Harrah's Metropolis, Gulf Coast Bloody Mary from Grand Biloxi Casino, Hotel & Spa, and Jewel of the Desert from Harrah's Ak-Chin.

I also sought to transform *The Seven Stars Cookbook* into every host's and hostess's secret weapon. Using this book as your new entertaining bible, you can now bring a Seven Stars flair to any meal or event, big or small, outside or inside, all to resounding effect.

Imagine your guests discovering your dinner or buffet table filled with an opulent Vegas smorgasbord: Colors of Caviar from Restaurant Guy Savoy at Caesars Palace Las Vegas; Peel & Eat Shrimp from Jimmy Buffett's Margaritaville at Flamingo Las Vegas; Blue Corn Muffins from Bradley Ogden at Caesars Palace Las Vegas; Seared Scallops with Tempura Ramps & Roasted Corn Custard from Búzios Seafood Restaurant at Rio All-Suite Hotel & Casino; Blue Corn–Crusted Red Snapper with Warm Tomato Relish from Bobby Flay's Mesa Grill at Caesars Palace Las Vegas; Parmesan-Crusted Orange Roughy from Embers at Imperial Palace; Eiffel Tower Raspberry Soufflés from the Eiffel Tower Restaurant at Paris Las Vegas; and Chocolate-Coconut Cake from Payard Pâtisserie & Bistro, also at Caesars Palace Las Vegas.

Or, how about dazzling your weekend guests with a first-class breakfast spread, boasting Boursin Cheese, Lobster & Cognac Omelets from Sterling Brunch at Bally's Steakhouse at Bally's Las Vegas; Poached Eggs with Bacon-Potato Hash & Hollandaise Sauce from Harrah's Chester Casino & Racetrack; and other selections from the Breakfast Buffet chapter? And nothing makes a more powerful statement, whether for business or for ladies and gentlemen who lunch, than selections from the VIP Luncheon menu, such as Duck with Porcini Mushrooms from Penazzi at Harrah's Las Vegas and Mahi Mahi & Grilled Shrimp with Black Beans & Mango from Seven Stars Lounge at Horseshoe Hammond.

However, if you're more the stay-at-home type, *The Seven Stars Cookbook* has the ultimate comfort food just for you. After all, at its core, this collection is all about treating you and your guests to the absolute best this life has to offer. Therefore, never hesitate to pamper yourself with Baja Blue Black Bean Dip from Baja Blue Restaurant & Cantina at Harrah's Laughlin; Leek, Sun-Dried Tomato, Shiitake Mushroom & Champagne Soup from Chef Paul Prudhomme's K-Paul's Louisiana Kitchen; the Range Crab Cocktail from The Range Steakhouse at Harrah's St. Louis; Premium Crab Cakes from Jack Binion's Steak House at Horseshoe Council Bluffs; Wild Mushroom Chowder from Caesars Windsor; Lobster Mac Casserole from Jack Binion's Steakhouse at Horseshoe Southern Indiana; Besh Steak Oysters Casino from Besh Steak at Harrah's New Orleans; Steak au Poivre from Jack Binion's Steak House at Horseshoe Bossier City; Ricotta Ravioli from Casa di

Napoli at Showboat Atlantic City; and Coconut Panna Cotta with Rum-Flamed Berries from The Pool at Harrah's Resort Atlantic City; topping it all off with an irresistible cocktail from the High Roller's Bar chapter, such as the star-studded Tahoe Wabo: Lake Tahoe's Trademark Margarita from Sammy Hagar's The Cabo Wabo Cantina at Harveys Lake Tahoe. You deserve every bite and sip of it.

There is also practicality amidst the scrumptious treasures in *The Seven Stars Cookbook.* More than thirty-five of Harrah's Entertainment's top chefs share their expertise in a series of Top 10 lists woven throughout the book. They advise, muse, and educate us on topics ranging from the ingredients and utensils every kitchen should always have on hand to choosing the best meat, fish, seafood, fruits, and vegetables and incorporating color, seasonality, and regional flair into your meals. And one of Harrah's Entertainment's premiere sommeliers serves as your private guide to pairing both wine and beer with food.

While epic in its creation and breadth, to say this book has been a labor of love for myself and the hundreds of chefs and other employees who have worked tirelessly to bring Harrah's Entertainment's unique brand of Seven Stars entertaining and dining into your kitchen would be a gross understatement. It has been that and so much more. For me, *The Seven Stars Cookbook* has been another opportunity to reach out my hand and take hold of yours and those of our fellow foodies who long for the perfect meal, exhilarating adventure, and laughter and to take you all along on that magic carpet ride with me once more.

So please join me now for this unforgettable journey that will allow your palate to crisscross the country and encounter some of the most visionary chefs and some of the most enlightened culinary masterpieces of our time. In doing so, I hope you will find your way through this book time and again over the years with the same starry-eyed enthusiasm you experienced when you, too, stepped into a casino for the first time and discovered a whole new world of possibilities awaiting your arrival.

Rock the kitchen!

—John Schlimm

Use the following tips to prepare for your next dinner party:

1   Food:

Choose the freshest foods available, from local farms, butchers, fish markets, or produce and gourmet markets. Look for those that are seasonal, unique, original, and have a story line, such as fresh-picked blueberries, sweet corn from New Jersey, vine-ripened tomatoes.

To decide on what to cook, ask yourself the following questions:

+   Who are my guests?

+   Where do they come from?

+   Are they into trying new foods?

+   Are they willing to have their food horizons broadened? (If the answer to this one is yes, then that's when it gets fun!)

2   Wording:

For the menu cards on your table, what you write is what you should eat. It's that simple! I love text that is clean and gives information on the food, such as origin, breed, season, age, etc. Your words should entice the palate and give a sense of comfort.

I am a firm believer that when you go to a restaurant and read through the menu, there should be at least one description there that will have you salivating. That's good writing.

3   Wine pairings:

There are no more rules! Wines are so complex these days that they have the character to stand up to any food combination, including those with flavors that are not dominant, such as tomatoes and sweet potatoes, and those with intense flavors, such as yuzu fruit or porcini mushrooms.

When pairing, be imaginative and be daring! California red table wine with sea urchin—why not?! Wine research is much easier with the Internet. Searching online will help you to find out what type of grape is used in a particular wine, which, in turn, will help you decide how daring you can be with flavors.

4   Creativity:

One of the most difficult things to teach anyone is creativity. In cooking, that means taking certain ingredients and seeing what evolves.

Flavor profiles play a large part in culinary creativity. Think about the ingredients you are using for your menu. However, the bottom line is Try! Try! Try! You may be surprised. I always am!

5   *Mise en place*:

French for "putting in place," *mise en place* refers to preparing and assembling all the necessary ingredients and equipment for cooking a dish before you begin. It includes not just physical objects, but also a knowledge of your ingredients and how to use them. This is a key tool to success in menu creativity.

6   Texture:

Food textures can be described as silky, crunchy, slimy, crispy, clean, spicy, soft, chewy, and so on. Your mouth seeks texture before it begins to define taste. Combining textures is one of the secrets to cooking interesting food.

7   Aroma and taste:

Like texture, aroma and taste are both very important. Aroma, of course, is the fragrance of the food, while taste is the mixture of flavors from all the ingredients used in a dish.

8   Contrast:

Contrast is the best way to achieve a sense of balance in a dish. A balance of tastes and textures is necessary to create memorable food.

9   Seasonality/origin:

In the culinary world, every season brings new gifts for the kitchen. For example, you can enjoy white asparagus in spring, Jersey tomatoes and corn during the summer, fall's abundance of root vegetables and wild mushrooms, and blood oranges in winter. And don't forget great oysters in all months ending in *r*.

Although many foods can be found in the markets year-round, sourced from different parts of the world, it's the foods you find in the backyards, farmers' markets, and local grocery stores that are best. Chef Alfred Portale says chefs have a twelve-season year, not a four-season one.

10   Guests:

Your table should be surrounded by family, friends, and colleagues who appreciate your passion for food and fun, because at the end of the day that is what it is all about!

++

Love, food, and wine—who needs more?
Guten appetit.

1

APPETIZERS

COLORS OF CAVIAR

RESTAURANT GUY SAVOY AT CAESARS PALACE LAS VEGAS
CHEF GUY SAVOY

Restaurant Guy Savoy at Caesars Palace Las Vegas has garnered numerous accolades, including two Michelin stars and the AAA Five Diamond Award. In doing so, famed French chef Guy Savoy's U.S. endeavor has set new standards for a fine-dining atmosphere. Now you can bring a little of Guy Savoy to your kitchen with his indulgent Colors of Caviar, a layered dish that will make you and your guests feel instantly transported to the City of Light.

CAVIAR VINAIGRETTE

½ sheet plain gelatin

1 cup very cold water

1 cup Sherry Vinaigrette
(see recipe facing page)

⅓ cup hackleback
(American sturgeon) caviar

Sea salt

CAVIAR CRÈME FRAÎCHE

½ sheet gelatin

1 cup very cold water

1¾ cups crème fraîche

⅓ cup hackleback caviar

Sea salt

CAVIAR SABAYON

1¼ cups haricots verts
(French green beans), trimmed

6 egg yolks

⅓ cup water

Salt

¼ cup golden osetra caviar

15 tablespoons golden osetra
caviar for garnish

SERVES 15

For the caviar vinaigrette: In a medium stainless-steel bowl, soak the gelatin in the cold water until it has softened, about 5 minutes. Drain the gelatin and add the Sherry Vinaigrette. Set the vinaigrette mixture over a saucepan with 2 inches of warm water. Stir until the gelatin dissolves and then remove from the heat. Add the caviar and blend with an immersion blender until most of the individual eggs are broken up and the mixture has turned a light gray color. Season with sea salt.

Spoon 2 tablespoons of the mixture into each *verrine* glass (a clear, cylindrical glass for layered desserts) or drinking glass. Gently tap each glass on a towel set on the work surface until the vinaigrette is evenly distributed. Refrigerate the glasses for at least 20 minutes in order to set.

For the caviar crème fraîche: In a medium stainless-steel bowl, soak the gelatin in the cold water until softened, about 5 minutes. Drain the gelatin and add the crème fraîche. Set the bowl over a saucepan with 2 inches of barely simmering water. Stir until the gelatin dissolves; remove from the heat. Gently fold in the caviar, season with sea salt, and transfer to a clean bowl.

Put 2 tablespoons caviar crème fraîche on top of the caviar vinaigrette in each glass and gently tap until it is evenly distributed. Refrigerate the glasses for at least 20 minutes to set.

For the caviar sabayon: In a large pot of salted boiling water, cook the beans until very tender, about 6 minutes. Transfer to a bowl of ice water to cool. Drain and coarsely chop the beans. In a blender, purée the beans until smooth. Transfer the purée to a pastry bag and set aside.

In a medium bowl set over a saucepan of 2 inches of barely simmering water, combine the egg yolks and water. Whisk vigorously, incorporating as much air as possible, until the mixture increases by at least 4 times the original volume. Continue to whisk until the sabayon is warm and forms a thick ribbon on the surface when the spoon is lifted. Season lightly with salt and carefully fold in the ¼ cup caviar.

To finish the dish, remove the glasses from the refrigerator and bring to room temperature. Carefully squeeze 2 tablespoons of the haricot vert purée into each glass. Gently tap the glasses until the purée is evenly distributed. Spread 1 tablespoon of the golden osetra caviar on top of the purée in each glass. Top each glass with a dollop of the sabayon. Serve with a small mother-of-pearl caviar spoon.

SHERRY VINAIGRETTE

¼ cup Dijon mustard
¼ cup sherry vinegar
1 egg yolk
2½ cups grapeseed oil
Salt and freshly ground white pepper

In a small bowl, whisk together the mustard, vinegar, and egg yolk. Gradually whisk in the oil in a thin stream to create an emulsion. Season with salt and white pepper.

MAKES ABOUT 3 CUPS

PEEL & EAT SHRIMP

Iconic singer Jimmy Buffett brings his island-hopping adventures and spirited rhythm for life to his Island-themed restaurant, Jimmy Buffett's Margaritaville, at Flamingo Las Vegas. Chef Phil Klinkenberg explains, "Jimmy Buffett's Peel & Eat Shrimp is an original Margaritaville recipe dating back to our first menu. For twenty-plus years it has been a favorite." In this recipe, everyone's favorite beverage, beer, is matched with everyone's favorite seafood, shrimp, in a delicious love fest that will turn you and your guests into the ultimate beach bums. Sand not included.

6 bottles Land Shark lager beer

2 teaspoons salt

¼ cup Old Bay Seasoning

12 lemons, halved

3½ pounds medium shrimp in the shell, preferably Key West pink shrimp

Cocktail sauce for serving

SERVES 8 TO 10

Fill a large pan half full with ice and set aside. In a large saucepan, combine the beer, salt, and Old Bay Seasoning. Squeeze the lemons into the pan and then add the lemon halves. Bring the beer mixture to a boil, add the shrimp, and cook for 1 minute. Turn off the heat and let the shrimp steep for 3 minutes. Drain the shrimp and empty them onto the ice; let cool, then drain again. Serve at once or cover and refrigerate. Serve with a favorite cocktail sauce.

BESH STEAK
OYSTERS CASINO

From one of the most celebrated chefs in America, John Besh, comes one of the favorite appetizers, a brilliant reimagining of the popular oysters Rockefeller, at his signature Besh Steak restaurant at Harrah's New Orleans. As is evidenced by Besh Steak Oysters Casino, the former U.S. Marine turned award-winning chef is dedicated to the "culinary riches of Louisiana, preserving and promoting ingredients, techniques, and heritage one mouth-watering dish at a time." Serve these on a bed of rock salt to hold the oysters in place.

1 cup (2 sticks) unsalted butter

1½ cups diced bacon

1½ cups minced shallots

¼ cup minced garlic

Pinch cayenne pepper

1 cup all-purpose flour

2 cups oyster liquor or water

½ cup grated Parmesan cheese

1 cup minced fresh flat-leaf parsley

8 ounces fresh lump crabmeat, picked over for shell

1 dozen oysters on the half shell

Kosher salt

Dry bread crumbs for sprinkling

SERVES 2

Preheat the oven to 350°F. In a heavy, medium saucepan, melt the butter over medium heat. Add the bacon, shallots, garlic, and cayenne and sauté for 5 minutes. Stir in the flour and cook, stirring, for 3 minutes; do not brown. Add the oyster liquor and cheese and cook, stirring occasionally, for 10 minutes. Remove from heat and stir in the parsley. Gently fold in the crabmeat. Remove from the heat, spread the mixture out on a baking sheet, and let cool. Place the oysters on a small jellyroll pan. Spoon 2 tablespoons of the crab mixture onto each oyster and spread the mixture evenly over the oyster. Sprinkle lightly with salt and bread crumbs. Bake at 400°F for 10 to 15 minutes, or until golden brown and bubbling around the edges.

BAJA BLUE BLACK BEAN DIP

BAJA BLUE RESTAURANT & CANTINA AT HARRAH'S LAUGHLIN
EXECUTIVE SOUS-CHEF JEREMY HUGHES

This dip has been a staple for years at Baja Blue Restaurant & Cantina, where it is an accompaniment to chips and salsa. Chef Jeremy Hughes explains, "We have had numerous customers over the years inquire about this recipe, and that is why I think it is a great addition to the Harrah's Laughlin collection in this cookbook."

4 slices bacon, chopped

½ yellow onion, diced

1 tablespoon minced garlic

1 pound (2 cups) dried black beans, rinsed and picked over

1 jalapeño chile, halved lengthwise and seeded

3 cups water

2 tablespoons chili powder

1 cup shredded Monterey jack cheese

Tortilla chips for serving

Salsa (optional)

MAKES 6 TO 8 CUPS

In a medium skillet, cook the bacon over medium heat until crisp. Transfer to paper towels to drain. Cook the onions in the bacon fat until translucent, about 3 minutes. Add the garlic and cook for 30 seconds. Add the beans, jalapeño, and water. Bring to a boil, reduce heat to a simmer, and cook until the beans are tender, about 1½ hours. Stir in the chili powder and cheese.

In a food processor, purée the beans (with their broth), in batches if necessary, until smooth. Serve with tortilla chips and top with your favorite salsa, if desired.

BRUSCHETTA POMODORO

ANDREOTTI AT HARRAH'S RENO
CHEF JASON HARRIS

This dish will allow you to experience the tastes of northern Italy, just like the guests who enjoy the bistro atmosphere of Andreotti at Harrah's Reno. Bruschetta Pomodoro is a classic Italian hors d'oeuvre. Its light combination of Roma tomatoes, garlic, and extra-virgin olive oil makes a great pairing with a glass of white wine. Chef Jason Harris notes, "Andreotti's guests like to start off with this appetizer because it's not too filling nor does it lack in flavor. I'm sure you will enjoy making this dish as well as eating it."

POMODORO SAUCE

1½ pounds Roma tomatoes, finely diced

5 tablespoons olive oil

1½ teaspoons salt

1½ tablespoons minced garlic

12 large fresh basil leaves, thinly sliced

Sixteen ¼-inch-thick sourdough baguette slices

Olive oil for brushing

4 slices prosciutto

8 ounces fresh mozzarella, finely diced

SERVES 4

For the pomodora sauce: In a small bowl, mix together all the ingredients.

Preheat the oven to 425°F. Put the baguette slices on a baking sheet and brush the tops with olive oil. Bake for about 5 minutes, or until golden brown. Remove and let cool on wire racks. Cut each slice of prosciutto into 4 pieces. Place a piece of prosciutto on top of each crostini and spoon the sauce on top. Finish with the mozzarella.

HARRAH'S RENO, THE COMPANY'S FIRST PROPERTY, WAS OPENED IN 1937 BY WILLIAM F. HARRAH.

FRIED PORTOBELLO MUSHROOMS

THE RANGE STEAKHOUSE & BAR AT TUNICA ROADHOUSE CASINO & HOTEL
CHEF DE CUISINE RAYMOND CARTER

Bite-sized pieces of portobello mushrooms will beckon you and your guests to dip them to your heart's content in your favorite ranch dressing or other sauce. This crisp and subtle dish is the most frequently ordered appetizer on the menu at The Range Steakhouse & Bar. Chef Raymond Carter explains, "Although there are more variations, we take pride in the decision to embellish the flavor of nature with the bold flavor of our vinegary marinade and perfectly seasoned batter to bring such a gentle yet elegant expression to our menu."

Note: The mushrooms need to be marinated the night before cooking.

BALSAMIC DRESSING

3 tablespoons balsamic vinegar

2 tablespoons fresh lemon juice

½ tablespoon Dijon mustard

1 garlic clove, minced

1 tablespoon minced shallot

½ cup olive oil

Salt and freshly ground pepper

3 portobello mushrooms, stemmed and cut into ¼-inch-thick slices

4 cups all-purpose flour

1 tablespoon kosher salt

2 teaspoons freshly ground pepper

2 teaspoons granulated garlic

Peanut oil for deep-frying

Buttermilk Dressing (recipe follows) or other dipping sauce for serving

SERVES 2

For the dressing: In a medium bowl, whisk together the vinegar, lemon juice, mustard, garlic, and shallot. Gradually whisk in the oil. Season with salt and pepper.

In a small bowl, soak the mushroom pieces in the balsamic dressing overnight and then drain. In a medium bowl, combine the flour, salt, pepper, and granulated garlic. Stir with a whisk to blend. Add the mushrooms and toss until well coated.

In a Dutch oven or large, heavy pot, heat 2 inches of the peanut oil to 375°F on a deep-fat thermometer. Add the mushroom pieces and cook until golden brown, 5 to 6 minutes. Using a wire skimmer, transfer to paper towels to drain. Serve hot, with buttermilk dressing or other dipping sauce of choice.

BUTTERMILK DRESSING

½ cup well-shaken buttermilk

2 tablespoons mayonnaise

2 tablespoons cider vinegar

2 tablespoons minced shallots

1 tablespoon sugar

½ teaspoon salt

¼ teaspoon freshly ground pepper

3 tablespoons minced fresh chives

In a large bowl, whisk together the buttermilk, mayonnaise, vinegar, shallots, sugar, salt, and pepper until the sugar is dissolved, then whisk in the chives.

MAKES ABOUT 1 CUP

RANGE CRAB COCKTAIL

THE RANGE STEAKHOUSE AT HARRAH'S ST. LOUIS
EXECUTIVE CHEF RAY LEUNG

Instead of serving the traditional shrimp cocktail, mix it up with this unique award-winning twist on a classic from Hawaii that combines crab salad, salsa, and microgreens, topped off with a garnish of star fruit. This dish will provide a colorful and memorable launch to your meal with what chef Ray Leung calls a "refreshing touch of aloha!"

Note: To make this dish, you will need four 3-inch ring molds.

CRAB COCKTAIL SALAD

1½ teaspoons minced shallot

1½ teaspoons minced fresh basil

4½ tablespoons crème fraîche

1½ teaspoons minced fresh mint

¼ teaspoon hazelnut oil

¼ teaspoon salt

¼ teaspoon minced garlic

¼ teaspoon freshly ground pepper

12 ounces fresh lump crabmeat, picked over for shell

SALSA

6 tablespoons finely chopped fresh pineapple

6 tablespoons finely chopped mango

3 tablespoons finely chopped red bell pepper

1½ teaspoons minced fresh chives

MICROGREEN SALAD

½ cup microgreens

1 teaspoon fresh lemon juice

2 teaspoons fresh mandarin orange juice

Salt and freshly ground pepper

Thirty-two ⅛-inch-thick half-moon slices cucumber

Eight ¼-inch-thick slices star fruit

SERVES 4

For the crab cocktail salad: In a medium bowl, combine all the ingredients except the crabmeat, stirring to blend. Add the crabmeat and toss gently to coat. Cover and refrigerate for at least 15 minutes or up to 30 minutes.

For the salsa: In a small bowl, combine all the ingredients and stir to blend. Cover and refrigerate for at least 15 minutes or up to 30 minutes.

For the microgreen salad: In a medium bowl, combine all the ingredients, tossing to combine.

In a 3-inch ring mold, evenly space 8 cucumber slices, standing upright, against the inside walls of the mold. Fill the mold with 2 tablespoons of the salsa and then spoon in the crab salad. Unmold gently by holding down the crab cocktail with your left index finger while pulling the mold up with your right hand. Repeat to make 4 servings. Top each serving with the microgreen salad and 2 star fruit slices. Serve immediately.

ACCORDING TO A 2006 SURVEY
CONDUCTED BY HARRAH'S ENTERTAINMENT, TABLE
GAMES ARE MORE THAN TWICE AS POPULAR AMONG
MEN THAN WOMEN.

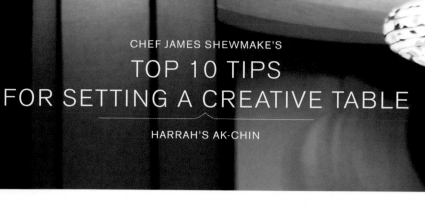

CHEF JAMES SHEWMAKE'S

TOP 10 TIPS
FOR SETTING A CREATIVE TABLE

HARRAH'S AK-CHIN

1   Use colorful linen napkins and experiment with different napkin folds. Books and online instructions are available to help you with these topics.

2   Learn proper silverware etiquette so you will know where and how to place the silverware.

3   Polish everything, from china to the flatware to the glassware, before using it.

4   Set the table with all the silverware and glassware needed for the meal so your guests will know what to expect.

5   There is a flower for every occasion, so use them whenever possible. Consult your local florist if you are not familiar with floral arrangements.

6   Lighting is key. It should be bright and sunny for breakfast and lunch, more subtle at dinner, and don't forget unscented candles for those romantic nights.

7   Use the elements of fire, air, and water whenever possible:

   + Air: Open a window or door for fresh air, turn on a ceiling fan, or eat outside, depending on the weather.

   + Fire: Light unscented candles or a fire in a fireplace.

   + Water: Use a clear water pitcher or a floating candle in a bowl of water.

8   Let the food aromas be the essence of your meal. Don't complicate aromas with incense and scented candles.

9   For multiple-course meals, choose adequately padded chairs for your guests' comfort.

10 Never forget that every meal is a gift. Enjoy it with friends and family. Cherish every meal with friends and family as though it were your last.

JUMBO LUMP CRAB CAKES

'37 AT HARRAH'S TUNICA / EXECUTIVE CHEF STEVE PAIROLERO

Chefs from every region of the country have their special recipe for the great American crab cake. This one from Harrah's Tunica, outside Memphis, is full of bright flavors. These are favorites at '37, which is named in tribute to the opening of the first Harrah's casino on October 30, 1937.

8 sea scallops

4 large egg yolks

2 tablespoons mayonnaise

1 teaspoon Dijon mustard

1½ pounds fresh lump crabmeat, picked over for shell

¼ cup finely chopped red bell pepper

½ teaspoon Old Bay Seasoning

1 tablespoon minced fresh flat-leaf parsley

1 teaspoon minced fresh dill

1 cup panko (Japanese bread crumbs)

½ cup clarified butter (recipe follows)

Cajun Rémoulade (recipe follows) or lemon vinaigrette for serving

MAKES 16 CRAB CAKES;
SERVES 6 TO 8

In a food processor, purée the scallops to a pastelike consistency. In a large bowl, mix together the scallops, egg yolks, mayonnaise, and mustard. In a medium bowl, combine the crabmeat, red bell pepper, Old Bay Seasoning, and herbs; toss to coat. Add the crabmeat mixture to the scallop mixture and gently stir to blend. Shape into 16 crab cakes and dredge each in the bread crumbs. Cook now, or place on a plate, cover in plastic wrap, and refrigerate for up to 1 hour.

In a large sauté pan or skillet, heat the clarified butter over medium-high heat and cook the crab cakes for 3 minutes on each side, or until golden brown. Serve immediately, with the rémoulade or vinaigrette.

CAJUN RÉMOULADE

2 cups mayonnaise

1 tablespoon chopped capers

1 teaspoon minced garlic

1 teaspoon minced fresh flat-leaf parsley

2 tablespoons fresh lemon juice

½ jalapeño chile, seeded and minced

2 tablespoons ketchup

1 teaspoon Dijon mustard

1 teaspoon anchovy paste

¼ teaspoon cayenne pepper

1 teaspoon Tabasco sauce

1 teaspoon Worcestershire sauce

½ teaspoon freshly ground pepper

1 teaspoon Cajun seasoning

In a food processor, combine all the ingredients and process until smooth.

MAKES 2½ CUPS

Clarifying butter: In a heavy saucepan, melt 1 cup (2 sticks) unsalted butter over low heat. Remove from the heat and skim the foam from the surface. Pour the clear yellow liquid into a glass container, leaving the milky residue behind (this can be added to soups and sauces). Cover and refrigerate indefinitely. Makes about ⅔ cup.

JACK BINION'S PREMIUM CRAB CAKES

JACK BINION'S STEAK HOUSE AT HORSESHOE COUNCIL BLUFFS
EXECUTIVE CHEF JAMES REBER

These classic crab cakes are one of Jack Binion's Steak House's original recipes. Chef James Reber and his team use sweet jumbo lump crabmeat, a touch of mayonnaise, and a secret blend of seasonings to make these tender golden cakes.

2 tablespoons mayonnaise

1 teaspoon dry mustard

2 teaspoons minced fresh flat-leaf parsley

½ teaspoon cayenne pepper

½ tablespoon minced garlic

2 dashes Worcestershire sauce

1 tablespoon fresh lemon juice

1 teaspoon kosher salt

1 teaspoon freshly ground black pepper

3 tablespoons panko (Japanese bread crumbs)

1 pound fresh lump crabmeat, picked over for shell

2 tablespoons extra-virgin olive oil

4 lemon wedges for garnish

Aioli Sauce for dipping (see recipe facing page)

SERVES 4

Preheat the oven to 350°F. In a medium bowl, whisk together the mayonnaise, mustard, parsley, cayenne, garlic, Worcestershire sauce, lemon juice, salt, and pepper. Add the panko and crabmeat. Using a rubber spatula, fold the mixture together gently to prevent breaking up the crabmeat too much. Mold the mixture into 4 cakes. In a large sauté pan or skillet, heat the oil over medium heat. Sauté the crab cakes for 3 minutes on each side, or until brown and crusty. Serve with the lemon wedges and aioli sauce.

WHEN IT'S TIME TO CUT LOOSE,
WHISKEY ROADHOUSE AT HORSESHOE CASINO COUNCIL BLUFFS
IS THE PLACE TO HEAR YOUR FAVORITE MUSIC UP CLOSE AND UNTAMED.
BO DIDDLEY PLAYED HIS LAST PERFORMANCE HERE
BEFORE HE DIED IN JUNE 2008. ERIC CHURCH, BETTER THAN EZRA,
AND GAVIN ROSSDALE
HAVE ALSO ALL PLAYED THE ROADHOUSE.

AIOLI SAUCE

1 cup mayonnaise

2 tablespoons fresh lemon juice

¼ teaspoon powdered garlic

1 teaspoon Worcestershire sauce

¼ teaspoon kosher salt

¼ teaspoon freshly ground pepper

In a medium bowl, combine all the ingredients and stir to blend.

MAKES ABOUT 1 CUP

GOAT CHEESE TRUFFLED BAKLAVA

BOA STEAKHOUSE AT THE FORUM SHOPS AT CAESARS PALACE LAS VEGAS
CHEF JOSE ALEMAN

Chef Jose Aleman at BOA Steakhouse has transformed the classic Greek dessert into an intriguing starter layered with goat cheese and flavored with truffles. Served on a bed of frisée tossed with a grapefruit dressing, it is an intriguing mixture of sweet and savory, crisp and creamy.

1 pound thawed frozen filo dough

1 cup (2 sticks) unsalted butter, melted

¼ cup honey

2 tablespoons truffle peelings

½ cup ground pistachios

16 ounces fresh white goat cheese

2 tablespoons truffle oil

SALAD

Leaves from 2 heads frisée lettuce

2 tablespoons grated grapefruit zest

2 tablespoons grapefruit juice

2 tablespoons extra-virgin olive oil

SERVES 12

Preheat the oven to 400°F. Line a baking sheet with parchment paper.

Cover the stack of filo dough with a cloth to keep it moist. Layer 1 sheet of filo dough on the prepared pan and brush it with butter. Repeat to layer 8 sheets of dough.

In a medium bowl, mix together the honey and truffle peelings. Drizzle the layered dough with 4 tablespoons of the honey mixture, followed by 6 tablespoons of the pistachios. Place another sheet of filo dough on top and brush it with melted butter. Repeat to layer 16 more sheets of dough, for a total of 24 sheets. Drizzle the top layer with 2 tablespoons of the remaining honey mixture and then sprinkle with the remaining pistachios. Bake for 45 minutes, or until golden brown.

Remove from the oven and let cool for 30 minutes on the pan. Drizzle with the remaining honey mixture. Let cool completely. Cut into twelve pieces.

In a medium bowl, combine the goat cheese and truffle oil. Stir to blend well. Transfer the mixture to a piping bag fitted with a ½-inch round tip. Lift off the top three-fourths of each pastry and pipe the goat cheese mousse into 3 rows along the length of the filo. Replace the tops.

For the salad: In a medium bowl, combine all the ingredients and toss to coat.

To serve, place each pastry on a salad plate and serve a mound of salad alongside.

JAPANESE YELLOWTAIL SASHIMI
WITH DICED CHILES

SUSHI ROKU AT THE FORUM SHOPS AT CAESARS PALACE LAS VEGAS
CHEF VERNON CARDENAS

In this appetizer, raw yellowtail is served with a ponzu sauce made with the juice of the yuzu, a sour citrus fruit. Ponzu sauce, a popular combination of sweet and sour flavors, is often used in Japanese cuisine. Here, it makes a tangy counterpoint to the tender, buttery fish.

4 ounces yellowtail fish fillet, cut into twelve ¹⁄₁₆-inch-thick diagonal slices

¼ teaspoon minced garlic

1 tablespoon shredded fresh ginger

1 tablespoon finely chopped green onion (white part only)

1 teaspoon minced red jalapeño chile

1 teaspoon minced green jalapeño chile

YUZU PONZU SAUCE

4 teaspoons ponzu sauce

1 teaspoon soy sauce

⅛ teaspoon yuzu juice

½ teaspoon olive oil

¼ teaspoon shredded daikon radish

Lemon slices for garnish

SERVES 2 TO 4

On a large serving dish, place the yellowtail slices in one layer. Brush the garlic over each slice. Evenly scatter the ginger, green onion, and red and green jalapeños on each slice of the yellowtail.

For the sauce: In a medium bowl, combine all ingredients and stir well. Drizzle the sauce over the yellowtail.

Just before serving, heat the oil in a small skillet over medium heat until shimmering. Pour it over the fish. Place the daikon radish on the center of the plate and garnish with the lemon slices.

AVOCADO SPRING ROLLS

AUGUSTUS CAFÉ AT CAESARS WINDSOR
EXECUTIVE CHEF PATRICK MCCLARY

These Asian-inspired spring rolls combine the best of East and West. Avocado, garlic, ginger, sun-dried tomatoes, and lime juice are the filling for crunchy morsels that will surprise your guests. Chef Patrick McClary comments, "This dish contains a great contrast of textures and just enough lime to enliven the senses. Spice it up with a Szechuan dip to complete the experience."

3 avocados, peeled and pitted

1 tablespoon roasted garlic
(see note)

½ tablespoon minced fresh ginger

3 tablespoons finely chopped
red onion

1 tablespoon finely chopped
oil-packed sun-dried tomato

2 tablespoons fresh lime juice

Salt and freshly ground pepper

Sixteen 4-inch-square
spring roll wrappers

1 large egg yolk beaten with
1 tablespoon water

Canola or peanut oil for deep-frying

Bottled spiced plum or
Szechuan sauce for serving

MAKES 16 PIECES

In a large bowl, combine the avocados, garlic, ginger, onion, and tomato and mash them coarsely with a fork. Add the lime juice and salt and pepper, mixing well.

Put the wrappers on a work surface and brush each with the egg mixture on two adjoining edges of the wrapper. Place 2 tablespoons of the mixture in the center of each wrapper and fold corner to corner to form a triangle. Press the edges together to form a seal. Brush one corner of the triangle with the egg mixture. Bring the opposite corners together and press to form a seal.

In a Dutch oven or large, heavy pot, heat 2 inches of the oil to 365°F on a deep-fat thermometer. Cook the spring rolls in batches for 4 minutes, or until golden brown. Using a wire skimmer, transfer to paper towels to drain. Serve hot, with plum or Szechuan sauce.

✦

Roasted garlic cloves: Cut a bulb of garlic in half and brush cut sides with olive oil. Roast in a preheated 400°F oven until tender and golden brown, about 20 minutes. Let cool. Press out the individual garlic cloves and chop.

SEARED SCALLOPS
WITH TEMPURA RAMPS & ROASTED CORN CUSTARD

BÚZIOS SEAFOOD RESTAURANT AT RIO ALL-SUITE HOTEL & CASINO
CHEF DE CUISINE TRANG TRAN

Although this appetizer is not on the regular menu at Búzios Seafood Restaurant, it often makes its appearance on the chef's tasting menu in some version. This dish is sure to impress your dinner guests with its vibrant colors and fresh combinations of flavors. Chef Trang Tran suggests, "A great wine pairing would be a Sauvignon Blanc or a Sancerre."

CITRUS VINAIGRETTE

Grated zest of 1 orange

2 tablespoons orange juice

½ teaspoon minced shallot

¼ teaspoon Dijon mustard

2 to 3 tablespoons canola oil

1 tablespoon chopped fresh chives

Salt and freshly ground pepper

ROASTED CORN CUSTARD

1 ear corn, shucked and roasted
(see note)

1 large egg, lightly beaten

4 tablespoons heavy cream

1 shallot, minced

1 garlic clove, minced

2 tablespoons cornmeal

1 tablespoon flour

½ teaspoon salt

Freshly ground pepper

TEMPURA RAMPS

¼ cup cornstarch

¼ cup all-purpose flour,
plus more for coating

1 teaspoon salt, plus more to taste

½ teaspoon freshly ground pepper, plus
more to taste

½ cup soda water

3 tablespoons canola oil, plus more
for frying

4 ramps (wild onions),
trimmed to 4 inches

4 sea scallops

1 tablespoon fresh lemon juice

1 blood orange, cut into 12 segments
(see note)

1 handful microgreens or
mixed baby greens for garnish

For the vinaigrette: In a medium bowl, combine the orange zest and juice, shallot, and mustard. Gradually whisk in the oil to emulsify. Stir in the chives and season with salt and pepper.

For the corn custard: Preheat the oven to 325°F. In a medium bowl, stir all the custard ingredients together. Pour the mixture into a buttered 10-ounce ramekin. Set the ramekin in a baking dish and add hot water to come halfway up the sides of the ramekin. Bake until the custard is set and lightly brown, about 20 minutes. Transfer to a wire rack.

For the ramps: In a medium bowl, combine the cornstarch, the ¼ cup flour, the 1 teaspoon salt, and the ½ teaspoon pepper; stir well. Whisk in the soda water. The batter should be thin. Set aside to rest for 1 hour.

In a Dutch oven or large, heavy pot, heat 2 inches of the oil to 365°F. Coat the ramps in flour, and then dip them into the batter. Fry the ramps for 1 minute, or until golden. Using a wire skimmer, transfer to a paper towel to drain. Sprinkle with salt and pepper. Keep warm in a low oven.

Pat the scallops dry with paper towels and season them lightly with salt and pepper. In a medium sauté pan or skillet, heat the 3 tablespoons oil over high heat until smoking. Add the scallops and sear on one side for 2 minutes, or until golden brown. Turn and cook until golden brown on the second side, 1 minute. Transfer to a plate and sprinkle with the lemon juice.

To serve, drizzle 1 tablespoon of the vinaigrette on each plate. Place a large spoonful of the corn custard in the center. Nestle a scallop on top of the custard. Set a tempura ramp on top, leaning on the scallop. Place 3 blood orange segments on the scallop. Garnish with the greens and serve at once.

SERVES 4

Roasting corn: Brush the ear lightly with canola oil and season with salt and pepper. Under a preheated broiler, on a hot grill, or in a hot grill pan, roast the corn, turning as needed, until browned on all sides. Let cool. Using a large knife, cut the kernels from the cob.

Segmenting citrus: Using a large knife, cut the peel off each end down to the flesh. Set the fruit, one end down, on a cutting board. Cut off the peel down to the flesh, following the curvature of the fruit. Hold the fruit over a bowl and cut on each side of each membrane to release the segments. Squeeze the empty fruit to release the juice.

ON A DAILY BASIS,
THE AWARD-WINNING CARNIVAL WORLD BUFFET
AT RIO ALL-SUITE HOTEL & CASINO:

✦ EMPLOYS MORE THAN FIFTY COOKS ✦

✦ OPERATES NINE COOKING STATIONS
IN A SERVICE LINE AS LONG AS A FOOTBALL FIELD ✦

✦ MAINTAINS TWELVE DIFFERENT
FOOD STATIONS SERVING A VARIETY OF FOODS
FROM AROUND THE WORLD ✦

✦ MAKES EVERYTHING FROM SCRATCH
IN THE RIO'S PASTRY SHOP,
INCLUDING NINE TYPES OF GELATO ✦

✦ CHANGES MENU ITEMS THREE TIMES A DAY,
SEVEN DAYS A WEEK ✦

2

SALADS

SEARED BEEF TENDERLOIN
& GOAT CHEESE SALAD

AUGUSTUS CAFÉ AT CAESARS WINDSOR
EXECUTIVE CHEF PATRICK MCCLARY

Whether served as a first-course salad or a light lunch, this layered dish is both easy and elegant. Chef Patrick McClary notes, "This salad has all it takes to make a great meal. It's well-balanced with the sharpness of the goat cheese, a sassy dressing, and the beef tenderloin. It's especially enjoyed by our guests on hot summer days."

2 teaspoons canola oil

1 pound beef tenderloin

1 teaspoon minced fresh rosemary

1½ teaspoons minced garlic

Salt and freshly ground pepper

4 Roma tomatoes, halved lengthwise

½ cup fresh white goat cheese

SPICY TOMATO DRESSING

1 cup plus ½ tablespoon canola oil

1 tablespoon coarsely chopped onion

½ ripe tomato, coarsely chopped

Grated zest of ½ lemon

½ teaspoon fresh lemon juice

¼ teaspoon Kashmiri mirchi chili powder or cayenne pepper

¼ cup tomato juice

Salt and freshly ground pepper

3 cups mixed baby greens

Twelve 4-inch squares focaccia bread, lightly toasted and cut into ¼-inch-thick slices

SERVES 4 AS A
MAIN-COURSE LUNCHEON
SALAD, 6 TO 8 AS A FIRST COURSE

Preheat the oven to 400°F. In a large sauté pan, heat the oil over medium-high heat and sear the beef on all sides. Season the beef with rosemary, garlic, and salt and pepper. Put on a rack in a roasting pan and roast for about 25 minutes for medium-rare. Remove from the oven, transfer to a carving board, and let cool to room temperature. Cut into 16 thin slices.

Preheat the broiler. Place the tomato halves on a broiler pan. Place 1 tablespoon of the goat cheese on each tomato half and broil 8 inches from the heat source until the cheese is melted and lightly browned, about 1 minute. Remove from the broiler and sprinkle with pepper.

For the dressing: In a medium skillet, heat ½ tablespoon of the oil over medium heat. Add the onion and sauté until golden brown, about 5 minutes. Add the tomato and sauté for 3 to 4 minutes. Add the lemon zest, juice, chili powder, and tomato juice. Pour the mixture into a blender and purée. Transfer the mixture to a medium bowl and gradually whisk in the remaining 1 cup oil. Add salt and pepper to taste.

To serve, toss the greens in just enough of the dressing to coat; there will be leftover dressing. On each plate, layer the ingredients as follows: Place ¼ cup of the greens in the center, followed by 2 focaccia slices and 2 beef slices. Repeat with a second layer of greens, bread, and beef, then top with a layer of ¼ cup greens. Place a tomato half on either side of the salad.

IN ONE YEAR, THE MARKET BUFFET AT CAESARS WINDSOR USES ALMOST 150,000 POUNDS OF PRIME RIB AND 50,000 POUNDS OF INSIDE ROUND.

TOP 10 TIPS FOR SERVING FOOD

HORSESHOE BOSSIER CITY

1 Always use hot plates for hot food and cold plates for cold food.

2 Never forget that people eat with their eyes first: Food should always be visually appealing. The use of color and height can catch a guest's eye, and lead to the success of the dish. If you create a dish that is beautiful, no matter what the ingredients, guests will probably enjoy it.

3 Think of the serving plate as a picture frame or blank canvas: Consider your food as art on the plate. Be sure to keep the rim of the plate clean to nicely frame your masterpiece.

4 Always use edible garnishes: Nothing should go on the plate that can't be eaten.

5 The use of nontraditional serving dishes can add excitement and flair to your dish: For example, when serving a cheese course, use a cheese box as a cheese plate. When serving seafood, use shells as vessels, or choose dishes with whimsical shapes and designs. Use one of the ingredients in the dish, such as a bell pepper or an orange shell, for serving the dish. Large leaves, such as fig leaves and sections of banana leaves, can be used in place of plates.

6 Fresh herbs can accent a dish as well as make it visually appealing: They add an alluring aroma that will capture your guests' attention and imagination. For example, fried basil looks like glass, has a clean, refreshing aroma, and will add a stylish touch to your dish.

7 Positioning is key: How you place the food on the serving plate is important because it brings the whole dish together. For example, if you're serving a dish like pan-seared halibut with root vegetable ragù, poached prawns, and a pepper fumet, you could position the ragù in the center of the plate and the fish on top. Then, you could place the prawns to the right of the fish and pool the fumet on the plate. This gives the dish a unified look, adds a dazzling visual appeal, and shows the love that was put into the dish.

8 Never use unnatural colors in a dish: Unnatural colors are those that invoke the wrong response from the guest. For example, one of my fellow chefs made a blueberry risotto, and many of our guests found the bright purple rice unappetizing.

9 Always highlight the key element of your dish: Place the main ingredient on the plate so that it becomes the central focus and is complemented by the side dishes.

10 KISS (Keep It Super Simple).

TENNESSEE PROSCIUTTO & WARM GOAT CHEESE SALAD

WITH HONEY-WALNUT TRUFFLE DRESSING

MAGNOLIA, A DELTA GRILLE AT HORSESHOE TUNICA

This tantalizing fall salad of warm goat cheese and prosciutto was inspired by an American-made version of prosciutto. The addition of fresh honey, walnut oil, and that slight hint of truffle provide the perfect balance to the salty prosciutto. To order Tennessee prosciutto, go to www.bentonshams.com.

DRESSING

5 tablespoons clover honey

¼ teaspoon white truffle oil

2 tablespoons walnut oil

Pinch of minced fresh lavender blossoms

Pinch of minced fresh rosemary

Juice of ½ lemon

Salt and freshly ground pepper

FRIED GOAT CHEESE

5 ounces fresh white goat cheese at room temperature

½ tablespoon minced fresh rosemary

½ tablespoon minced fresh thyme

½ tablespoon freshly ground pepper

1 large egg

4 large eggs, beaten

4 cups all-purpose flour

4 cups panko (Japanese bread crumbs)

Peanut oil for deep-frying

Herb flowers or edible flowers, such as pansies, violas, and nasturtiums

6 cups mixed baby greens

6 thin slices prosciutto, preferably Benton's

SERVES 6

For the dressing: In a small bowl, combine all the ingredients and whisk to emulsify. Taste and adjust the seasoning.

For the goat cheese: In a small bowl, combine the goat cheese, rosemary, thyme, pepper, and the 1 egg. Stir well to blend. Shape the mixture into six ½-inch-thick disks.

Put the 4 beaten eggs, the flour, and the panko in each of 3 separate shallow bowls. Dip a goat cheese disk first into the eggs, coating evenly all over, then in the flour, and back into the eggs again, coating evenly all over with each layer. Coat the disk evenly all over with the panko. Repeat with the remaining disks.

In a Dutch oven or heavy pot, heat 2 inches of the oil to 350°F on a deep-fat thermometer. Gently add the goat cheese and cook until golden brown, 2 to 3 minutes. Using a wire skimmer, transfer to paper towels to drain. Set aside and keep warm.

Soak the flowers in ice water for 2 to 3 minutes; drain and dry on paper towels.

Reserve 1 tablespoon of the dressing. In a medium bowl, toss the greens with the remaining dressing to coat. On a work surface, lay out the prosciutto slices. Place one-sixth of the greens on one end of each slice and roll up. Pool a small amount of dressing on each plate. Place a goat cheese disk on top, then top the cheese with the prosciutto roll. With a soup spoon, drizzle more of the dressing around the stack. Garnish with the flowers.

MAGNOLIA, A DELTA GRILLE FEATURES LOCALLY SOURCED FOODS, INCLUDING ALLEN BENTON'S TENNESSEE BACON AND HAM.

CUCUMBER & MINT SALAD

HARRAH'S LAKE TAHOE & HARVEYS LAKE TAHOE
EXECUTIVE CHEF JOE WELLS

This refreshing dish is derived from the famous Thai cucumber salad. At Harrah's Lake Tahoe and Harveys Lake Tahoe, it is served as a side dish for some of their Hawaiian fish specials. Chef Joe Wells advises how to vary the dish: "Sometimes, for a change, we mix it up and add julienned carrots and daikon."

4 cucumbers, peeled every other pass with a vegetable peeler, halved lengthwise, and seeded

1 white onion, halved and thinly sliced

10 radishes, thinly sliced

30 fresh mint leaves, coarsely chopped

20 fresh cilantro leaves, coarsely chopped

2 teaspoons red pepper flakes

1½ cups seasoned rice vinegar

8 butter leaf lettuce cups

Cut the cucumbers into diagonal slices. In a medium bowl, mix together all the ingredients except the leaf lettuce cups. Divide the mixture equally among the leaf lettuce cups and serve at once.

SERVES 8

HARRAH'S LAKE TAHOE WAS THE FIRST HOTEL IN THE WORLD TO FEATURE TWO FULL BATHROOMS IN EVERY ROOM.

FRESH MARKET POTATO SALAD

FRESH MARKET SQUARE BUFFET AT HARRAH'S CHEROKEE
EXECUTIVE CHEF KEITH ANDREASEN

When you visit the Fresh Market Square Buffet, you will encounter three things: great food, a friendly staff, and their famous potato salad. Chef Keith Andreasen says, "The chefs at Fresh Market Square Buffet have been making this salad since the day the buffet opened, and for more than ten years the guests have loved every bite of it."

1 pound Yukon gold potatoes, peeled and diced

¼ cup finely diced celery

¼ cup finely diced yellow onion

3 large eggs, hard-cooked and cut into ½-inch dice

½ cup sweet pickle relish

¾ cup mayonnaise

2 teaspoons salt

2 teaspoons ground white pepper

1 tablespoon diced pimiento

2 teaspoons minced fresh flat-leaf parsley

Put the potatoes in a medium saucepan of salted cold water. Bring to a boil and cook for 8 to 10 minutes, or until just tender. Drain.

In a large bowl, combine the potatoes, celery, onion, and eggs. Stir gently to mix. Gently stir in the sweet relish and mayonnaise, then the salt and pepper, pimientos, and parsley, mixing well. Cover and refrigerate for 1 hour before serving.

SERVES 4 TO 6

SALADS

APPLE & BLOOD ORANGE VINAIGRETTE OVER BIBB LETTUCE & WATERCRESS

HARRAH'S JOLIET
CHEF PETER JESCHKE

This is a lovely vinaigrette to use in late fall and winter when blood oranges are in season. The apple balances the acidity of the vinaigrette and complements the sliced apples, Gorgonzola, and walnuts in this satisfying salad.

APPLE & BLOOD ORANGE VINAIGRETTE

Juice of 1 blood orange

1 tablespoon Dijon mustard

½ Granny Smith apple, peeled, cored, and chopped

1 teaspoon minced fresh thyme

⅓ cup apple cider vinegar

⅔ cup extra-virgin olive oil

Salt and freshly ground pepper

Leaves from 2 heads Bibb lettuce

2 bunches watercress, stemmed

1 cup crumbled Gorgonzola cheese

1 Granny Smith apple, peeled, cored, and sliced

½ cup walnuts, toasted (see note)

SERVES 4

For the vinaigrette: In a blender or food processor, combine the orange juice, mustard, apple, and thyme and pulse for 15 seconds. Add the vinegar and pulse quickly. With the machine running, gradually add the oil in a thin stream to emulsify. Season with salt and pepper. Use now, or cover and refrigerate for up to 24 hours.

In a medium bowl, combine the lettuce and watercress. Use ½ cup of vinaigrette to toss and serve the remainder on the side. The vinaigrette may be kept refrigerated for up to 1 week. Divide the Gorgonzola, sliced apples, and toasted walnuts among the salads.

✦✦

Toasting nuts: Spread the nuts in a pie pan and toast in a preheated 350°F oven until fragrant, 5 to 8 minutes. Remove from the oven and pour into a bowl to let cool.

TOP 10 KNIVES
EVERY KITCHEN SHOULD HAVE

HARRAH'S ATLANTIC CITY

No chef, at home or in a professional kitchen, can execute even the most basic of tasks without the correct tools. And of all the tools used in the kitchen, knives are a hallmark of our profession. It is imperative to have a small arsenal of knives that will cover the many requirements of chopping, dicing, and slicing. A good knife essentially becomes an extension of your own hands.

The following is my dream team of knives that will be the foundation to your success in the kitchen.

1   A 10-inch chef's knife (also called a French knife): If you were only able to have one knife in your kitchen, this all-purpose culinary tool would be it.

2   A 3½-inch paring knife: This short knife is used for trimming and paring vegetables and fruits.

3   A 5- to 7-inch utility knife: This is a smaller, lighter chef's knife that is used for light cutting chores.

4   A 6-inch boning knife: As the name suggests, this rigid knife is used to separate raw meat from bones.

5   A 9-inch fillet knife: This flexible knife is perfect for filleting fish, both round and flat, and for steak cuts.

6   A 10- to 14-inch carving/scimitar knife: This knife usually has a long blade with a rounded tip and a fluted edge with hollow-ground ovals for easier slicing of cooked meats.

7   An 8½-inch bread knife: This serrated knife cuts soft and hard breads without damaging their structure.

8   A 7-inch santoku knife: The extremely sharp blade of this Japanese-style knife is tapered and looks similar to a cleaver. It is used for sushi cookery and precise slicing.

9   A 10- to 12-inch cleaver: This is a bone-breaking chopper.

10 A 12- to 16-inch sharpening steel: Although this is not a knife, it is a necessity. Sharp knives are the safest and easiest to use.

TOP 10 UTENSILS
EVERY KITCHEN SHOULD HAVE

BALLY'S LAS VEGAS AND PARIS LAS VEGAS

1   Paring knife: The most versatile knife in a chef's kitchen. It can be used to cut almost anything.

2   French knife: Also called a chef's knife, the French knife has a broad, tapered shape and fine edge and is perfect for chopping all types of food.

3   Digital scale: A digital scale is more accurate when weighing smaller amounts, and accuracy is everything in cooking.

4   Wooden spoon: The handle of a wooden spoon stays cool so you won't burn yourself as you could with a metal spoon.

5   Wire whisk: This hand whip can be used for everything from whipping egg whites to smoothing out sauces.

6   Kitchen tongs: Tongs are gentle on your food and will never pierce your steaks the way a fork will.

7   Corkscrew: This one is pretty self-explanatory: No corkscrew, no wine.

8   Vegetable peeler: Choose a swivel-head peeler, which cuts on both downward and upward strokes and gets the job done in half the time.

9   Offset spatula: An offset spatula is identical to the palette knife except that the blade is bent at a 90-degree angle from the handle. It is great for spreading, flipping, and lifting all types of foods.

10 Rolling pin: Every baker needs a good, sturdy rolling pin. Some of the best and most cherished are those handed down through the generations.

PECAN HERBED ORZO SALAD

HARRAH'S NORTH KANSAS CITY
CHEF ROY ASKREN

Guests at Harrah's North Kansas City come back multiple times to savor this pasta salad made with fresh orange juice, cranberries, and mint. Chef Roy Askren comments, "Our guests always ask how to make this salad at home for their families and parties."

3 quarts chicken stock

2 cups (14 ounces) orzo pasta

2 cups chopped pecans

1 shallot, minced

1 tablespoon minced garlic

1 orange, scrubbed and quartered

1 cup dried cranberries

2 tablespoons minced fresh chives

DRESSING

½ cup white wine vinegar

½ cup extra-virgin olive oil

½ cup fresh orange juice

¼ cup sugar

1 tablespoon Dijon mustard

Salt and freshly ground pepper

1 tablespoon minced fresh flat-leaf parsley

1 tablespoon minced fresh mint

2 tablespoons finely diced red bell pepper

SERVES 4 TO 6

In a large stockpot, bring the chicken stock to a boil. Reduce the heat to a low boil and add the orzo, stirring constantly to prevent the pasta from sticking. Add the pecans, shallot, garlic, and orange, continuing to stir the pasta to prevent sticking. Cook until al dente, 10 to 12 minutes. Drain and transfer to a bowl of ice water to cool for 1 to 2 minutes. Drain again for 10 minutes. Remove and discard the orange. Empty into a medium bowl and add the cranberries and chives, lightly tossing until blended. Set aside.

For the dressing: In a medium bowl, combine all the ingredients and whisk until thoroughly blended.

Add the dressing to the pasta mixture and toss to coat well. Garnish with the parsley, mint, and bell pepper. Let stand at room temperature for 1 to 2 hours before serving.

SALADS

62   63

FENNEL, ENDIVE & ARUGULA SALAD
WITH A CITRUS-BASIL VINAIGRETTE & PARMESAN CHEESE TWISTS

REFLECTIONS CAFÉ AT HARRAH'S RESORT ATLANTIC CITY
CHEF JAMES COOMBS

Reflections Café is regarded by guests as one of the best eateries in Atlantic City, and this salad's sophisticated blend of flavors and textures is one of the reasons. Chef James Coombs explains, "Our guests would always request this salad after we offered it as a special. The fresh fennel with its licorice flavor balances the sharpness of the endive and arugula greens. This salad can be a great starter for an Italian dinner or be served as a luncheon meal."

PARMESAN CHEESE TWISTS

½ sheet thawed frozen puff pastry dough

1 large egg, beaten

½ cup grated Parmesan cheese

¼ cup minced fresh flat-leaf parsley

Coarsely ground pepper

1 fennel bulb, cored and thinly sliced

Leaves from 2 heads Belgium endive, thinly sliced

4 cups arugula leaves

CITRUS-BASIL VINAIGRETTE

¼ cup fresh orange juice

¼ cup fresh lime juice

¼ cup fresh lemon juice

1 tablespoon Dijon mustard

¼ bunch basil, stemmed

2 tablespoons honey

½ cup extra-virgin olive oil

1 cup canola oil

Salt and freshly ground pepper

8 thin slices prosciutto

8 thin slices Manchego cheese

SERVES 4

For the cheese twists: Preheat the oven to 375°F. Lay the puff pastry dough on a work surface and lightly roll it out with a rolling pin. Using a fork, dock the dough all over. Brush the dough with the egg. Sprinkle the Parmesan cheese, parsley, and pepper over it. Fold the dough in half and roll it lightly with the rolling pin. Cut the dough into 8-inch crosswise strips about ¾ inch thick and twist each one into a spiral. Place the twists 2 inches apart on a baking sheet. Bake for 12 minutes, or until golden brown. Remove from the oven and transfer the twists to a wire rack.

In a large bowl, combine the fennel, endive, and arugula.

For the vinaigrette: In a blender, combine all three juices, the mustard, basil, and honey and blend. With the machine running, gradually add the olive oil and canola oil until emulsified. Stir in salt and pepper.

To serve, alternately lay 2 slices each of prosciutto and Manchego cheese on each plate. Add 2 cups of the vinaigrette to the salad greens and toss lightly. Place 1½ to 2 cups of the salad over each serving of prosciutto and Manchego cheese. Garnish with cheese twists.

REFLECTIONS CAFÉ HAS BEEN VOTED THE BEST CAFÉ IN ATLANTIC CITY FOR THE PAST THREE YEARS BY *CASINO PLAYER* MAGAZINE.

GARDEN BASKET-WEAVE SALAD

WITH HEIRLOOM TOMATOES & FRESH MOZZARELLA

HARRAH'S METROPOLIS
EXECUTIVE CHEF JON M. KELL

Woven thin slices of carrot, squash, and cucumber make a cunning presentation for this salad, which will allow each of your guests to have his or her own edible favor.

4 yellow squash

4 zucchini

2 cucumbers

2 carrots, peeled

4 cups arugula

4 heirloom tomatoes, quartered

Four 3-ounce fresh mozzarella balls, sliced and halved

½ cup finely sliced fresh basil

4 tablespoons extra-virgin olive oil

4 tablespoons balsamic vinegar

SERVES 4

Using a mandoline or a large sharp knife, cut the squash, zucchini, cucumber, and carrots into paper-thin lengthwise slices. Cut the squash and zucchini strips in half lengthwise. Lay 4 yellow squash slices next to each other on a cutting board with the short ends facing you and the skin sides facing left. Take a slice of zucchini with the long side facing you and the skin side facing away from you. Weave the zucchini into the squash as if you were making a woven lattice pie pastry top by lifting the first slice of yellow squash and placing the zucchini beneath it. Lay the zucchini on top of the second slice of yellow squash. Lift the third slice of yellow squash and lay the zucchini under it. Repeat until the zucchini has gone over, then under, each of the yellow squash slices. Repeat with slices of zucchini until a woven sheet is formed.

Next, place one cucumber slice in the center of the sheet. Place 2 carrot slices in the center of the sheet on top of the cucumber. Place some arugula on the sheet. Roll up the sheet and place it seam side down. Cut each end on the diagonal and transfer the roll to a salad plate. Repeat with the remaining sliced vegetables and arugula.

Place 4 tomato quarters and 2 cheese slices on each plate. Sprinkle with the basil. Drizzle each serving with 1 tablespoon oil and 1 tablespoon balsamic vinegar.

FRIED GREEN TOMATOES

THE RANGE STEAKHOUSE & BAR AT TUNICA ROADHOUSE CASINO & HOTEL
EXECUTIVE CHEF & DIRECTOR OF FOOD & BEVERAGE CHRISTOPHER J. HENCYK

In this fabled Southern dish from Tunica Roadhouse Casino & Hotel in the heart of Mississippi, fried tomatoes are accented with mustard vinaigrette and onion jam. Chef Christopher J. Hencyk sums up this treat, "Fix ya up some of mama's sweet tea, fry ya up some tomatoes, and watch the sunset. What more can you ask for?"

MUSTARD VINAIGRETTE

½ tablespoon coarse-grain mustard

1 tablespoon minced shallot

½ teaspoon sugar

⅛ teaspoon salt

Pinch of freshly ground pepper

2 tablespoons white wine vinegar

3 tablespoons extra-virgin olive oil

4 firm green (unripe) tomatoes, cut into crosswise slices

Salt and freshly ground pepper

1 cup finely ground cornmeal

1 teaspoon sweet paprika

2 large eggs

Canola oil, as needed

1 cup spinach leaves

1 slice applewood-smoked bacon, cooked and crumbled

¼ cup Onion Jam (see recipe facing page)

SERVES 4

For the vinaigrette: In a small bowl, whisk together the mustard, shallot, sugar, salt, pepper, and vinegar. Gradually whisk in the oil until emulsified.

Sprinkle the tomato slices with salt and pepper and set aside. In a shallow bowl, combine the cornmeal and paprika. In another shallow bowl, beat the eggs.

In a large, heavy skillet, heat ½ inch of the oil over medium-high heat. Coat the tomato slices in the egg, then dredge them in the cornmeal mixture. Fry the tomatoes in batches until nicely browned, about 2 minutes per side. Using a slotted spatula, transfer to paper towels to drain.

In a large bowl, toss the spinach in 2 tablespoons of the vinaigrette. Arrange the tomatoes on a plate and put the tossed spinach on top of them. Sprinkle some of the bacon pieces over the spinach and dot the spinach with spoonfuls of Onion Jam. Pass the remaining vinaigrette alongside. Serve at once.

THE SHERATON HOTEL & CASINO, NOW TUNICA ROADHOUSE CASINO & HOTEL, WAS AMONG THE FIRST CASINOS TO ADOPT THE DOCKSIDE ARCHITECTURAL APPROACH PREVALENT AMONG MISSISSIPPI CASINOS TODAY. EARLY MISSISSIPPI CASINOS WERE ACTUAL WORKING RIVERBOATS.

ONION JAM

8 ounces red onions, very thinly sliced

2 cups dry red wine

2 tablespoons honey

1 tablespoon chopped fresh thyme

2 tablespoons red wine vinegar

1 tablespoon water (optional)

Salt and pepper

In a large skillet, combine the onions, wine, honey, and thyme. Bring to a boil over medium-high heat. Reduce the heat to medium-low and simmer, stirring occasionally, until the wine is almost absorbed, about 55 minutes. Mix in the red wine vinegar. Simmer, stirring frequently, for 10 minutes to blend the flavors, adding water as needed and stirring often (the onions will still be slightly crunchy). Season with salt and pepper. Remove from the heat. Use now, or cover and refrigerate for up to 3 days.

Before using, rewarm over medium heat until just warm, adding more water by tablespoonfuls if the jam is dry.

MAKES ½ CUP

TOP 10 TIPS
FOR PREPARING MEMORABLE, FAST, AND EASY MEALS

TUNICA ROADHOUSE CASINO & HOTEL

1   Involve the entire family in the preparation of the meal. You'll have more fun and share quality time with loved ones while cutting down on the preparation time.

2   Use your slow cooker.

3   Keep the total number of ingredients in each dish to six or fewer.

4   Create or use recipes that can be prepared in one pot or pan.

5   Plan your menu for the entire week and utilize leftovers for lunch or breakfast.

6   Make use of pantry foods, such as pasta and rice, as a base and vary the sauce, vegetable, or protein.

7   Use leftover fresh vegetables and meats to create an awesome salad.

8   Chop vegetables or meats in the morning or the day before your meal.

9   Use high-quality canned, frozen, or packaged vegetables or fruits to save preparation time.

10 Simply adding a single fresh herb or glaze of butter can bring a whole new dimension to a meal without a lot of additional work.

TOP 10 TIPS
FOR CREATING A BALANCED DISH
THAT YOUR GUESTS WILL LOVE

HORSESHOE HAMMOND

1 Budget: First, consider what you are willing to spend on food.

2 Know your guests: Ask yourself such questions as: What are my guests' likes and dislikes? Do any of my guests have allergies? Are any of my guests vegetarians?

3 Menu planning: Creating a dish can be fun and challenging at the same time. Many factors should be considered first. For example: What is the occasion? What season of the year is it? What foods are now in season?

4 Variety: Because we all have different tastes, you need to ensure that you have a good variety of dishes on your menu.

5 Freshness: The freshness of your ingredients is the key to a quality and memorable meal.

6 Spices: Choose the correct spices to complement your ingredients.

7 Cooking equipment: Make sure you have the right equipment to cook the meal you have in mind.

8 Wine selection: This could make or break your dinner. The flavor profiles of the wine and the food should complement each other.

9 Timing: Timing when your food is ready to be served is a vital part of preparing a great meal, especially if the menu includes dishes that need to be served at once.

10 Presentation! Presentation! Presentation! Always remember, people eat with their eyes first. If the food looks great, it will taste great.

ROASTED PEPPER ANTIPASTO

CAESARS ATLANTIC CITY
CHEF DE CUISINE JOHN MEJLAK

An antipasto (Italian for "before the meal") is a first course that traditionally combines several colorful ingredients. For your next dinner party, dazzle your guests with this vibrant array of red, yellow, and green bell peppers. Chef John Mejlak comments, "This is a nice, easy salad that I like to make for my family."

3 red bell peppers

2 yellow bell peppers

2 green bell peppers

2 tablespoons balsamic vinegar

5 tablespoons extra-virgin olive oil

Tabasco sauce

Kosher salt and freshly ground pepper

Four 12-ounce cans artichoke hearts, drained and quartered

½ cup oil-packed sun-dried tomatoes, drained and julienned

1 garlic clove, thinly sliced

8 basil leaves, stemmed and coarsely chopped

SERVES 6

Preheat the oven to 400°F. Line a baking sheet with aluminum foil and oil the foil. Place the peppers on the prepared pan and roast for 45 minutes, or until blackened. Put the peppers in a medium bowl, cover, and let cool for 15 minutes.

Meanwhile, in a small bowl, whisk together the balsamic vinegar, oil, and Tabasco sauce to taste. Season with salt and pepper.

Peel, seed, and devein the peppers. Cut them into strips about 1 inch wide. In a large bowl, combine the peppers with the artichokes, tomatoes, and garlic. Pour the dressing over and toss gently to coat. Serve garnished with the basil.

FIORE TOMATO CAPRESE

FIORE AT HARRAH'S RINCON CASINO & RESORT
EXECUTIVE CHEF VESA LEPPALA

Fiore Tomato Caprese is Fiore's variation of a classic salad from the island of Capri. Serve this at the height of summer, when tomatoes are at their most flavorful, with the best mozzarella you can find.

BALSAMIC REDUCTION

1 cup balsamic vinegar

¼ cup ruby port

**4 ripe tomatoes, cut into
¼-inch-thick slices**

Salt and freshly cracked peppercorns

12 fresh basil leaves

**10 ounces fresh mozzarella,
cut into ¼-inch-thick slices**

3 tablespoons extra-virgin olive oil

SERVES 4

For the balsamic reduction: In a small nonreactive saucepan, combine the vinegar and port. Bring to a boil over medium heat, reduce to a simmer, and cook until reduced by half. Remove from the heat and let cool. The mixture will thicken as it cools. Pour into a squeeze bottle and set aside at room temperature.

To serve, place 1 slice of tomato on a plate and sprinkle with a little salt and pepper. Layer the tomato slice with a basil leaf, then a slice of mozzarella. Repeat the process to make three layers. Sprinkle the top layer with salt and pepper and drizzle with the balsamic reduction, then the olive oil. Repeat to make 4 servings. Serve at once.

3
SOUPS

LEEK, SUN-DRIED TOMATO, SHIITAKE MUSHROOM & CHAMPAGNE SOUP

K-PAUL'S LOUISIANA KITCHEN
CHEF PAUL PRUDHOMME

This is a unique recipe of flavors, which in concert create a rich and mouthwatering soup suitable for the chilly fall and winter months. The splash of Champagne adds a festive touch!

Note: Chef Prudhomme's sauces and seasonings are available at www.ChefPaul.com.

½ cup dry-packed sun-dried tomatoes

2 pounds leeks

3 tablespoons unsalted butter

1 cup chopped onions

1½ tablespoons Chef Paul Prudhomme's Vegetable Magic (see note)

4 cups shiitake mushrooms, sliced

¾ cup Champagne or dry sparkling wine (optional)

2 cups unsalted chicken stock

2 cups heavy cream

1 cup shredded Gouda cheese

SERVES 8

Soak the sun-dried tomatoes in warm water for 30 minutes. Drain and julienne. Trim off the dark green leaves (leaving the white and light green parts) and the root ends of the leeks and discard. Split the remaining leeks in half lengthwise and wash thoroughly under running water, making sure that all the dirt is removed from between the sections. Slice the leek halves crosswise into very thin half-rounds. You should have about 3 cups.

In a medium saucepan, melt the butter over medium-high heat. Add the leeks and onions and cook, stirring frequently, until the onions are wilted and soft, about 8 minutes. Add the Vegetable Magic and stir well. Continue to cook until the seasoning begins to darken slightly, about 2 minutes. Add the shiitake mushrooms and the sun-dried tomatoes. Cook, stirring frequently, until the mushrooms begin to darken, about 4 minutes. Add ¼ cup of the Champagne, if using, and stir to scrape up the browned bits from the bottom of the pan. Add the chicken stock. Bring to a boil, then reduce the heat to medium-low and simmer for 20 minutes. Add the cream, stir well, and return to a boil. Reduce heat and simmer until the soup has reduced slightly, about 10 minutes. Gradually stir in the cheese and continue stirring until it has melted. Add the remaining ½ cup of the Champagne and stir briefly. Remove from the heat and serve.

GRILLED SHRIMP GAZPACHO

RESERVE AT HARRAH'S JOLIET
CHEF DE CUISINE TYE NIELSEN

Gazpacho, that hot-weather standby, is here made more substantial with the addition of grilled shrimp. The simple flavors blend together to create a harmony of vegetables and cool broth, leaving you fulfilled and invigorated. Look for the best vine-ripened tomatoes to make this refreshing dish.

Note: The gazpacho needs to be prepared the day before serving.

GAZPACHO

1 small to medium red onion, diced

2 small celery stalks, diced

3 small to medium tomatoes, diced

15 red grapes

Grated zest and juice of 1 lime

Juice of 1 lemon

3 fresh basil leaves, chopped

½ bunch cilantro, stemmed and chopped

½ cup sweet white wine

4 cups water

Salt and freshly ground pepper

2 garlic cloves, crushed

3 tablespoons canola oil

8 to 12 jumbo shrimp, shelled and deveined

5 cilantro sprigs for garnish

SERVES 4 TO 6

For the gazpacho: In a large glass or ceramic bowl, combine the vegetables, grapes, lime zest, lime and lemon juices, basil, chopped cilantro, wine, water, and a pinch of salt. Cover and refrigerate overnight. Season with salt and pepper.

Soak 2 wooden skewers in water to cover for 30 minutes. Prepare a hot fire in a charcoal grill, preheat a gas grill to high, or heat a grill pan over high heat. In a medium bowl, combine the garlic and oil. Add the shrimp and toss to coat. Thread the shrimp on the skewers and grill them for 2 to 3 minutes on each side, or until evenly pink.

To serve, ladle the gazpacho into martini glasses or bowls and top each serving with 2 to 3 shrimp. Garnish with the sprigs of cilantro.

THE RESERVE AND MOSAIC RESTAURANTS
AT HARRAH'S JOLIET
SUPPORT CHARITIES SUCH AS BIG BROTHERS
BIG SISTERS AND MARCH OF DIMES.

HARRAH'S STEAK HOUSE CREAMY FIVE-ONION SOUP

HARRAH'S STEAK HOUSE AT HARRAH'S RENO
EXECUTIVE CHEF KLAUS FEYERSINGER

Voted Reno's No. 1 Steak House, Harrah's is not only legendary for its steaks, but also for its side dishes and soups. Five different members of the onion family go into this soup, which is complemented with sweet basil and Burgundy wine and served in a dramatic presentation. Chef Klaus Feyersinger explains, "This longtime favorite will start your dining experience off right. The creamy, hot soup is ladled into a hollowed-out colossal onion and crowned with a golden brown Swiss cheese crust. This is Harrah's Steak House's most requested menu item. One taste and you'll know why."

1 cup (2 sticks) unsalted butter

1 large white onion, julienned

1 red onion, julienned

4 shallots, finely diced

1½ cups chopped green onions, white and light green parts only

1 small leek, white part only, cut into crosswise slices and washed well

1 tablespoon dried basil

½ teaspoon freshly ground pepper

1 cup all-purpose flour

1 cup Burgundy or other dry red wine

8 cups beef consommé

2 cups heavy cream

8 large onions, hollowed out (optional)

8 large round croutons, 2 inches in diameter

8 slices Swiss cheese

8 slices Gruyère cheese

SERVES 8

Preheat the oven to 450°F. In a large stockpot, melt the butter over medium heat and sauté the white onion, red onion, shallots, ½ cup of the green onions, the leek, basil, and pepper until the onions are tender, about 5 minutes. Stir in the flour and cook, stirring constantly, for 1 minute. Add the wine, consommé, and cream. Bring to a boil, then reduce the heat to a simmer and cook, stirring frequently, for 10 minutes.

Ladle the soup into the onions or ovenproof soup bowls. Top each with a crouton and 1 slice of each cheese. Bake for 10 minutes, or until the cheese is melted and browned. Remove from the oven, sprinkle with the remaining green onions, and serve.

HARRAH'S STEAK HOUSE HAS HELD THE FOUR-DIAMOND RATING FROM THE AMERICAN AUTOMOBILE ASSOCIATION (AAA) LONGER THAN ANY OTHER RESTAURANT IN RENO.

WILD MUSHROOM CHOWDER

CAESARS WINDSOR
EXECUTIVE CHEF PATRICK MCCLARY

Add a woodsy aura to your entertaining with this hearty chowder, which will have mushroom lovers coming back again and again. Don't let the long list of ingredients intimidate you; the preparation is minimal and the result is an intensely flavorful, satisfying dish.

¼ cup dried morels

¾ cup dried porcini mushrooms, or 2 tablespoons porcini powder

8 cups chicken stock

⅓ cup unsalted butter

4 shallots, minced

2 garlic cloves, chopped

½ cup all-purpose flour

¼ cup canola oil

1½ ounces oyster mushrooms, sliced

1½ ounces shiitake mushrooms, stemmed and sliced

1½ ounces chanterelle mushrooms, sliced

¾ cup dry white wine

¼ cup cooked wild rice

½ cup diced cooked potatoes

¼ cup cooked black beans

¼ cup cooked white beans

3 tablespoons honey

1 tablespoon minced fresh rosemary

2 cups heavy cream

Salt and cracked pepper

SERVES 10

Soak the morels in warm water to cover for 30 minutes, then drain and slice. In a blender, grind the dried porcini to a powder. Bring the chicken stock to a boil, reduce the heat, and maintain at a simmer.

In a large soup pot, melt the butter over medium heat and sauté the shallots and garlic until the shallots are translucent, about 3 minutes. Stir in the flour and cook, stirring constantly, for about 3 minutes; do not brown.

Gradually whisk the hot chicken stock into the flour mixture. Reduce the heat to medium-low and stir in the porcini powder. Let the soup simmer.

In a large skillet, heat the oil over medium-high heat and sauté the oyster, shiitake, and chanterelle mushrooms for 5 to 7 minutes, or until tender. Stir in the morels, then add the wine, stirring to scrape up the browned bits from the bottom of the pan. Cook for 10 minutes.

Add the mushrooms and wine mixture to the simmering soup base, reduce the heat to a simmer, and cook for 45 minutes. Add the rice, potatoes, beans, honey, rosemary, and cream. Cook for 15 minutes. Season with salt and pepper. Serve in deep soup bowls.

TOP 10 HERBS EVERY KITCHEN SHOULD HAVE AND WHY

1 Thyme: My favorite herb, thyme, is used in a wide range of dishes, including stews, meats, poultry, and seafood. Thyme adds a savory touch to every dish and is a standard ingredient in bouquet garnis. It can be added to hot teas to help get rid of a cough and bronchitis, or to various cocktails to bring out savory notes. Buy a plant and keep it on your back porch or in a sunny window.

2 Basil: Basil adds a fresh note to every dish made with it. The leaves can be stacked, rolled, and cut into fine shreds, or used whole or minced. Add it to food just before serving, as basil is pungent and delicate. Basil can also be used as a garnish and is even added to many drinks in Asian cultures, where it's noted for its medicinal properties.

3 Chives: Fresh and delicate, chives instantly remind me of springtime on the farm. This herb will add a light touch of onion flavor to your cooking. Minced chives are added to sauces, soups, potatoes, and seafood just before serving and are very often used as a garnish.

4 Cilantro: Also known as fresh coriander, cilantro adds an undeniable energy to every dish it's used in, and perhaps most famously to many salsas. I have a cilantro plant in my yard and use it for fruit salsas, seafood, and my favorite spicy Vietnamese soup, pho. When the plant flowers and seeds, I collect the seeds and dry them. I then grind the seeds and use the coriander to flavor seafood and sauces.

5 Flat-leaf, or Italian, parsley: I love this herb for its deep color and palate-cleansing notes. My mother used this herb in her salads. Flat-leaf parsley has more flavor than the more common curly-leaf parsley.

6 Bay leaf: Bay leaves come from California, from the California laurel tree, or from Turkey. The ones from California have a stronger flavor. Although the prized, distinct flavor develops after several weeks of drying, I like to buy this herb fresh and freeze it. I use bay leaves daily, in stocks, étouffée, gumbos, jambalaya, red beans, and much more. This hardy leaf should be added early in the cooking process to develop its flavor. Be sure to remove it before serving the dish.

7 Rosemary: Use this highly aromatic herb with assertively flavored foods like lamb and game. Rosemary can be overpowering, so use it lightly. I like to keep the branches and use them for flavorful skewers in grilling and roasting.

8 Thai basil: This basil has small leaves, purple stems, and flavors of licorice and mint. It is used in Thai dishes and is a refreshing addition to the Vietnamese soup pho; it also adds a fresh note to fried rice and stir-fried noodles.

9 Chervil: Also known as gourmet's parsley and garden chervil, this delicate herb adds a faint licorice flavor to seafood, omelets, soups, salads, and vegetables.

10 Spearmint: Spearmint has serrated, wrinkly leaves and a milder flavor than peppermint. Use it in cooking, to garnish desserts, and to make the perfect mojito.

PICKLES' FAMOUS MUSHROOM-BARLEY SOUP

PICKLES AT BALLY'S ATLANTIC CITY
CHEF ROLF BECHTOLD

Straight from Atlantic City's favorite deli, this hearty soup is one of the town's favorite indulgences. A rustic mixture of garden vegetables and comforting grain, it's somehow right at home among the bright lights of the big city.

5 tablespoons unsalted butter

2 cups pearl barley

1½ cups finely diced onions

1½ cups finely diced celery

1½ cups finely diced carrots

1 pound white mushrooms, cleaned and sliced

1 bay leaf

1 tablespoon dried thyme

8 cups chicken stock

Salt and freshly ground pepper

SERVES 8 TO 10

In a large soup pot, melt the butter over medium heat. Add the barley and sauté for 5 minutes. Add the onions, celery, and carrots and sauté until tender, 4 to 5 minutes. Add the mushrooms, bay leaf, thyme, and stock. Bring the mixture to a boil, then reduce the heat to a simmer. Cook until the barley is tender, 20 to 25 minutes. Season with salt and pepper.

SEVEN STARS SPLIT PEA SOUP

FRESH MARKET BUFFET AT HARRAH'S NORTH KANSAS CITY
CHEF JEFF CRAIG

This mouthwatering take on a classic soup is a favorite at Harrah's North Kansas City. Chef Jeff Craig says, "Our Seven Stars Split Pea Soup is not only fast to make and tastes great, but it's a great recipe for cold weather."

1 tablespoon olive oil

2 cups chopped yellow onions

Salt and freshly ground black pepper

Red pepper flakes

1 tablespoon minced garlic

1 bay leaf

1 pound green split peas, picked over and rinsed

8 cups chicken stock

1 cup milk

SERVES 6 TO 8

In a large soup pot, heat the oil over medium heat. Add the onions and salt, black pepper, and red pepper flakes to taste. Sauté for 2 minutes. Add the garlic, bay leaf, and split peas and cook, stirring, for 1 minute. Add the stock and bring to a boil, then reduce the heat to a simmer and cook, stirring occasionally until the peas are tender, about 45 minutes. Remove from the heat and let cool slightly. Remove the bay leaf and discard. Add the milk. Working in batches, purée in a blender until smooth. Taste and adjust the seasoning. Serve hot.

CLASSIC GUMBO

HARRAH'S LOUISIANA DOWNS
EXECUTIVE CHEF J. RYAN GILLESPIE

Gumbo is eaten year-round in Louisiana. Chef J. Ryan Gillespie explains, "This is an item that we offer every day. We couldn't pull it off the menu even if we wanted to. This recipe isn't considered a traditional gumbo due to the fact that it has both okra and filé. Normally, it is one or the other, but we have such die-hard gumbo connoisseurs here that we like to keep them all happy—no matter their preference." He also warns, "Be careful not to burn the roux, as a large part of this classic dish's flavor comes from it."

¾ cup canola oil or ¾ cup (1½ sticks) unsalted butter

¾ cup all-purpose flour

3 bell peppers, seeded, deveined, and diced

1 large tomato, seeded and diced

½ cup diced onion

½ cup diced celery

1 tablespoon plus 2 teaspoons filé powder, preferably Cajun Chef brand

4 bay leaves

1 tablespoon crawfish boil, preferably LaDon's brand

1 tablespoon Durkee Hot Sauce or other hot sauce

1 tablespoon Worcestershire sauce

½ tablespoon minced garlic

2 teaspoons red pepper flakes

2 teaspoons onion powder

7 cups chicken stock

8 ounces medium shrimp, shelled and deveined

8 ounces smoked sausage, cooked and sliced

8 ounces okra, sliced

8 ounces diced cooked chicken meat, diced

Steamed white rice for serving

SERVES 10 TO 12

In a heavy, medium saucepan, heat the oil or melt the butter over medium heat and stir in the flour until blended. Cook, stirring frequently, until the roux has turned a dark brownish red and has a nutty fragrance, about 25 minutes; take care not to burn. Remove from the heat and set aside.

In a large soup pot, combine the bell peppers, tomato, onion, celery, seasonings, and stock. Bring to a low boil and cook until the vegetables are very tender, about 20 minutes. Stir in the roux until thoroughly blended. Reduce the heat to a simmer and cook for about 30 minutes, or until thickened and flavorful.

Stir in the shrimp, sausage, and okra; cook for about 3 minutes, or until the shrimp is evenly pink. Stir in the chicken and cook another minute or two until heated through.

Serve in deep bowls, spooned over the rice.

FOOD USAGE PER YEAR AT
HARRAH'S LOUISIANA DOWNS:
8,875 GALLONS OF MILK,
2,184 GALLONS OF VANILLA ICE CREAM,
2,063 GALLONS OF KETCHUP,
1,208 GALLONS OF MAYONNAISE,
AND 75,420 EGGS.

GUMBO

THE RANGE STEAKHOUSE & BAR AT TUNICA ROADHOUSE CASINO & HOTEL
EXECUTIVE CHEF & DIRECTOR OF FOOD & BEVERAGE CHRISTOPHER J. HENCYK

Chef Christopher J. Hencyk's version of Southern gumbo earned a top award at the 2008 Porter-Leath Rajun Cajun Crawfish Festival in Memphis. One taste, and you'll know why this distinctive blending of flavors is a winner.

¾ cup canola oil

¾ cup all-purpose flour

½ cup (1 stick) unsalted butter

1 green bell pepper, seeded, deveined, and diced

1 white onion, diced

2 celery stalks, diced

5 garlic cloves, chopped

1 teaspoon dried basil

1 teaspoon dried thyme

1 teaspoon dried oregano

1 bay leaf

1 teaspoon cayenne pepper

1 tablespoon Tabasco sauce

2 teaspoons Worcestershire sauce

2 tablespoons seafood base

2 tablespoons chicken base

1 teaspoon crab boil (liquid)

1 teaspoon filé powder

¼ pound shredded cooked chicken

¾ pound andouille sausage

¼ pound crawfish tail meat

1¼ pounds shrimp meat (bay shrimp)

½ pound lump crabmeat, picked over for shell

2 dozen oysters, shucked

One 14-ounce can crushed tomatoes

1 pound frozen okra

3 quarts water

Salt and freshly ground pepper

Steamed white rice for serving

SERVES 12 AS A MAIN COURSE

In a medium saucepan, heat the oil over medium heat and gradually stir in the flour. Cook, stirring frequently, until well browned, about 20 minutes; the roux should have a rich, nutty aroma. Remove from the heat and set aside.

In a large soup pot, melt the butter over medium heat and sauté the pepper, onion, and celery until the onion is translucent, about 3 minutes. Add the garlic, herbs, cayenne, Tabasco, Worcestershire, bases, crab boil, filé powder, chicken, sausage, seafood, tomatoes, and okra and cook for 10 minutes. Add the water and bring to a boil. Stir in the roux until smooth. Season with salt and pepper. Reduce the heat to a simmer and cook for 30 minutes.

Serve in deep bowls, spooned over the rice.

OF THE NINE CASINO BRANDS CURRENTLY OPERATING IN TUNICA, TUNICA ROADHOUSE CASINO & HOTEL WAS THE FIFTH TO OPEN ITS DOORS, IN 1994, AS THE SHERATON HOTEL & CASINO.

NEW ORLEANS GUMBO

THE BUFFET AT HARRAH'S AT HARRAH'S NEW ORLEANS
CHEF HOYCE OATIS

Chef Hoyce Oatis says, "When you talk about Southern cuisine, gumbo is usually the theme. This recipe is one of our most famous and tastiest delights, and can be served as a first, second, or third course. Gumbo is on every menu of all New Orleans restaurants and is truly the favorite meal of many local households."

½ cup canola oil for frying

2 fresh or frozen blue crabs

¾ cup (1½ sticks) unsalted butter

1¼ cups all-purpose flour

1 small onion, diced

½ large bell pepper, seeded, deveined, and diced

2 celery stalks, diced

⅓ cup tomato paste

1 cup canned crushed tomatoes

1 bay leaf

½ tablespoon dried thyme

8 cups shrimp stock (page 202)

4 ounces chicken gizzards, halved

¼ cup diced pickle meat (pickled pork) or tasso, sliced

4 ounces smoked sausage

1 cup sliced okra

½ cup filé powder

¼ cup water

8 ounces medium shrimp, shelled and deveined

Salt and freshly ground pepper

Steamed white rice for serving

SERVES 8

In a large sauté pan, heat the oil over low heat and fry the crabs until golden brown, about 2 minutes on each side. Remove from the heat and set aside.

In a large soup pot, melt the butter over low heat. Gradually stir in the flour and continue to cook the roux, stirring constantly, until it becomes the color of peanut butter. Stir in the onion, bell pepper, and celery, mixing well, then the tomato paste, tomatoes, bay leaf, thyme, and shrimp stock. Add the crabs, then the chicken gizzards and pickle meat. Stir very well and let simmer for 30 minutes. Add the smoked sausage and okra. Increase the heat to medium-high and bring to a rolling boil. Mix the filé powder with the water and pour it into the boiling pot. Add the shrimp. Stir for 2 minutes, then season with salt and pepper.

Serve in deep bowls spooned over the rice.

LOCATED IN THE HEART OF THE CRESCENT CITY, STEPS FROM THE HISTORIC FRENCH QUARTER, HARRAH'S NEW ORLEANS CASINO RIVALS THE GRANDEUR OF A VEGAS-STYLE CASINO. THE SOLE LAND-BASED CASINO IN DOWNTOWN NEW ORLEANS, WITH MORE THAN 2,100 OF THE NEWEST SLOTS, IT HOSTS ACTION-PACKED TABLE GAMES TWENTY-FOUR HOURS A DAY EVERY DAY OF THE WEEK.

BEEF & ONION SOUP
WITH SHORT RIB CROUTONS & FIVE-ONION SALAD

THE STEAKHOUSE AT HARRAH'S RESORT ATLANTIC CITY
CHEF RICHARD LEADBETTER

Chef Richard Leadbetter says, "One of my favorite cuts of beef is the short rib. The rich baritone flavors that are derived from the short ribs make for robust stocks and tender beef. The combination of a deconstructed onion soup of hearty broth, crispy crostini, pulled short rib meat, and onion salad takes the traditional French onion soup to the next level. Served as a soup and salad course or as a meal, this combination will always satisfy."

2 pounds bone-in beef short ribs

Kosher salt and freshly ground pepper

2 cups all-purpose flour

1 cup olive oil

1 cup diced celery

2 pounds sweet white onions, such as Vidalia, sliced, plus 1 cup diced white sweet onion

1 cup diced carrots

6 garlic cloves

3 cups dry red wine

2 cups tomato juice

8 cups beef stock

8 thyme sprigs

1 rosemary sprig

2 cups dry sherry

FIVE-ONION SALAD

2 shallots, finely shaved

1 small bunch chives, minced

1 tablespoon finely chopped red onion

2 green onions, green parts only, julienned

1 tablespoon finely chopped sweet white onion, such as Vidalia

1 tablespoon minced fresh flat-leaf parsley

1 tablespoon extra-virgin olive oil

Salt and freshly ground black pepper

SERVES 8

CROUTONS

1 loaf French or Italian bread

Olive oil for brushing

2 cups shredded white Cheddar cheese

Preheat the oven to 300°F. Prepare the short ribs by cutting between each bone to separate them. Season with salt and pepper. Dredge each piece of short ribs in the flour and set aside.

In a large, heavy sauté pan, heat ½ cup of the olive oil over medium-high heat until shimmering. Sear the short ribs on all sides until well browned. Transfer the short ribs to a small roasting pan.

Immediately add the celery, the 1 cup diced onions, the carrots, and garlic to the sauté pan that the short ribs were seared in. Sauté the mixture over medium heat for 10 minutes, or until caramelized. Add 2 cups of the red wine and cook to reduce by half. Add the tomato juice and 3 cups of the beef stock. Simmer the mixture for about 5 minutes. Add 4 sprigs of the thyme and the rosemary.

Pour the braising liquid over the seared short ribs in the roasting pan. Cover the pan with aluminum foil and braise in the oven for at least 4 hours, or until the meat falls off the bone. Remove the short ribs from the braising liquid and let cool to the touch.

Pull the meat from the ribs, being careful not to pull the gristly part close to the bone. Add some of the braising liquid to the pulled meat. Strain the braising liquid and set aside.

In a large, heavy soup pot, heat the remaining ½ cup olive oil over high heat and sauté the 2 pounds sliced onions, stirring occasionally, until caramelized, about 10 minutes. Add the remaining 1 cup red wine and the sherry, and cook to reduce by half. Add the remaining beef stock and the reserved braising liquid. Let the mixture simmer for about 30 minutes. Add the remaining thyme sprigs. Taste and adjust the seasoning.

For the salad: In a medium bowl, combine all the ingredients and toss to coat.

For the croutons: Preheat the oven to 325°F. Cut the bread into eight to ten ¼-inch-thick slices. Brush the slices with the olive oil and season with salt and pepper. Place on a baking sheet and bake for 15 minutes, or until crisp. Remove from the oven.

Increase the oven temperature to 375°F. Top each crouton with some pulled short rib and Cheddar cheese. Bake at 375°F for 20 minutes, or until golden brown.

To serve, ladle the soup into deep soup bowls. Place a crouton on top of each. Garnish the croutons with the salad and serve at once.

CHICKEN & SHRIMP JAMBALAYA

FRENCH QUARTER BUFFET AT SHOWBOAT ATLANTIC CITY
CHEF TODD BANNAN & CHEF ARMANDO CORTES

Like gumbo, jambalaya is one of Louisiana's culinary superstars. The co-creator of this one, chef Todd Bannan, explains, "It is believed that the word 'jambalaya' comes from the French word *jambon*, meaning 'ham'; the Acadian language, where everything is *à la*; and the African *ya*, meaning 'rice.' Most purists believe that a jambalaya should be brown in color." In this recipe, the color is achieved by browning the sausage and the chicken in a cast-iron Dutch oven.

2 boneless, skinless chicken thighs, diced

1 teaspoon dried oregano

1 teaspoon dried thyme

1 teaspoon onion powder

½ teaspoon ground cumin

¼ teaspoon cayenne pepper, or to taste

2 tablespoons olive oil

8 ounces andouille sausage, sliced

½ cup sliced onion

½ cup diced green bell pepper

¼ cup diced celery

2 tablespoons minced garlic

½ cup chopped tomatoes

3 bay leaves

1 teaspoon Louisiana hot sauce

¾ cup rice

3 cups chicken stock

12 extra-large shrimp, shelled and deveined

Salt and freshly ground pepper

Warm French bread for serving

SERVES 4

In a medium bowl, combine the chicken, herbs, and spices. Coat the chicken well. In a large cast-iron Dutch oven, heat the oil over medium-high heat. Add the sausage and chicken and cook until seared on all sides, about 2 minutes per side. Add the onion, bell pepper, and celery, and sauté for about 3 minutes. Add the garlic, tomatoes, bay leaves, and hot sauce. Stir in the rice and then gradually stir in the stock. Reduce the heat to medium and cook until the rice absorbs the liquid and becomes tender, about 15 minutes. Add the shrimp about 3 minutes before the rice is done and cook until evenly pink. Season with salt and pepper. Serve with warm French bread.

TO SATISFY THE MEAT-AND-POTATO CROWD THAT IS SHOWBOAT ATLANTIC CITY'S RIB AND CHOPHOUSE CUSTOMER BASE, MORE THAN 4,200 POUNDS OF PRIME RIB WERE SERVED IN 2008. ACCOMPANYING THE RIBS WERE 7,800 ORDERS OF POTATOES, VARYING FROM TRUFFLE PARMESAN FRIES TO FORK-SMASHED AND THE EVER-CLASSIC BAKED.

ROASTED EGGPLANT SOUP

WATERFRONT BUFFET AT HARRAH'S RESORT ATLANTIC CITY
CHEF DAVID SUSCAVAGE

Eggplant stars in this class act of a soup with a supporting cast of flavorful ingredients, such as celery, onion, garlic, and white wine. Chef David Suscavage comments, "Roasted eggplant soup is a family favorite and a great summer soup. The firmness and earthy flavors of the eggplant make for a versatile ingredient in the kitchen. This soup can be served piping hot or finished with fresh cream and served chilled."

¾ cup olive oil

4 cups diced celery

1 pound onions, diced

3 pounds eggplant, diced

1 pound potatoes, peeled and diced

3 garlic cloves

¾ cup dry white wine

1 cup tomato purée

1 cup cooked kidney beans

4 cups low-salt chicken broth or vegetable stock

Salt and freshly ground pepper

Red pepper flakes

1 bunch basil, stemmed and chopped

SERVES 4 TO 6

In a soup pot, heat the oil over medium heat. Add all the vegetables and garlic and sauté until the vegetables turn golden brown, about 12 minutes. Add the white wine and cook to reduce by half. Add the tomato purée and kidney beans and simmer for 10 minutes. Add the chicken broth and simmer until the vegetables are tender, about 15 minutes. Working in batches, purée the soup in a blender. Return to the pan and season with salt, black pepper, and red pepper flakes to taste. Reheat for a minute or two, then pour into shallow bowls and garnish with the basil.

THE WATERFRONT BUFFET FEATURES
ELEVEN FOOD STATIONS:
BRAZILIAN, AMERICAN, ITALIAN, ASIAN, MONGOLIAN,
SUSHI, CRÊPES, DESSERT, DIM SUM, SALAD,
AND GELATO, AND HAS BEEN *CASINO PLAYER*
MAGAZINE'S PICK AS THE NO. 1 BUFFET IN ATLANTIC
CITY FOR THE PAST THREE YEARS.

SELU TURKEY & ROASTED CORN SOUP

SELU GARDEN CAFÉ AT HARRAH'S CHEROKEE
EXECUTIVE CHEF KEITH ANDREASEN

Chef Keith Andreasen explains the Native American inspiration for his soup: "Selu is known as the mother of corn and Kanati as the great hunter. They were married, and their story is the basis of many Cherokee legends. In the Cherokee language, *selu* means 'corn.' Corn is held in high regard among Native peoples and continues to occupy a special place in Cherokee traditions. Native Americans have indeed given the world the most precious of our blessings, corn."

¾ cup corn kernels (about 1½ ears)

½ tablespoon canola oil

8 cups water

⅓ cup diced carrot

1½ cups diced raw turkey breast

6 tablespoons chicken base or
2 chicken bouillon cubes

⅓ cup diced onion

⅓ cup diced celery

¼ cup diced red bell pepper

¼ teaspoon granulated onion

¼ teaspoon ground white pepper

¼ teaspoon dried thyme

SERVES 6 TO 8

Preheat the oven to 350°F. In a cast-iron skillet, toss the corn in the oil to coat and roast in the oven for 20 minutes, or until lightly browned. Remove from the oven and set aside.

In a large soup pot, combine the water and carrot and bring to a boil over medium-high heat. Add the turkey and return to a boil. Add the chicken base, onion, celery, bell pepper, granulated onion, white pepper, thyme, and corn. Return to a boil, reduce to a simmer, and cook for 30 minutes. Serve in deep soup bowls.

ITALIAN MEATBALL & SAUSAGE CHILI

BREAKAWAY CAFÉ AT BALLY'S ATLANTIC CITY
FOOD SERVICE DIRECTOR ROLF J. WEITHOFER

Until now, employees of Bally's Atlantic City have enjoyed this Italian version of chili all to themselves in the employee dining room they've named Breakaway Café. Hot and sweet Italian sausages are matched with such Mediterranean favorites as cannellini beans, cremini mushrooms, and roasted garlic to make a hearty, spicy stew to enjoy year-round.

½ cup extra-virgin olive oil

2 pounds cremini mushrooms, quartered

4 red bell peppers, seeded, deveined, and diced

4 white onions, finely diced

3 pounds ground beef

2 pounds hot Italian sausage, casings removed

2 pounds sweet Italian sausage, casings removed

One 4-ounce can tomato paste

1 tablespoon red pepper flakes

4 cups canned diced Italian tomatoes

2 cups cooked cannellini beans

1 cup dry red wine

2 bunches flat-leaf parsley, stemmed and minced

1 cup fresh basil, cut into fine shreds

½ cup minced fresh oregano

2 cups roasted garlic cloves (see page 48)

Salt and freshly ground pepper

Toasted or grilled Italian bread slices, rubbed with garlic

Grated Parmesan cheese for serving

SERVES 20

In a medium sauté pan, heat the oil over medium heat and sauté the mushrooms, bell peppers, and onions until tender and lightly browned, about 8 minutes. Using a slotted spoon, transfer to a large soup pot. Add the beef and sausage to the pan and sauté over medium heat, cooking meat until cooked through, about 10 minutes, and then skim off excess grease. Stir in the tomato paste and red pepper flakes, then the tomatoes, beans, red wine, herbs, and garlic. Reduce the heat to low and simmer for about 1 hour. Season with salt and pepper. Serve with the garlic bread and Parmesan cheese alongside.

THE DENNIS HOTEL WAS ONE OF THE MOST MAGNIFICENT HOTELS IN THE COUNTRY WHEN CONSTRUCTED IN 1921. CURRENTLY, IT IS PART OF BALLY'S ATLANTIC CITY AND IS STILL IN USE AS A HOTEL.

4

SIDE
DISHES

BRADLEY OGDEN'S
BLUE CORN MUFFINS

BRADLEY OGDEN AT CAESARS PALACE LAS VEGAS
CHEF BRADLEY OGDEN

Celebrated San Francisco Bay Area chef Bradley Ogden has earned numerous awards and other national accolades for his version of American cuisine. Bradley Ogden at Caesars Palace Las Vegas is his first restaurant outside of California. These muffins will bring the memory of simpler times and country cooking into your kitchen, whether you live down on the farm or in the city. This recipe makes enough for a large gathering or for extras that your guests can take home with them.

6¼ cups all-purpose flour

3 cups sugar

3 tablespoons baking powder

5 tablespoons baking soda

4 cups blue corn flour

3 bunches dill, stemmed and minced

4 cups corn kernels (from 8 ears corn)

4 tablespoons salt

Pinch of ground pepper

2 pounds unsalted butter at room temperature

8 cups sour cream

6 cups buttermilk

1 cup heavy cream

20 large eggs, beaten

MAKES 30 MUFFINS

Preheat the oven to 350°F. Butter 30 muffin cups.

In a large bowl, combine the dry ingredients and stir with a whisk to blend. Add the dill, corn, salt, and pepper. Cut in the butter. In another large bowl, mix together the sour cream, buttermilk, heavy cream, and eggs and fold into the dry mixture until just mixed. Fill the prepared muffin cups three-fourths full. Bake for 6 minutes, then rotate them, and bake for 6 more minutes, or until golden brown. Remove from the oven and unmold onto wire racks. Serve warm or at room temperature.

PAULA DEEN'S HOECAKES

PAULA DEEN BUFFET AT HARRAH'S TUNICA
PAULA DEEN & EXECUTIVE SOUS-CHEF TAMMY WILLIAMS-HANSEN

A classic from Paula Deen's famed Savannah restaurant, The Lady & Sons, as well as Paula Deen Buffet at Harrah's Tunica, her Hoecakes prove to be a perfect Southern side for incorporating a yummy touch of Paula's unique charm into your next party or family dinner. A type of cornbread, Paula Deen's Hoecakes are irresistible when served hot off the griddle with some maple syrup.

1 cup self-rising flour

1 cup self-rising cornmeal or corn bread mix, such as Aunt Jemima's

1 tablespoon sugar

2 large eggs

¾ cup buttermilk

⅓ cup plus 1 tablespoon water

¼ cup canola oil or bacon grease

Canola oil, clarified butter (see page 43), or unsalted butter for frying (enough to generously cover the entire cooking surface)

MAKES 16 HOECAKES

In a medium bowl, combine the flour, cornmeal, and sugar. Stir with a whisk to blend. In a small bowl, whisk the eggs, buttermilk, water, and canola oil together until blended. Stir the wet ingredients into the dry ingredients until blended.

In a large skillet, heat the oil or clarified butter or melt the butter over medium heat. Drop 2 tablespoons batter per hoecake 1 to 2 inches apart into the skillet and fry until golden brown and crisp on both sides, 3 to 5 minutes per side. Using a slotted metal spatula, transfer to paper towels to drain. Keep warm in a low oven while cooking the remaining hoecakes. Serve hot.

Note: The batter can be covered and refrigerated for up to 2 days.

PAULA DEEN BUFFET'S SOUTHERN CUISINE NATURALLY CALLS FOR GREAT ICED TEA. SINCE OPENING IN MAY 2008, THE BUFFET HAS SERVED MORE THAN 40,000 GALLONS OF LUZIANNE ICED TEA, PAULA'S FAVORITE, WHICH IS SERVED WITH FRESH MINT.

MASHED SWEET POTATOES

THE RANGE STEAKHOUSE AT HARRAH'S NORTH KANSAS CITY
CHEF WILLIAM DWORZAN

Chef William Dworzan says, "These sweet potatoes garner a lot of compliments at the Steakhouse. But then, how in the world can you go wrong with ingredients like brown sugar, cinnamon, and butter? This side dish is especially popular during the holiday season."

2 pounds sweet potatoes
½ cup packed brown sugar
2 tablespoons mascarpone cheese
1 tablespoon unsalted butter
2 tablespoons maple syrup
Dash of ground cinnamon
Salt and ground white pepper

SERVES 4 TO 6

In a large pot of boiling water, cook the sweet potatoes until they are tender when pierced with a knife. Transfer to a platter and let cool to the touch. Peel and put the potatoes in a large bowl. Beat in all the remaining ingredients until smooth. Serve hot.

HARRAH'S NORTH KANSAS CITY
WON THE *KANSAS CITY BUSINESS JOURNAL*'S
BEST PLACE TO WORK AWARD IN 2007 AND 2008.

CAULIFLOWER PURÉE

NEROS STEAKHOUSE AT CAESARS WINDSOR
CHEF DERON LEPORE

A high-quality white truffle oil brings out the robust flavor of cauliflower in this dish, which is equally at home with fish, lamb, and game fowl such as partridge. Chef Deron Lepore comments, "Our guests love its velvety texture, and its unique flavor is surprising because of its impressive white color, making this a favorite of mine given the lack of natural white produce found in nature."

1 cup chicken stock
1 cauliflower, cored and chopped (about 2 cups)
½ cup heavy cream
2 tablespoons unsalted butter
Sea salt and cracked pepper
½ teaspoon white truffle oil

SERVES 4

In a medium saucepan, bring the chicken stock to a boil and add the cauliflower. Reduce the heat to a simmer and cook until tender, about 10 minutes. Drain the cauliflower, reserving the stock.

In a blender, purée the cauliflower and ¼ cup of the reserved stock. Return to the pan over low heat. Add the heavy cream and butter and heat until the butter melts. Stir in salt and pepper. Divide among serving plates and drizzle each serving with a few drops of the white truffle oil.

TOP 10 TIPS
FOR CHOOSING FRUITS AND VEGETABLES

1   Grow your own: There is nothing better than homegrown fruits and vegeta-
    bles. You have complete control of the growing process, including how to fer-
    tilize. Gardening is also a fun activity that can save a lot of money. At Harrah's
    Metropolis, we're working on a rooftop garden to help supply our kitchen.

2   Buy from a farmers' market that sells local produce: When you support local
    growers, you're not only helping the farmers, but you are most likely getting
    produce that is much fresher than what is available at the grocery store.

3   Buy produce that is in season: While nearly every kind of produce is avail-
    able year-round these days, fruits and vegetables that are in season will have
    the best quality and will usually be more affordable. For example: In spring,
    buy apricots, artichokes, asparagus, avocados, beets, cauliflower, cherries,
    radishes, rhubarb, and spinach. In summer, buy berries, corn, cucumbers,
    eggplant, garlic, and tomatoes. In fall, buy apples, broccoli, Brussels sprouts,
    squash, pears, sweet peppers, and sweet potatoes.

4   Look closely, smell, and touch: In other words, use your senses to choose the
    best fruits and vegetables.

    Following are some tips for selecting my six favorite kinds of produce:

5   Asparagus: Asparagus should be firm and bright green, with purple-tinted
    buds. The thinner asparagus stalks are more tender and flavorful than thicker
    ones.

6   Avocados: Avocados should be slightly soft and squeezable, but not mushy.
    If you buy hard avocados, let them sit on a kitchen windowsill for a few days
    to ripen, or put them in a closed brown paper bag to expedite the process.

7   Corn: Look for tightly wrapped, grass green, slightly damp husks. Many
    grocery stores will allow you to partially open the husks to check for rotten
    kernels.

8   Tomatoes: These should be bright red, firm, and free of bruises.

9   Berries: Look for those with a bright, vivid color and a fruity aroma. Check the
    berries in the bottom of the container for signs of mold. Blueberries, one of
    my favorites, should be plump, firm, and uniform in color, with a silvery frost.

10 Mushrooms: All types of mushrooms should be smooth and even in color,
    without blemishes or brown spots. Avoid presliced, slimy, or wrinkled
    mushrooms.

POTATOES AU GRATIN

THE RANGE STEAKHOUSE AT HARRAH'S NORTH KANSAS CITY
CHEF HUGH RENO

This recipe from chef Hugh Reno takes comfort food to a new level. The many layers of flavors work together to create a warm, soothing richness. Serve with your favorite steak or, perhaps, smoked chicken.

3 tablespoons softened unsalted butter

2 pounds russet potatoes, peeled and cut into ⅛-inch-thick slices

8 ounces Swiss cheese, sliced

½ cup heavy cream

1 teaspoon minced garlic

Salt and freshly ground pepper

SERVES 4 TO 6

Preheat the oven to 325°F. Rub the sides and bottom of a 12-cup gratin dish with the butter. Alternately layer with the potatoes and Swiss cheese, ending with the Swiss cheese on top. In a medium bowl, mix together all the other ingredients and pour the mixture over the layers. Cover with aluminum foil and bake for 45 minutes. Remove the foil and bake for 25 minutes, or until the potatoes are tender and the cheese is browned. Remove from the oven and let stand for 10 minutes. Cut into squares or spoon out sections to serve.

PARMESAN & GARLIC POTATO CHIPS

BALLY'S STEAKHOUSE AT BALLY'S LAS VEGAS
CHEF JOSHUA SIERGEY

Serve these addictive chips with any steak or burger, or alone in a bowl for almost any occasion. Chef Joshua Siergey says, "This recipe has been a fixture at Bally's Steakhouse for many years for one reason: It is as timeless and classic as Bally's Steakhouse itself. Although basic, the complexity of flavors and textures is remarkable. The natural sweetness of the potato is concentrated with slow frying. The combination of the flavorful garlic and cheese with the salty crunch of kosher salt provides a contrast to the potato."

Canola oil for deep-frying

2 large russet potatoes, peeled and cut paper thin

½ cup grated Parmesan cheese

6 minced roasted garlic cloves (see page 48)

2 tablespoons minced fresh flat-leaf parsley

Kosher salt for sprinkling

SERVES 4

In a Dutch oven or large, heavy pot, heat 4 inches of the oil to 325°F on a deep-fat thermometer. Meanwhile, rinse the potato slices to remove the excess starch. Drain well and dry on paper towels to remove as much water as possible.

Add the potato slices to the hot oil in 2 batches. Fry, stirring constantly to ensure even cooking, until golden brown, 6 to 8 minutes. Using a wire skimmer, transfer to dry paper towels to drain. Transfer to a large bowl and sprinkle with the Parmesan cheese, garlic, parsley, and salt. Toss to coat and serve at once.

TOMATO CONFIT CHIPS

ARTURO'S AT BALLY'S ATLANTIC CITY
CHEF MAURIZIO DIMARCO

Bring a touch of Italy to your table with these chips from Arturo's at Bally's Atlantic City. Their deep, rich color will add a spark to your meal, and their flavor will complement other foods. Chef Maurizio Dimarco says, "Tomato confit chips are a great garnish for salads, entrées, and appetizers."

1 teaspoon olive oil

One large tomato (about 5 inches in diameter), cut into ⅛-inch-thick slices

1 teaspoon sugar

MAKES ABOUT 10 CHIPS

Preheat the oven to 250°F. Line a small baking sheet with parchment paper or a Silpat baking mat. Brush the paper or mat with the oil. Add the tomato slices in one layer. Lightly sprinkle the sugar on top of the tomato slices. Wait for 10 seconds, then turn them over. Bake for 45 minutes to 1 hour, or until caramelized and semi-crisp. Remove from the oven and, using a metal spatula, transfer to a plate lined with paper towels and let cool completely.

Serve now, or store the chips in an airtight container for up to 1 week, placing a paper towel between the layers.

CRISPY FRIED GREEN BEANS

AH SIN AT PARIS LAS VEGAS
CHEF THIERRY MAI-THANH

These crisp green beans are served at Ah Sin with the guest's sauce of choice, such as sweet chile, Thai peanut, or hoisin. Serve as a side dish or a crunchy anytime treat.

2 pounds green beans, trimmed

1 cup plus 2 tablespoons cornstarch

2 large eggs

1 cup ice water

1 cup all-purpose flour

About 1 cup chilled soda water

Canola oil or peanut oil for deep-frying

Salt and freshly ground pepper

SERVES 4 TO 6

In a large bowl, toss the green beans lightly in the 2 tablespoons cornstarch. In a shallow bowl, beat the eggs with the ice water. In a medium bowl, combine the flour and the 1 cup cornstarch. Stir the egg mixture into the dry ingredients just until blended. Gradually whisk in the soda water to the consistency of heavy cream.

In a wok, Dutch oven, or large, heavy pot, heat 2 inches of the oil to 350°F on a deep-fat thermometer. Dip the beans in the batter, one at a time, coating evenly. In batches, deep-fry the coated beans for 4 minutes, or until golden. Using a wire skimmer, transfer to paper towels to drain. Put all the beans in a bowl and toss with salt and pepper. Serve at once.

BUTTERMILK POTATOES

HARRAH'S LOUISIANA DOWNS
EXECUTIVE CHEF J. RYAN GILLESPIE

These deep-fried potato wedges are a wonderful alternative to French fries, and go well with almost any chicken, beef, or pork dish. The buttermilk and flour batter makes a crunchy contrast to the tender potatoes.

12 cups buttermilk

1 tablespoon cayenne pepper

½ cup minced fresh rosemary

¼ cup kosher salt

5 Idaho potatoes, scrubbed, dried, and cut into wedges

Canola oil for deep-frying

3 cups all-purpose flour

In a large saucepan, combine 8 cups of the buttermilk, the cayenne, rosemary, salt, and potatoes and bring to a simmer over medium heat. Cook until the potatoes are almost tender, 30 to 40 minutes. Using a wire skimmer, transfer to baking sheets to cool completely.

In a Dutch oven or large, heavy pot, heat 2 inches of the oil to 350°F on a deep-fat thermometer. Pour the remaining 4 cups of buttermilk into a medium bowl and put the flour in another medium bowl. Dip the potato wedges in the buttermilk first and then the flour. Add the wedges to the oil in batches and fry until golden brown, 3 to 5 minutes. Using a wire skimmer, transfer to paper towels to drain. Serve at once.

SERVES 10 TO 12

TELEVISION PERSONALITY LARRY KING WAS THE DIRECTOR OF PUBLIC RELATIONS AT HARRAH'S LOUISIANA DOWNS IN THE 1970S.

SWEET IOWA CREAMED CORN

360 STEAKHOUSE AT HARRAH'S COUNCIL BLUFFS
EXECUTIVE CHEF CHRISTOPHER COLELLO

The state of Iowa produces some of the heartland's best sweet corn. This spin-off of a classic Iowa dish is the perfect blend of savory, creamy, and sweet. Chef Christopher Colello advises, "Always taste the corn before cooking, as its sweetness varies. If the corn is very sweet, you may want to reduce the amount of sugar."

15 ears sweet Iowa corn, shucked

3½ cups heavy cream

2 bay leaves

¾ cup sugar

2 tablespoons kosher salt

8 tablespoons (1 stick) unsalted butter at room temperature

2 tablespoons minced fresh chives

Cut the corn kernels from the cobs and reserve the kernels and 5 of the cobs. In a large, heavy saucepan, combine the reserved cobs, the cream, bay leaves, sugar, and salt. Place over medium heat, bring to a simmer, and cook for 45 minutes.

Drain the corn, reserving the cream, and return the reserved cream to the pan. Add one-third of the corn kernels and cook for 12 minutes, or until tender. In batches, purée the corn mixture until smooth. With the machine running, add the butter, 2 tablespoons at a time. Strain the mixture through a fine-mesh sieve, pressing on the solids with the back of a large spoon. Return the mixture to the pan, add the remaining corn kernels, and cook until tender, about 12 minutes. Taste and adjust the seasoning. Remove from the heat and sprinkle the chives on top of each serving. Serve at once, in shallow soup bowls.

SERVES 6

SIDE DISHES

HARRAH'S COUNCIL BLUFFS'
STIR CONCERT COVE, THE MIDWEST'S
PREMIERE OUTDOOR CONCERT VENUE,
WAS RANKED ONE OF THE TOP 100 AMPHITHEATERS
IN THE WORLD BY *POLLSTAR* MAGAZINE.

CAULIFLOWER GRATIN

LE VILLAGE BUFFET AT PARIS LAS VEGAS
CHEF STEVEN KISNER

Walking into Le Village Buffet in Paris Las Vegas is like entering a quaint French village. The cuisine stations are housed in country-style homes, and each one represents a different French culinary region. Chef Steven Kisner says, "On the Brittany station, we offer this rich and luxurious gratin. With subtle horseradish and yellow curry highlights, the natural flavors of cauliflower, aged cheese, and fresh cream marry together beautifully. Few things are more enticing than pulling a browned and bubbling gratin dish out of a hot oven on a cool day."

2 cauliflowers (about ½ pound each)

5 tablespoons unsalted butter

2 garlic cloves, smashed

Salt and freshly ground pepper

1 teaspoon grated fresh horseradish

¼ cup milk

3 thyme sprigs

1 sage sprig

1 cup heavy cream

Freshly grated nutmeg

¼ teaspoon curry powder

⅓ cup grated Parmesan cheese

⅔ cup shredded Swiss cheese

¼ cup fresh bread crumbs

SERVES 4 TO 6

Trim the leaves and stems from the cauliflowers. Cut the cauliflowers into ½-inch-long florets. Reserve all the trimmings. Finely chop all the trimmings, including the leaves.

In a medium sauté pan, melt 2 tablespoons of the butter over medium heat and sauté the garlic until the butter starts to foam. Add the florets and toss to coat. Sprinkle with salt and pepper and cook until tender, 8 to 10 minutes. Using a slotted spoon, transfer to a baking sheet and let cool. Transfer to the refrigerator.

In a medium saucepan, melt the remaining 3 tablespoons butter over medium heat. Add the horseradish and a little salt. Sauté for 1 minute. Add the chopped cauliflower trimmings, the milk, thyme, and sage. Simmer over very low heat until the cauliflower is very soft and the milk has mostly evaporated, 5 to 6 minutes. Add the cream, nutmeg to taste, and curry powder and simmer for 2 more minutes. Remove and discard the thyme and sage. In batches, purée the mixture until smooth. Taste and adjust the seasoning. Fold in the florets and Parmesan cheese.

Preheat the oven to 400°F. Butter a 6-cup gratin dish. Pour the mixture into the prepared dish and top with the Swiss cheese, then the bread crumbs. Bake for 20 to 30 minutes, or until browned and bubbling hot.

PATATE ARROSTITE
(ROASTED POTATOES WITH SPECK)

POLISTINA'S ITALIAN RISTORANTE AT HARRAH'S RESORT ATLANTIC CITY
CHEF MIKE LAURENZA

Polistina's is a celebration of the foods from Venice, Florence, and Rome, right in the heart of Atlantic City. The main attraction of this authentic potato dish is the speck. Chef Mike Laurenza explains, "Speck is a juniper-flavored ham that originated in the Tyrol region, which lies in both Austria and Italy. Speck's distinctive flavor comes from a time-honored combination of salt-curing and smoking."

2 pounds Yukon gold potatoes, unpeeled and quartered

½ cup olive oil

2 rosemary sprigs

1 garlic clove, chopped

Kosher salt and cracked black pepper

4 ounces speck or prosciutto, sliced

1 bunch flat-leaf parsley, stemmed and minced

1 cup grated Parmigiano-Reggiano cheese

Preheat the oven to 350°F. In a roasting pan, combine the potatoes, oil, rosemary, garlic, and salt and pepper. Toss well to coat. Roast for 30 minutes, then stir in the speck. Return to the oven for 4 minutes. Remove from the oven and transfer to a large bowl. Add the parsley and cheese and toss well to mix. Serve at once.

SERVES 4 TO 6

POLISTINA'S ITALIAN RISTORANTE SERVES OVER EIGHT THOUSAND POUNDS OF CALAMARI ANNUALLY.

GARLIC BREAD FINGERS

MOSAIC AT HARRAH'S JOLIET
CHEF MATTHEW E. SECKO

Serve these treats with your favorite pasta dish or on their own. Chef Matthew E. Secko comments, "As a variation, the bread fingers can be transformed into a nice appetizer by spreading the garlic and butter on top and toasting them in the oven. Serve the tomato mixture alongside as a dipping sauce."

1 large garlic clove, coarsely chopped

¼ teaspoon salt

5 tablespoons unsalted butter at room temperature

2 tablespoons minced fresh flat-leaf parsley

2 tablespoons finely chopped green onion, white part only

2 tablespoons finely chopped pitted kalamata olives

2 tablespoons finely chopped oil-packed sun-dried tomatoes

12 slices firm white bread, crusts trimmed

Preheat the broiler. In a food processor, combine all the ingredients, except the bread, and process until a smooth paste forms. Spread the tomato mixture on top of the bread slices. Cut each bread slice into 3 pieces and put them on a broiler pan 6 to 8 inches from the heat source. Toast for 45 seconds to 1 minute, or until the mixture starts to bubble and melt into the bread and is golden brown. Serve immediately.

SERVES 6

SIDE DISHES

PAULA DEEN'S CHEESE BISCUITS

PAULA DEEN BUFFET AT HARRAH'S TUNICA
PAULA DEEN & EXECUTIVE SOUS-CHEF TAMMY WILLIAMS-HANSEN

Paula Deen takes a beloved Southern treat to a new level with her cheese biscuits, a favorite at the Paula Deen Buffet. Chef Tammy Williams-Hansen says, "The secret of these biscuits is that you must brush them with butter and serve them right out of the oven. We scoop over three thousand a day in the Paula Deen Buffet! Hey, y'all, I think you will agree these are a great accompaniment to any Southern meal."

2 cups self-rising flour
1 teaspoon baking powder
1 teaspoon sugar
½ teaspoon salt
⅓ cup vegetable shortening
¾ cup shredded sharp Cheddar cheese
1 cup buttermilk
4 tablespoons unsalted butter, melted

MAKES 16 TO 20 BISCUITS

Preheat the oven to 350°F. Grease a baking sheet.

In a medium bowl, mix together the flour, baking powder, sugar, and salt using a fork. Cut in the shortening with a pastry cutter or your fingers until it resembles cornmeal. Add the cheese. Stir in the buttermilk all at once, just until blended. Do not overstir. Drop by tablespoonfuls, or use an ice cream scoop, onto the prepared pan. Brush the dough with the butter. Bake for 12 to 15 minutes, or until golden brown. Transfer to wire racks to cool slightly. Serve warm.

SWEET POTATO & RAISIN PANCAKES

HARRAH'S JOLIET
EXECUTIVE CHEF SCOTT D. LECOMPTE

Potato pancakes have been one of chef Scott D. LeCompte's favorite morning indulgences for as long as he can remember. He credits his grandmother with making some of the best he has ever eaten. In this recipe, the chef has created a variation on potato pancakes to pair with his version of pork chops and applesauce.

1 Idaho potato, peeled and shredded
1 sweet potato, peeled and shredded
½ small red onion, thinly sliced
1 large egg
Pinch of dried thyme
¼ cup golden raisins
Salt and freshly ground pepper
1 tablespoon all-purpose flour
2 tablespoons canola oil
Apple compote and crème fraîche or sour cream and minced fresh chives for serving

MAKES 10 PANCAKES;
SERVES 2 TO 3

In a medium bowl, combine the Idaho and sweet potatoes, onion, egg, thyme, raisins, and salt and pepper. Add the flour and toss to coat.

In a large sauté pan or skillet, heat the oil over medium heat. Form ¼ cupfuls of the potato mixture into pancakes about 2½ inches in diameter. Put the pancakes into the heated pan and brown on both sides for a total of 3 to 4 minutes. Serve with apple compote and crème fraîche, or sour cream and chives.

TOP 10 TIPS
FOR COOKING SEASONALLY

HARRAH'S TUNICA

1   Spring means new vegetables, but it also brings some of the best fish, including wild salmon, scallops, and brown crabs. When purchasing seafood, check for firmness and aroma. Fish should spring back when pressed and have a fresh aroma.

2   Visit a local farmers' market and build your menu around the vegetables that you find in season. For example, during spring, you may find some beautiful watercress that can be used with a seared salmon and drizzled with blood orange vinaigrette.

3   Like vegetables, meats are seasonal; visit your local butcher to see what is available. Lamb is a spring meat and can be served in a hearty dish or a light one. For example, marinate lamb with rosemary, mint, and garlic, roast it to perfection, and serve sliced with roasted spring potatoes.

4   Summer brings berries and stone fruits to add to sauces and salads. Think about pairing meats with the kinds of food the animal eats, such as accompanying venison dishes with currants and loganberries.

5   Spring and summer are the times for light, refreshing foods, such as lettuces, citrus fruits, berries, fish, tomatoes, and peppers. Season them with light oils, vinegars, and citrus juices.

6   Tomatoes are one of the most versatile summer foods. Look for firm vine-ripened fruit with no blisters or bruises, especially heirloom tomatoes, which come in a wide variety of colors, shapes, and sizes.

7   Fresh corn, available in summer and fall, can be used grilled or roasted or cut from the cobs in dishes from a Southwestern black bean and corn relish to corn pudding.

8   Fall and winter bring long-cooked dishes that use such seasonal ingredients as mushrooms, salsify, turnips, chestnuts, apples, and pears. Many of these foods complement not only pork, but also duck and pheasant.

9   The hearty foods of fall and winter make us feel warm inside when it is cold outside. Squashes, root vegetables, greens, apples, pears, and nuts are great additions to roasted and braised meats. Warm spices like cinnamon, nutmeg, and cardamom complement many cold-weather dishes.

10 The seasonality of dishes can be enhanced with the addition of special drinks to complement foods. During spring and summer, choose fruit drinks, citrus fruit juices, ice teas, and lemonades. During fall and winter, choose coffees, hot chocolates, hot tea, and hot apple cider.

EXECUTIVE CHEF JOHN MALTBY'S

TOP 10 TIPS FOR COOKING LOCALLY WHEREVER YOU ARE

HARRAH'S LAS VEGAS

1 Shop at small local grocery stores and farmers' markets.

2 Talk to your local butcher about locally grown livestock and which is best.

3 Patronize local wine and cheese shops. They love to share their knowledge with free tastings and newsletters and have access to all the best from the local providers.

4 Many restaurants and hotels have cooking demonstrations where you can watch chefs prepare your favorite dishes and then eat them! This is a great way to see firsthand what ingredients are used and how to prepare the food correctly.

5 Ask the chef of your favorite restaurant what restaurants he or she likes, then visit those places.

6 Go to the small restaurants frequented by the locals. Ask the server or chef how specific dishes are made. They may even give you the recipe.

7 If you really want to find out about local food, find a local club, church, or school cookbook. They can usually be found at used bookstores and the library.

8 Talk to older people in your neighborhood about what foods they grew up with and how they were prepared.

9 Look for traditional local recipes and vary them to create your own regional specialty.

10 Learn about the herbs and spices traditionally used in your area and use them to make your own dishes.

5

BEEF + PORK

TOP 10 TIPS FOR CHOOSING MEAT

1   Build a friendly relationship with your local butcher:

Ask your butcher questions, respect his or her opinions, see what the specials are, and find out when new shipments of meat are coming in. Following are some questions to ask your butcher:

+   How fresh is the meat? Was it just put out in the case that day?

+   Was the meat previously frozen? If so, for how long?

+   Explain what you intend to use the meat for and ask if it is the best choice or what the butcher would recommend.

+   Why is the meat at a reduced price? Is it old?

+   Where does the butcher get his or her meat from?

2   Inspect the meat:

Always check to make sure the label on beef, poultry, ham, veal, and other meats says that the meat was inspected by the United States Department of Agriculture (USDA). If this is not noted on the label, ask the butcher why.

Also, look for bruising, blood clots, and irregular discolorations, such as freezer burn, which is a grayish color, and dark spots on red meat, which may indicate it is a few days old. All these signs may mean the meat was mishandled in production or transportation.

Check the label for an expiration date.

3   Color:

If the meat looks discolored in any way, ask the butcher why. The color could be perfectly natural or a sign the meat is old. For example, fresh beef should be ruby red with no bruising or brownish or dark spots.

4   Cut:

The basic cuts of meat are called primal cuts. Each cut lends itself to various cooking techniques. Always use the proper cut for your specific preparation.

Primal cuts and their uses include:

+   Chuck: Pot roast and hamburgers

+   Rib: Ribs, rib-eye steak, and prime rib loin for strip steaks, T-bone, porterhouse, and tenderloin

+   Round: Roast beef

+   Brisket: Barbecued brisket, corned beef, pot roast

+   Plate: Short ribs for braising cuts, such as the outside skirt steak for fajitas and hanger steak (this is typically a cheap, tough, and fatty meat)

+   Shank for broth, stews, and soup (this is the toughest of the cuts)

+   Flank: Ground meat, flank steak

5   Marbling:

The white, speckled fat found in meat. The more marbling in beef, the higher the grade of the beef and the more tender it will be.

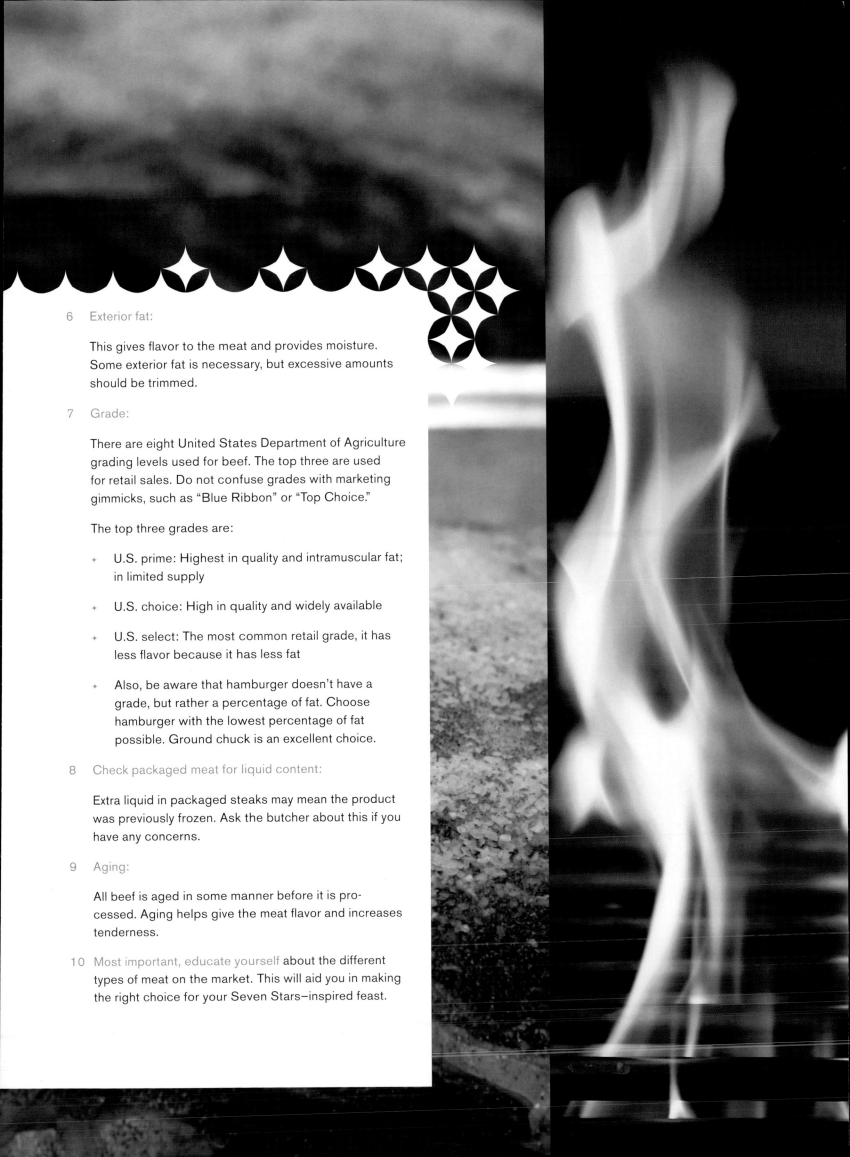

6   Exterior fat:

This gives flavor to the meat and provides moisture. Some exterior fat is necessary, but excessive amounts should be trimmed.

7   Grade:

There are eight United States Department of Agriculture grading levels used for beef. The top three are used for retail sales. Do not confuse grades with marketing gimmicks, such as "Blue Ribbon" or "Top Choice."

The top three grades are:

+   U.S. prime: Highest in quality and intramuscular fat; in limited supply

+   U.S. choice: High in quality and widely available

+   U.S. select: The most common retail grade, it has less flavor because it has less fat

+   Also, be aware that hamburger doesn't have a grade, but rather a percentage of fat. Choose hamburger with the lowest percentage of fat possible. Ground chuck is an excellent choice.

8   Check packaged meat for liquid content:

Extra liquid in packaged steaks may mean the product was previously frozen. Ask the butcher about this if you have any concerns.

9   Aging:

All beef is aged in some manner before it is processed. Aging helps give the meat flavor and increases tenderness.

10 Most important, educate yourself about the different types of meat on the market. This will aid you in making the right choice for your Seven Stars–inspired feast.

SAGE STEAK

SAGE ROOM STEAK HOUSE AT HARVEYS LAKE TAHOE
EXECUTIVE CHEF JOE WELLS

This signature steak is one of the most popular dishes on the menu at the Sage Room. Poblano chiles and Gorgonzola are surprising partners in this intensely flavorful sauce. Chef Joe Wells advises, "roasted-shallot mashed potatoes are a very good side with this dish."

Four 12-ounce New York steaks, trimmed and lightly pounded

Salt and freshly ground pepper

1½ cups clarified butter (see page 43)

1 cup julienned red onion

2 teaspoons minced garlic

1 cup julienned red bell pepper

2 large poblano chiles, roasted, peeled, and julienned (1 cup; see page 196)

¾ cup dry red wine

1 cup veal demi-glace

½ cup crumbled Gorgonzola cheese

4 watercress sprigs for garnish (optional)

SERVES 4

Season both sides of the steaks with salt and pepper. Heat 2 large sauté pans or skillets over high heat. Add ½ cup clarified butter to each pan. Add 2 steaks to each pan and reduce the heat to medium. Cook the steaks for 3 to 4 minutes on each side for medium-rare. Transfer the steaks to a platter and keep warm.

Pour off the fat from one of the pans. Add the remaining ½ cup clarified butter and melt over medium heat. Add the red onion to the pan and sauté for 2 to 3 minutes. Add the garlic, bell pepper, and chiles and sauté for 2 to 3 minutes. Season the vegetable mixture with salt and pepper. Transfer the vegetables to a bowl and keep warm.

Add the red wine to the pan and stir over medium heat to scrape up the browned bits from the bottom of the pan. Cook to reduce the wine to about ½ cup. Add the demi-glace and cook for 2 to 3 minutes. Taste and adjust the seasoning.

To serve, preheat the broiler to 550°F. Top each steak with one-fourth of the vegetable mixture, then the cheese. Place under the broiler about 6 inches from the heat source for 2 minutes, or until the cheese is melted. Pool ¼ cup of the sauce on each plate and place a steak on top. Garnish with the watercress sprigs, if desired, and serve at once.

SINCE 1947, THE SAGE ROOM STEAK HOUSE HAS BEEN WORLD RENOWNED FOR ITS OLD WEST AMBIANCE AND ITS FINE CUISINE. HERE, DINERS CAN PERUSE ARTWORKS BY RUSSELL AND REMINGTON WHILE ENJOYING TRADITIONAL STEAK HOUSE DINING WITH TABLESIDE SERVICE.

THE BEST STEAK IN KANSAS CITY

THE RANGE STEAKHOUSE AT HARRAH'S NORTH KANSAS CITY
CHEFS HUGH RENO, ANDY SPARKS, JEFF CRAIG & WILLIAM DWORZAN

In 2008 chefs Hugh Reno, Andy Sparks, Jeff Craig, and William Dworzan joined forces as Team Harrah's and entered this dish in the prestigious Great American Barbecue Contest in Kansas City. When the smoke cleared, this dynamic team was the grand-prize winner for the Best Steak in Kansas City, and a new Kansas City legend was born. Follow the recipe below to re-create it in your own kitchen.

MARINADE

2 cups Jack Daniel's Black Label whiskey

1 cup (2 sticks) unsalted butter

2 teaspoons beef base

3 shallots, minced

8 garlic cloves, minced

2 teaspoons kosher salt

2 teaspoons freshly ground pepper

Six 12-ounce Kansas City strip steaks or
New York strip steaks
(depending on what part of
the country you are in)

COMPOUND BUTTER

1 cup (2 sticks) unsalted butter
at room temperature

2 tablespoons dry white wine

2 tablespoons white truffle oil

6 shallots, julienned

1 teaspoon minced fresh
flat-leaf parsley

1 teaspoon minced fresh basil

1 teaspoon minced fresh rosemary

1 teaspoon minced fresh thyme

SERVES 6

For the marinade: Add the whiskey to a medium saucepan and warm over medium heat. Turn off the heat, stand back from the stove, and light the whiskey with a long match or long-handled lighter. Once the alcohol is lit, do not stir or shake the saucepan. Let the flame burn itself out naturally. Stir in the butter, beef base, shallots, garlic, salt, and pepper. Let the mixture cool to room temperature.

Put the steaks in a nonreactive bowl or heavy self-sealing plastic bag and add the marinade. Cover the bowl or close the bag and refrigerate for 24 hours.

Remove the steaks from the refrigerator about 30 minutes to 1 hour before cooking. Light a very hot fire in a charcoal grill, or preheat a gas grill to high.

Meanwhile, make the compound butter: Put the butter in a medium bowl. In a medium sauté pan or skillet, heat the white wine and truffle oil over medium heat. Add the shallots and sauté, stirring constantly, until well browned, 2 to 3 minutes. Pour the mixture into a bowl and let cool, then cover and refrigerate for at least 30 minutes. Mince the shallots and stir into the butter. Stir in the herbs until well blended.

Grill the steaks for about 5 minutes on each side for medium-rare. Transfer to plates and let rest for 5 minutes. Place a dollop of the compound butter on each steak and serve at once.

GRILLED CITRUS-MARINATED SKIRT STEAK

WITH SAFFRON–HEIRLOOM TOMATO SALAD

RIB & CHOPHOUSE AT SHOWBOAT ATLANTIC CITY
RESTAURANT CHEF EDWARD LEDWON

This feast for your eyes and palate starts with marinating skirt steaks in a mixture of fresh orange and lime juice, garlic, shallots, and cilantro. It's crowned with a tomato salad that could also be served on its own as a side dish for many other main courses. Chef Edward Ledwon says, "The skirt steak is an amazing cut of beef. Its tenderness and light gaminess allow you to play with bold flavors and textures. The marriage of saffron and coffee would overpower any other steak. Our guests are always surprised and delighted by this dish. In fact, there is no other item on our menu that brings me out to the table more often."

Note: The steak must be marinated overnight before cooking.

MARINADE

Juice of 3 oranges

Juice of 4 limes

1 tablespoon minced garlic

2 tablespoons minced shallots
or red onion

1 bunch cilantro, stemmed and
coarsely chopped

3 cups extra-virgin olive oil

Four 8-ounce skirt steaks, trimmed

TOMATO SALAD

6 heirloom tomatoes, each cut
into 6 wedges

2 red onions, thinly sliced

1 bunch basil, stemmed and leaves torn

2 tablespoons minced fresh chives

Pinch of powdered saffron

½ cup extra-virgin olive oil

Juice of 1 lemon

Salt and freshly ground pepper

½ cup extra-virgin olive oil

1 cup finely ground coffee

Salt

SERVES 4

For the marinade: In a medium bowl, combine all the marinade ingredients and stir to blend. Put the steaks in a nonreactive bowl or heavy self-sealing plastic bag and add the marinade. Cover the bowl or close the bag and refrigerate overnight.

For the salad: In a large ceramic or glass bowl, combine all the ingredients. Toss well. Cover and refrigerate overnight.

Remove the steaks from the marinade 30 minutes to 1 hour before cooking. Light a very hot fire in a charcoal grill, or preheat a gas grill to 500°F. (Since the steaks are thin, they need to be grilled over a high flame.)

Rub the steaks with the olive oil, coffee, and salt. Grill the steaks for 1 to 2 minutes on each side for medium-rare. Transfer to a carving board and let rest for about 5 minutes.

To serve, cut the steaks into thin diagonal slices and top with the tomato salad and some of its dressing.

CONDIMENTS ARE A HUGE PART OF THE STEAK HOUSE APPEAL, ALLOWING CUSTOMERS TO PERSONALLY CRAFT THEIR DINING EXPERIENCE. OVER THE YEARS, THE RIB & CHOPHOUSE HAS DOLED OUT EVERYTHING FROM 1,100 BOTTLES OF WORCESTERSHIRE SAUCE, 600 BOTTLES OF TABASCO SAUCE, 4,000 POUNDS OF BUTTER IN VARIOUS FLAVORED FORMS, 200 POUNDS OF BLUE CHEESE, AND AN ASTOUNDING 400 GALLONS OF THE CLASSIC BORDELAISE SAUCE.

EXECUTIVE CHEF KEITH MITCHELL'S

TOP 10 TIPS FOR MAINTAINING AN ORGANIZED KITCHEN

CAESARS ATLANTIC CITY

1 Keep cabinets and pantries well stocked and clutter-free.

2 Stock your pantry with your favorite staples and must-haves.

3 Keep knives sharp and hand tools where you can find them when you need them.

4 Keep your refrigerator well stocked with fresh fruits, vegetables, and herbs.

5 Buy spices in small amounts and replace them frequently.

6 Get rid of kitchen clutter, such as old pans and containers, and tools that don't work.

7 Clean up as you go.

8 Make cooking a family affair; get the kids into the kitchen to help.

9 Think green and recycle.

10 Plan your meals and events, then stick to your plan!

PAN-ROASTED DRY-AGED RIB-EYE STEAK

WITH FINGERLING POTATOES & ASPARAGUS-MOREL RAGOUT

VOODOO STEAK & LOUNGE AT RIO ALL-SUITE HOTEL & CASINO
CHEF DE CUISINE HONORIO MECINAS

VooDoo Steak & Lounge guests always rave about their steaks. Chef Honorio Mecinas's dry-aging process gives the meat superior tenderness and flavor. The chef advises, "Currently, you can find dry-aged beef in gourmet stores. Always look for center cuts and marbling." In this recipe, fingerling potatoes and a spring ragout of morels and white asparagus complement the rich beef.

ROASTED POTATOES

1 pound fingerling potatoes, halved

10 garlic cloves, sliced

3 thyme sprigs

2 slices bacon, cut into bite-sized pieces

¼ cup canola oil

Salt and freshly ground pepper

Four 18-ounce dry-aged bone-in rib-eye steaks

Sea salt and cracked pepper

Canola oil for brushing

ASPARAGUS AND MOREL RAGOUT

1 cup (2 sticks) unsalted butter

2 shallots, sliced

16 morel mushrooms, rinsed

8 stalks white asparagus, trimmed, peeled, and cut into matchsticks

1 cup dry sherry

SERVES 4

For the potatoes: Preheat the oven to 350°F. Combine the potatoes, garlic, thyme, and bacon in a medium bowl. Add the oil and salt and pepper to taste; toss to coat. Put the mixture in a roasting pan and roast for about 20 minutes, or until tender. Remove from the oven and keep warm.

While the potatoes are cooking, season the steaks with sea salt and cracked pepper. Heat a large cast-iron pan over high heat and brush with a little oil. Sear the steaks until well browned, about 3 minutes on each side. Transfer the pan to the oven and roast for 6 minutes for medium-rare. Transfer the steaks to a carving board and let rest for about 5 minutes.

For the ragout: In a medium saucepan, melt half of the butter over low heat. Add the shallots and morels and cook for about 4 minutes. Add the asparagus and cook for 2 minutes, or until tender. Add the sherry and stir well. Remove from the heat and stir in the remaining ½ cup butter.

To serve, divide the potatoes and ragout among 4 plates. Add the steaks. Drizzle the pan juices over the steaks and sprinkle with a little more sea salt. Serve at once.

THE AWARD-WINNING VILLAGE SEAFOOD BUFFET
AT RIO ALL-SUITE HOTEL & CASINO:

• OPERATES 5 COOKING STATIONS •

• MAKES EVERYTHING FROM SCRATCH IN THE RIO'S PASTRY SHOP,
INCLUDING 12 FLAVORS OF GELATO •

• HOSTS A FULL SUSHI BAR,
WHICH PRODUCES 3,000 PIECES OF SUSHI ROLLS,
NIGIRI SUSHI, AND SASHIMI •

• PREPARES MORE THAN 2,100 POUNDS OF
PEEL AND EAT SHRIMP AND 5,000 POUNDS OF
CRAB LEGS PER WEEK •

• PREPARES MORE THAN 2,000 POUNDS OF BEEF RIBS AND
1,250 POUNDS OF PRIME RIB PER WEEK •

STEAK AU POIVRE

JACK BINION'S STEAK HOUSE AT HORSESHOE BOSSIER CITY
EXECUTIVE SOUS-CHEF ROBERT BROOKS

This classic French dish has become a staple at Jack Binion's Steak House. The magical combination of a rich brandy cream sauce, fresh-cracked pepper, and tender, buttery filet proves that some things never go out of style.

Four 7-ounce filet mignons

Kosher salt and crushed pepper

3 tablespoons extra-virgin olive oil

1 teaspoon minced shallot

¼ cup brandy

1 cup veal demi-glace or your favorite brown gravy

1 tablespoon Dijon mustard

½ cup heavy cream

4 tablespoons unsalted butter

SERVES 4

Season the filets on both sides with salt and pepper. In a medium sauté pan or skillet, heat the oil over medium-high heat until it begins to smoke. Add the filets and sear for 4 to 5 minutes. Turn and cook on the second side for 4 minutes for medium-rare. Transfer to 4 plates and keep warm.

Drain the excess oil from the pan and add the shallot. Remove the pan from the heat and add the brandy. Standing back from the stove, light the brandy with a long match or long-handled lighter. Once the alcohol is lit, do not stir or shake the pan. Let the flames subside, then add the demi-glace, mustard, and heavy cream. Cook over medium heat for 1 to 2 minutes, stirring well. Add the butter and swirl until melted.

To serve, pour the sauce over the filet mignons and serve at once.

GARY W. LOVEMAN BECAME CHIEF EXECUTIVE OFFICER OF HARRAH'S ENTERTAINMENT IN 2003. SINCE THEN, *INSTITUTIONAL INVESTOR* MAGAZINE 4 TIMES NAMED HIM "BEST CEO" IN THE GAMING AND LODGING INDUSTRY.

TOP 10 SPICES
THAT SHOULD BE IN EVERY KITCHEN

FLAMINGO LAS VEGAS

Each of the following spices can be used in a variety of different dishes. Having this collection in your spice rack means you have the flavors of the world right at your fingertips.

1 Curry powder

2 Chili powder

3 Paprika

4 Cumin

5 Sesame seeds

6 Fennel seeds

7 Black peppercorns

8 Szechuan pepper

9 Red pepper flakes

10 Coriander

GRILLED BOURBON PORK CHOPS

THE RANGE STEAKHOUSE AT HARRAH'S METROPOLIS
EXECUTIVE CHEF JON M. KELL

The thick pork chops at The Range Steakhouse receive a stellar treatment: First they're grilled over charcoal, then dipped in a mixture of maple syrup, molasses, bourbon, and mango-chili sauce and grilled again. Juicy inside, dark and flavorful outside— that is the essence of these unparalleled chops, which are one of the restaurant's most popular specials.

BOURBON SAUCE

1 cup pure maple syrup

1 cup molasses

1 cup bourbon

¼ cup bottled mango-chili sauce
(available in specialty foods stores)

Four 12-ounce bone-in pork chops

Salt and freshly ground pepper

SERVES 4

Prepare a medium fire in a charcoal grill, or preheat a gas grill to 400°F.

For the sauce: In a medium saucepan, combine all the ingredients. Heat over low heat, stirring well. Pour half of the mixture into a shallow dish. Cover the remaining sauce; set aside and keep warm.

Season the chops on both sides with salt and pepper. Grill the pork chops for 5 to 7 minutes on each side. Dip the chops in the pan of sauce to coat both sides. Move the chops to the edge of the fire, not over direct heat, and cook for 15 to 20 minutes, or until an instant-read thermometer inserted in the center of a chop registers 160°F.

Transfer to plates and serve with the remaining sauce alongside.

THE REAL CITY OF METROPOLIS IN ILLINOIS SHARES ITS NAME WITH THE FICTIONAL CITY (ORIGINALLY MODELED AFTER TORONTO) THAT IS THE HOME OF THE MAN OF STEEL— SUPERMAN! JUST A FEW BLOCKS FROM THE CASINO, THE FAMED BRONZE STATUE OF SUPERMAN STANDS IN THE TOWN SQUARE.

VEAL CHOPS PORTOBELLO

MURANO'S AT HARRAH'S TUNICA
EXECUTIVE CHEF STEVE PAIROLERO

This dish of portobello mushrooms, veal loin chops, and asparagus tips will transport you and your guests to Tuscany. Chef Steve Pairolero says, "This is definitely one of my favorite flavor combinations. The heartiness from the portobello mushrooms and the mild flavor of the veal make for a fantastic meal. To further enhance this dish, serve it with a really nice glass of Pinot Noir."

4 portobello mushrooms, stemmed

4 tablespoons extra-virgin olive oil

½ teaspoon salt

½ teaspoon freshly ground pepper

Four 10-ounce veal loin chops

2 teaspoons minced garlic

4 ounces sliced porcini mushrooms

1 bunch asparagus, cut into tips

1 cup dry red wine

¼ cup veal demi-glace

1 cup diced tomatoes for garnish

4 rosemary sprigs for garnish

SERVES 4

Preheat the oven to 350°F. Using a spoon, scrape the underside of the portobello mushroom caps to remove the gills. Rub the caps with 2 tablespoons of the olive oil and sprinkle with ¼ teaspoon of the salt and ¼ teaspoon of the pepper. Place the mushrooms on a baking sheet and roast for about 10 minutes, or until tender. Remove from the oven and set aside.

Light a charcoal or wood fire in a charcoal grill, or preheat a gas grill to 400°F. Season the veal chops with the remaining ¼ teaspoon salt and ¼ teaspoon pepper. Grill the chops 6 to 8 minutes on each side for medium-rare. Remove from the heat and keep warm.

In a medium sauté pan or skillet, heat the remaining 2 tablespoons oil. Add the garlic, porcini mushrooms, and asparagus tips and sauté for 4 to 6 minutes, or until the asparagus turns bright green and you can pierce it with a fork. Add the red wine and stir to scrape up the browned bits on the bottom of the pan. Stir in the demi-glace and cook for 3 to 5 minutes, or until slightly thickened.

To serve, place a roasted portobello mushroom in the center of each plate and top with a veal chop. Ladle the sauce over the chop. Garnish with the tomatoes and rosemary.

BRAISED SHORT RIB SLIDERS
WITH GOAT CHEESE, RICOTTA & HORSERADISH GREMOLATA

PREVIEW BAR AT BALLY'S ATLANTIC CITY
FOOD SERVICE DIRECTOR ROLF J. WEITHOFER

Preview Bar at Bally's Atlantic City is known for both its outstanding cocktails and its great bar food, like these sliders. For your next picnic or casual get-together, kick it up a notch with short ribs topped with goat cheese and horseradish gremolata.

BRAISED SHORT RIBS

10 boneless beef short ribs, cut into about 3-inch pieces

1 tablespoon salt

1 ½ teaspoons freshly ground pepper

¼ cup canola oil

4 ounces pancetta, diced

2 cups diced mixed onions, carrots, and celery

¼ cup tomato paste

½ cup plus ⅓ cup dry red wine

1 cup brown veal stock

2 cups veal demi-glace

2 bay leaves

Pinch of minced fresh thyme

GOAT CHEESE, RICOTTA & HORSERADISH GREMOLATA

1 cup crumbled fresh white goat cheese

½ cup ricotta cheese

1 teaspoon grated lemon zest

1 teaspoon minced fresh oregano

1 teaspoon grated fresh horseradish

Salt and freshly ground pepper

2 tablespoons extra-virgin olive oil

2 tablespoons minced fresh chives

10 mini-hamburger buns, toasted

SERVES 10

For the short ribs: Preheat the oven to 275°F. Season the short ribs with the salt and pepper. In a large ovenproof sauté pan, heat the oil over medium-high heat until shimmering. Sear the short ribs on all sides until a deep golden brown. Transfer the short ribs to a plate.

Add the pancetta and chopped vegetables to the pan and sauté until golden brown, 8 to 10 minutes. Add the tomato paste and cook for 3 to 5 minutes, or until it turns a deeper color and gives off a sweet aroma; do not burn. Stir in the ½ cup wine and cook to reduce by one-fourth.

Return the short ribs and any juices to the pan. Add the stock and demi-glace. Bring to a gentle simmer, cover, and braise in the oven for 45 minutes. Spoon the fat from the top of the liquid and add the bay leaves and thyme. Return to the oven and braise for another 45 minutes, or until fork-tender.

Using a wire skimmer, transfer the short ribs to a plate. Spoon off the fat from the top of the pan liquid, stir in the remaining ⅓ cup wine, and bring to a simmer. Taste and adjust the seasoning. Strain the sauce into a bowl and add the short ribs; set aside and keep warm.

For the gremolata: In a small bowl, combine all the ingredients and stir to blend.

To serve, toast the buns and place a short rib on top of the bottom half of each bun and dollop with the gremolata. Drizzle a little of the sauce over the gremolata. Close the buns and serve at once.

BLACKENING SPICE

2 tablespoons red pepper flakes

3 tablespoons garlic powder

3 tablespoons onion powder

2 tablespoons dark chili powder

3 tablespoons sweet paprika

1 tablespoon salt

1 teaspoon dried parsley

1 teaspoon dried thyme

1 teaspoon celery powder

Pinch of cayenne pepper

In a medium bowl, combine all the ingredients, mixing well. Store in an airtight container.

MAKES ABOUT 1 CUP

CAJUN SKILLET FILETS

360 STEAKHOUSE AT HARRAH'S COUNCIL BLUFFS
EXECUTIVE CHEF CHRISTOPHER COLELLO

The ultimate taste of this dish comes from its many layers of flavor. The wave of flavor starts with the bacon fat and the blackening spice and ends at the tiger shrimp with just a splash of cream to blend everything together. Serve with a favorite side dish.

Four 8-ounce center-cut beef filets

**¾ cup blackening spice
(see recipe facing page)**

6 tablespoons bacon fat

12 jumbo shrimp, shelled and deveined

6 tablespoons unsalted butter

**¾ cup lobster stock or shrimp stock
(page 202)**

¼ cup heavy cream

SERVES 4

Season the filets with all but 1 tablespoon of the blackening spice, making sure to completely cover the meat on all sides. Reserve the 1 tablespoon blackening spice for the shrimp. In a large sauté pan or skillet, melt the bacon fat over medium-high heat. Cook the filets for 9 minutes on each side for medium-rare. Transfer to a plate and keep warm. Discard the bacon fat.

Season the shrimp with the reserved blackening spice. In the same pan used to cook the meat, melt 4 tablespoons of the butter over medium heat until lightly browned. Immediately add the shrimp and cook for about 1½ minutes on each side, or until evenly pink. Using a slotted spoon, transfer to a plate and keep warm.

Using the same pan, add the lobster stock to the butter in the pan and cook over medium heat to reduce to about ½ cup. Add the cream and cook to reduce slightly. Add the remaining 2 tablespoons butter and simmer until the sauce is thick.

To serve, place each filet on a plate with 3 shrimp on top. Evenly drizzle the sauce among the 4 plates.

THE GREEN AND BLUE FAÇADE OF
HARRAH'S COUNCIL BLUFFS HOTEL REPRESENTS ITS
LOCATION NEAR THE MIGHTY MISSOURI RIVER AND
THE RIVERBANKS OF OMAHA, NEBRASKA,
AND COUNCIL BLUFFS, IOWA.

TOP 10 DREAM KITCHEN APPLIANCES FOR CHEFS

SHOWBOAT ATLANTIC CITY

1 TurboChef Oven: This oven rapidly and evenly browns the outside of food while evenly cooking the inside without compromising food quality. In laymen's terms, it cooks really fast and kicks . . . well, you know. Especially important in high-volume restaurants.

2 Beurre mixer: Also known as the stick blender, hand blender, or, as some chefs affectionately refer to it, "the happy stick." And why not? It has 750 watts of power that spins at 18,000 RPMs. For anyone who needs to purée about fifty gallons of soup, this immersion blender is the right tool for that job.

3 Jade Infrared Broiler: Its four 26,000-BTU burners will perfectly char a magmalike crust on a twenty-eight-ounce porterhouse and cook it to medium-rare in seven minutes flat. It's like standing next to the sun. However, it's not for beginners; experienced riders only, please!

4 Rational Combi Oven: This oven allows you to roast, steam, bake, oven-poach, reheat, or execute a combination of the aforementioned. You can auto-program it to cook specific foods with specific settings, times, and various methods of cooking. You may even be able to program it to wake you up and make coffee, I just haven't found that button yet.

5 Cleveland Tilting Skillet: Also known as the braiser. It's very versatile. You can sauté, braise, poach, and sear meat in it. It will handle almost any task. Make sure you get the manual hand-crank model; it will last for centuries. The electric tilt models are junk.

6 Commercial smoker: Nothing to do for twelve hours or so? What's better than a smoker full of cured pork bellies going low and slow?

7 Vertical chopper and mixer (VCM): It's like a Cuisinart on steroids. If the Cuisinart had a big brother, this would be it. As a young aspiring saucier, I was amazed at the sight of my first one. If you ever need to purée a brick, this could probably handle it.

8 Cryovac machine: This machine is great for storing any perishable food. We mostly use it for portion-cut meat, as it creates an airtight environment. It's also great for marinating meat, as it penetrates the protein faster, giving a consistent flavor throughout.

9 Treif Puma industrial meat slicer: I strongly suggest that if you have 45K laying around, you get one of these slicers. We produce deli meat for two large properties, and it blows through a day's worth of work in about two hours. At four hundred cuts per minute, this thing will pay for itself. When you are slicing lunch meat in thousand-pound increments, it beats the conventional slicing method.

10 iPod docking station with Bose speakers: Okay, technically this is not a kitchen appliance, but I do consider it a necessity during prep times. Nothing like a little Disturbed, Metallica, or if you are having "one of those days," "Break Stuff" by Limp Bizkit to get you through some rather monotonous tasks. Prepping for four-thousand customers a day in the buffet requires much caffeine and heavy metal music.

TOP 10 POTS AND PANS
EVERY KITCHEN SHOULD HAVE AND WHY

1   Teflon omelet pan: A great omelet screams for an unscratched Teflon pan. Unless you're from the generation that grew up without Teflon, you probably have never had to cope without it, which is a good thing. Teflon allows easy-in and easy-out for crêpes, eggs, meats, and so on, without sticking.

2   Half-sheet pan, also known as a baking sheet: One of my favorite pans in the kitchen is the half-sheet pan, mostly because it fits in home ovens and refrigerators. It is nice for baking and for roasting lightweight meats and fish.

3   Roasting pan: For larger cuts of meat, the roasting pan is very durable and able to withstand the weight of larger cuts of meat and fish. The roasting pan also allows for added vegetables and liquid for making great pan gravy.

4   Saucepans: You will need these in small, medium, and large sizes. Small saucepans are perfect for reductions and blanching small quantities of vegetables or garnishes, and for small amounts of soup and sauce.

5   Stockpot: For making large quantities of soups and stocks, these range in size from small to large. A stockpot is also great for cooking pasta.

6   Sauce pot, also known as a soup pot: For larger quantities of soups and sauces, the sauce pot is the next gradation up from the saucepan. This pot is also used for cooking pasta and blanching vegetables.

7   Sautoir, also known as a sauté pan: A great pot for panfrying. It has straight sides and is versatile for both stove-top and oven cooking. Covered with a lid, it can be used for braising in the oven or on the stove top.

8   Sauteuse: Like a sauté pan, but with two short side handles instead of one long handle, which allows for easier storage. Curved sides allow the food in the pan to be tossed back and forth with small amounts of oil. This pan is very versatile; it comes in various sizes and has a place in every kitchen.

9   Wok: There are many different types of woks made of different materials. I prefer a thin-gauge steel wok that can fit on a home burner. A wok heats quickly and maintains heat so that food can be cooked quickly. There are two ways to manage the wok on the stove top: (1) Use wok utensils and stir the food; (2) Use the wok handles and flip the food from back to front. Both are effective, but the flipping method takes a bit of time to master.

10 Paella pan: One of my favorite dishes is a great paella. This type of pan is typically made of thin-gauge steel and is meant to be used on the stove top and in the oven.

APPLEWOOD-SMOKED MOLASSES & FIVE PEPPERCORN–CRUSTED PORK LOIN

FOREST BUFFET AT HARRAH'S LAKE TAHOE
EXECUTIVE CHEF JOE WELLS

Year after year, the Forest Buffet is voted Best Buffet in the annual Best of Tahoe readers' poll conducted by the *Tahoe Daily Tribune. Casino Player* magazine readers have also selected the restaurant as Lake Tahoe's Best Buffet. One reason for these glowing accolades is the following dish: boneless pork loin, brined in a sweet and salty mixture to keep it juicy, then smoked lightly over applewood, is brushed with molasses and spiced with peppercorns before being roasted to perfection and finished with more warmed molasses.

Notes: You will need ¾ cup applewood chips to make this recipe. The pork must be brined 48 hours and refrigerated overnight prior to cooking.

BRINE

8 cups cold water

¾ cup molasses

½ cup brown sugar

3 garlic cloves, crushed

½ cup kosher salt

¼ cup five-peppercorn blend

One 5- to 6-pound boneless pork loin roast

½ cup molasses

¾ tablespoon coarsely ground pepper mixed with 3 pinches onion powder

SERVES 15

For the brine: In a large pot, combine all the ingredients and bring to a boil. Remove from the heat and let cool.

Add the pork loin to the pot; it should be submerged in the liquid. Cover and refrigerate for 48 hours. Remove from the brine. Rinse and dry the pork well with paper towels. Refrigerate, uncovered, overnight. Remove from the refrigerator 30 minutes before cooking.

Soak ¾ cup applewood chips in water for 30 minutes. Drain.

Open the kitchen windows and turn on the exhaust fan. Add the drained chips to a pan smoker and place a wire rack over the chips. Or, to use a wok, line the wok with aluminum foil first, then add the drained chips and wire rack. Turn on the burner to medium heat. When the chips begin to smoke, reduce the heat to low, add the pork to the pan, and cover. Smoke for 1 hour and check, being sure not to go over 155°F.

Preheat the oven to 350°F. In a small saucepan, warm the molasses over low heat. Brush the warm molasses over the top of the pork loin, then sprinkle with the cracked pepper and onion powder mixture. Transfer the pork to a rack set in a roasting pan and roast 30 minutes, or until an instant-read thermometer inserted in the center of the meat registers 155°F. Transfer to a carving board, tent with aluminum foil, and let rest for 15 minutes. Cut into slices to serve.

HARRAH'S/HARVEYS LAKE TAHOE IS THE HOME OF THE *TAHOE STAR* (PICTURED ON PAGE 307), A 54-FOOT YACHT THAT WAS CUSTOM BUILT FOR WILLIAM F. HARRAH IN 1978, JUST BEFORE HE DIED. SPECIFICALLY DESIGNED FOR MR. HARRAH TO TAKE GUESTS OUT ON THE LAKE DURING THE SUMMER MONTHS, IT IS STILL USED FOR THIS PURPOSE TODAY.

MING'S GLAZED CHINESE PORK SPARERIBS

MING'S TABLE AT HARRAH'S LAS VEGAS
CHEF WINSTON CHUNG

Ming's Table boasts some of the finest Asian cuisine in Las Vegas. Chef Winston Chung is especially known for his pork spareribs, marinated in a mixture that includes soy sauce, hoisin sauce, and ginger.

Notes: The ribs need to be marinated for at least 8 hours before cooking. You can find ground bean sauce and malt sugar in most Asian markets.

2 pounds pork spareribs

MARINADE

¼ cup soy sauce

3 tablespoons hoisin sauce

3 tablespoons Shaoxing wine

2 garlic cloves, minced

¼ teaspoon five-spice powder

1 teaspoon minced fresh ginger

6 tablespoons sugar

3 pieces fermented bean curd, chopped

4 large eggs, beaten

1 tablespoon red food coloring

½ cup ground bean sauce (see notes)

GLAZE

1 teaspoon malt sugar (see notes)

1 tablespoon soy sauce

1 teaspoon Shaoxing wine

½ cup malt sugar for brushing the ribs
Sesame seeds for sprinkling (optional)

SERVES 4

Separate the ribs and trim off the excess fat. Put the ribs in a large baking dish.

For the marinade: In a medium bowl, combine all the ingredients and stir well. Pour the marinade over the ribs, cover, and refrigerate for at least 8 hours or overnight, turning occasionally. Remove from the refrigerator 30 minutes before cooking. Remove the ribs from the marinade and discard the marinade. Preheat the oven to 350°F.

For the glaze: In a small bowl, combine all the glaze ingredients, mixing well. Brush half of the glaze on the ribs.

Line a large roasting pan with aluminum foil. Put a wire rack in the pan and place the ribs on the rack. Roast for 30 minutes, then turn the ribs, brush with the remaining glaze, and roast for about 40 minutes more, or until tender when pierced. Remove from the oven.

To serve, brush the ribs with the malt sugar and sprinkle with sesame seeds, if you like.

BLACK FOREST HAM & GRUYÈRE CHEESE FEUILLETÉES

HARRAH'S LAKE TAHOE & HARVEYS LAKE TAHOE
EXECUTIVE CHEF JOE WELLS

A spectacular brunch dish: savory ham and cheese enclosed in crisp, golden puff pastry packets. A refreshing mesclun salad is just the right counterpoint. Chef Joe Wells and his team serve this as a special dish at Harrah's Lake Tahoe and Harveys Lake Tahoe.

3 sheets thawed frozen puff pastry

12 thin slices Black Forest ham (18 ounces total)

12 tablespoons (¾ cup) German mustard

2 cups shredded Gruyère cheese

5 large egg yolks beaten with 3 tablespoons heavy cream or water

9 ounces mesclun lettuce

1 apple, peeled, cored, and cut into thin slices

1 pear, peeled, cored, and cut into thin slices

12 walnut halves

¾ cup vinaigrette of choice

SERVES 6

Preheat the oven to 375°F. Line a baking sheet with parchment paper.

Lay a sheet of puff pastry on a work surface. Using a 6-inch round pastry cutter, cut out 12 rounds of pastry (4 per sheet). Place 1 slice of the ham on the puff pastry and brush with 1 tablespoon of the German mustard. Place ⅓ cup of the Gruyère cheese on the ham and top with another slice of ham and 1 tablespoon of the mustard. Brush another piece of puff pastry with the egg wash around the edge to use as a seal and place it on top. Press gently with a fork to seal the top pastry to the bottom pastry. Repeat this process to create 6 stacks. Brush the top of each with the egg wash and prick with a fork. Using a metal spatula, transfer to the prepared pan and bake for 10 minutes, or until puffed and golden. Remove from the oven and keep warm.

Divide the mesclun among 6 plates and top with the apple and pear slices. Sprinkle with the walnuts and drizzle with the vinaigrette. Place 1 pastry on each plate next to the salad and serve at once.

MOST OF THE 740 ROOMS AND SUITES
AT HARVEYS LAKE TAHOE OFFER STRIKING VIEWS OF
EITHER LAKE TAHOE OR
THE MAJESTIC SIERRA NEVADA MOUNTAINS.

MONTE CRISTO SANDWICH

BALLY'S ATLANTIC CITY
EXECUTIVE SOUS-CHEF RON ULCZAK

A variation on the croque monsieur, the traditional Monte Cristo is a ham or turkey sandwich that is battered and fried. Chef Ron Ulczak's version hews close to the original while adding refinements that make all the difference: He uses both ham and turkey; he adds beer, soda water, and baking powder to the batter to make it extra light; he uses rich and delicate challah for the bread; and he adds a little raspberry jam and confectioners' sugar for the perfect touch of sweetness.

BATTER

2 cups all-purpose flour

1 cup cornstarch

1 tablespoon baking powder

¼ teaspoon cayenne pepper

1 teaspoon salt

One 12-ounce bottle beer,
preferably Heineken

1 cup club soda

4 tablespoons raspberry jam

8 slices challah bread

4 slices Swiss cheese

4 slices ham

4 slices turkey

¾ cup canola oil for frying

Confectioners' sugar for dusting

SERVES 4

For the batter: In a large bowl, combine all the dry ingredients and stir with a whisk. Gradually whisk in the beer and club soda until smooth. Set aside.

For each sandwich, spread ½ tablespoon of the jam on 2 slices of bread. Cut the sliced cheese, ham, and turkey to the same dimensions as the bread slices. Top a slice of bread with 1 slice of cheese, then ham, and then turkey and a second slice of bread. Cut each sandwich in half.

In a large skillet, heat the oil over medium heat. Dip 2 sandwich halves in the batter to coat completely. Drop a little of the batter in the oil to see that it begins to cook. Once ready, add the sandwich and fry until golden brown, about 2 minutes on each side. Transfer to a low oven to keep warm. Repeat to fry the remaining sandwiches. Dust sandwiches with confectioners' sugar and serve.

SMOKED BABY BACK RIBS

TOBY KEITH'S I LOVE THIS BAR & GRILL & THE RANGE STEAKHOUSE AT HARRAH'S NORTH KANSAS CITY
TOBY KEITH & CHEF WILLIAM DWORZAN

These back ribs are a big seller at both of the Harrah's North Kansas City restaurants: A versatile dish, they can be ordered as appetizers, half slabs, and full slabs. They're also a favorite among Harrah's North Kansas City employees, who often enjoy them as a take-home meal. As chef William Dworzan says, "Everyone likes smoked ribs in Kansas City!"

Notes: The barbecue sauce needs to be prepared the day before the ribs are cooked. You will need 2 pounds hickory chips for this recipe. You can purchase Toby Keith's signature sauces and seasonings at his restaurant and at www.tobykeith.com.

MUSTARD-STYLE BARBECUE SAUCE

1 cup yellow mustard

½ cup sugar

¼ cup packed brown sugar

½ cup apple cider vinegar

¼ cup water

2 tablespoons chili powder

¾ teaspoon ground black pepper

¾ teaspoon ground white pepper

½ teaspoon soy sauce

2 tablespoons unsalted butter

1½ teaspoons liquid smoke

PORK DRY RUB

¼ cup ground black pepper

¼ cup sweet paprika

2 tablespoons sugar

1 teaspoon salt

½ tablespoon chili powder

1½ teaspoons garlic powder

1½ teaspoons onion powder

4 slabs pork baby back ribs

For the sauce: In a medium saucepan, mix together the mustard, sugar, brown sugar, apple cider vinegar, water, chili powder, black pepper, and white pepper. Bring to a simmer over medium-low heat and cook for 30 minutes. Stir in the soy sauce, butter, and liquid smoke and simmer for 10 more minutes. Remove from the heat and let cool. Cover and refrigerate overnight to allow the flavors to blend.

For the rub: In a small bowl, combine all the ingredients and stir to blend.

To cook the ribs, soak 2 pounds of hickory wood chips in water to cover for 1 hour. Score the back side of the ribs with a sharp knife moving across the bones. Rub the ribs completely and liberally with the dry rub on both sides.

Light a low fire in a charcoal grill. Move the coals to opposite sides of the grill for indirect heat. Place a disposable aluminum pan in the center of the fuel bed of the grill to catch drips. Drain the wood chips and sprinkle half of them over the coals. Place the ribs, bone side up, on the grill grids. Cover the grill and cook for 1 hour. Replenish the coals with live coals lighted in a charcoal chimney starter. Sprinkle the remaining wood chips over the coals and cook the ribs for 1 more hour. Replenish the coals again. Wrap the ribs completely with aluminum foil and cook them for 2 more hours, moving the coals together or replenishing them to maintain low heat as necessary.

Take the ribs out of the aluminum foil and baste them with the barbecue sauce. Serve immediately.

SERVES 4 TO 6

6

POULTRY

CHANTERELLE & PARMESAN–CRUSTED CHICKEN
WITH LEMON-BASIL CREAM SAUCE

HARRAH'S STEAK HOUSE AT HARRAH'S RENO
CHEF JEFFREY GALICK

Leave it to an award-winning steakhouse to serve the best chicken dish in town. If you're looking for a new way to serve chicken, chef Jeffrey Galick at Harrah's Steak House in Reno has the solution: Coat it in an intensely flavorful mixture of dried mushrooms and Parmesan, pan-roast it, and serve on a bed of sautéed spinach, topped with a tangy and velvety sauce.

1 cup all-purpose flour

Salt and freshly ground pepper

2 large eggs

½ cup heavy cream

2 cups grated Parmesan cheese

½ cup finely chopped dried black or golden chanterelle mushrooms

4 skinless, boneless chicken breast halves

5 tablespoons canola oil

LEMON-BASIL CREAM SAUCE

4 cups heavy cream

¼ cup water

2 tablespoons cornstarch

Juice of 3 lemons

Salt and freshly ground pepper

5 fresh basil leaves, julienned

1 tablespoon olive oil

2 cups spinach leaves, rinsed

SERVES 4

Preheat the oven to 400°F. In a shallow bowl, combine the flour and salt and pepper to taste and stir with a whisk to blend. In a second shallow bowl, whisk the eggs and heavy cream until blended. In a third shallow bowl, stir the Parmesan and mushrooms together.

Coat the chicken in the seasoned flour and shake off the excess. Next, dip the chicken in the egg mixture and let the excess run off. Lastly, coat the chicken well in the Parmesan and chanterelle mixture. In a large ovenproof sauté pan or skillet, heat the canola oil over medium heat and cook the chicken for 1 minute on each side. Transfer to the oven and bake for 12 minutes, or until opaque throughout.

For the sauce: In a small, heavy saucepan, simmer the cream over medium heat to reduce by half. In a small bowl, stir the water and cornstarch together until the cornstarch is dissolved. Gradually whisk the cornstarch mixture into the simmering cream until it thickens. Whisk in the lemon juice until smooth. Cook for 2 more minutes and season with salt and pepper. Remove from the heat. Stir in the basil just before serving.

In a small sauté pan, heat the olive oil over medium heat and sauté the spinach until wilted. Season with salt and pepper.

To serve, divide the spinach among 4 plates and place a chicken breast on each serving. Top with the cream sauce and serve at once.

PORTOBELLO CHICKEN CHARDONNAY

HARRAH'S JOLIET
EXECUTIVE CHEF SCOTT D. LECOMPTE

This is one of those appealing dishes that looks complicated but is really quite simple to prepare. Chef Scott D. LeCompte says, "While some preparations can be done ahead of time, you will be able to cook and finish this dish while still hosting your guests around the kitchen counter. The end result is a harmonious balance of quality fresh ingredients, which complement each other very well."

2 portobello mushrooms, stemmed

1 bunch asparagus, trimmed

1 teaspoon balsamic vinegar

Salt and freshly ground pepper

Four 10-ounce boneless chicken breasts, skin on and wing bone attached

4 ounces buffalo mozzarella, sliced

4 tablespoons olive oil

2 teaspoons minced garlic

2 teaspoons minced shallot

¼ cup Chardonnay or Pinot Grigio wine

¼ cup chicken stock

½ cup diced tomatoes

1 pound angel hair pasta, cooked

2 teaspoons sliced green onion

2 tablespoons cold unsalted butter, cut into bits

2 tablespoons grated Parmesan cheese

SERVES 4

Heat a grill pan over medium-high heat; oil the pan. Rub the mushrooms and asparagus with the balsamic vinegar and season them with salt and pepper. Grill the mushrooms for 4 to 5 minutes on each side and transfer to a plate; grill the asparagus for 3 to 4 minutes on each side and transfer to a plate. Let the mushrooms cool and cut them into thin slices.

Preheat the oven to 350°F. Using your fingers, make a pocket under the skin of each chicken breast. Stuff the mushrooms and mozzarella equally under the skin of each breast. Season the chicken with salt and pepper.

In a large ovenproof sauté pan or skillet, heat 2 tablespoons of the oil over medium-high heat and sauté the chicken, skin side down, for 3 to 4 minutes. Using tongs, transfer the chicken to a plate.

In the same pan, sauté the garlic and shallot until golden, about 4 minutes. Add the wine and chicken stock and stir to scrape up the browned bits from the bottom of the pan. Return the chicken to the pan and transfer the pan to the oven. Roast for 15 minutes, or until opaque throughout. Remove from the oven; transfer the chicken to a cutting board and keep warm.

Place the pan on the stove top over medium heat and cook to reduce by half. Add the tomatoes, asparagus, and pasta and cook for 2 minutes. Add the green onions. Taste and adjust the seasoning. Using a wire skimmer, transfer the pasta and vegetables to a platter and keep warm. Gradually whisk the butter into the sauce a few pieces at a time over low heat. Stir in the Parmesan cheese until melted. Cut the chicken into diagonal slices, place it on top of the pasta, pour the sauce over, and serve.

THE RESERVE RESTAURANT AT HARRAH'S JOLIET HAS RECEIVED *WINE SPECTATOR* AWARDS TWO YEARS IN A ROW FOR ITS DIVERSE MENU AND GRAND SELECTION OF WINES.

TOP 10 STAPLES THAT SHOULD BE IN EVERY KITCHEN AND WHY

HARRAH'S CHESTER CASINO & RACETRACK

1 Kosher salt or sea salt: You need to season your food. It doesn't come to you already seasoned.

2 Pepper mill with peppercorns: You will need this to properly season your food.

3 Coffee beans and a French coffee press: This produces the best coffee ever.

4 Soy sauce: A staple in every Asian kitchen.

5 Tabasco sauce: What else are you going to put on your eggs at 4 A.M.?

6 Instant noodles: When you don't know what to eat, you eat instant noodles.

7 Nishiki rice: This is a great short-grain rice. I eat this every day.

8 Rice wine vinegar: You need this when eating pot stickers, lumpia, or dumplings.

9 Instant brown gravy: This is necessary for loco moco: a large bed of rice, hamburger on top of that, gravy on top of that, and an over-easy egg on that. It's a Hawaiian delicacy that you can have right in your own kitchen whenever you want it!

10 Scotch: In case your recipes don't work out so well.

CHICKEN ROMANO

CARVINGS BUFFET AT HARRAH'S RENO
EXECUTIVE CHEF KLAUS FEYERSINGER

Chicken breasts, breaded and sautéed until golden brown, are topped with a long-cooked tomato sauce and served on buttered pasta for a satisfying dish. Carvings Buffet's time-tested version of the classic marinara sauce is equally good with seafood, pasta, and red meats.

MARINARA SAUCE

5 tomatoes

1½ cups olive oil, plus 3 tablespoons

2 teaspoons kosher salt

10 roasted garlic cloves (see page 48)

10 raw garlic cloves, peeled

½ cup finely chopped carrot

1 cup finely chopped celery

1½ cups finely chopped onions

1½ cups dry Marsala wine

4 cups canned San Marzano tomatoes

¼ cup sugar

2 teaspoons whole fresh thyme leaves

1 tablespoon minced fresh rosemary

2 tablespoons minced fresh oregano

3 tablespoons minced fresh basil

2 cups water

½ cup shredded fresh basil leaves

1 cup panko (Japanese bread crumbs), seasoned with a little salt and pepper

1 cup grated Romano cheese

1 cup all-purpose flour

Salt and freshly ground pepper

1 large egg

Four 6-ounce boneless, skinless chicken breast halves

2 tablespoons canola oil

Buttered cooked pasta for serving

Grated Parmesan cheese for garnish

SERVES 4

For the sauce: Preheat the oven to 400°F. Put the tomatoes in a small roasting pan. Coat with the 3 tablespoons olive oil and sprinkle with 1 teaspoon of the salt. Roast for 25 minutes, or until soft. Remove from the oven, let cool to the touch, and pull off the skins. Purée the tomatoes in a blender and set aside.

In a large, heavy saucepan, heat the 1½ cups olive oil over medium heat and sauté the roasted garlic, raw garlic, carrot, celery, and onions for about 8 minutes, or until the vegetables are tender. Add the wine and stir to scrape up the browned bits from the bottom of the pan. Add the canned tomatoes, roasted-tomato purée, sugar, thyme, rosemary, oregano, minced basil, remaining 1 teaspoon salt, and water. Bring to a boil over high heat, then reduce the heat to a simmer and cook for 1 hour. Working in batches, purée in a blender until smooth. Return to the pan and fold in the basil leaves.

In a shallow bowl, stir the panko and Romano cheese together. In a second shallow bowl, combine the flour with salt and pepper to taste; stir to blend. In a third shallow bowl, whisk the egg until blended. Dredge each chicken breast in the seasoned flour, then the egg, then the panko mixture.

In a large sauté pan or skillet, heat the oil over medium-high heat and sauté the chicken for 2 to 3 minutes on each side, or until golden brown on the outside and opaque throughout.

To serve, place some buttered pasta on each serving plate. Top with some of the sauce, then a chicken breast. Sprinkle with Parmesan cheese and serve at once.

WILLIAM F. HARRAH OPENED HIS FIRST BINGO PARLOR IN RENO IN 1937.

TOBY KEITH'S WHO'S YOUR DADDY? CHICKEN WINGS

TOBY KEITH'S I LOVE THIS BAR & GRILL AT HARRAH'S NORTH KANSAS CITY
TOBY KEITH & CHEF WILLIAM DWORZAN

At country music star Toby Keith's restaurant, these fiery classics can be purchased by the dozen or by the hundreds. Now, you can enjoy them at home for any occasion, from football games to backyard parties.

Note: You can purchase Toby Keith's signature sauces and seasonings at his restaurant and at www.tobykeith.com.

1 teaspoon cayenne pepper

½ cup hot pepper sauce

2½ pounds chicken wings, tips removed, halved at the joint

Canola oil for deep-frying

SERVES 4 TO 6

In a small bowl, mix the cayenne pepper with the hot sauce. In a large pot of boiling water, cook the chicken wings for 10 minutes. Drain and let cool.

In a large, shallow ceramic or glass bowl, combine the chicken with half of the hot sauce and toss well to combine. Cover and refrigerate for at least 1 hour or up to 3 hours.

In a Dutch oven or large heavy pot, heat 3 inches of the oil to 360°F on a deep-fat thermometer. In two batches, add the chicken and cook, turning occasionally, for 3 to 4 minutes, or until brown on all sides. Using a wire skimmer, transfer to paper towels to drain. Toss the chicken wings with the remaining hot sauce and serve immediately.

NEXT TIME YOU'RE AT TOBY KEITH'S RESTAURANT AT HARRAH'S NORTH KANSAS CITY OR HARRAH'S LAS VEGAS, DON'T BE SURPRISED TO SEE TOBY HIMSELF THERE SOME NIGHT. TOBY USUALLY STOPS BY THE RESTAURANT WHENEVER HE IS IN TOWN AND HAS ALSO BEEN KNOWN TO SING A SONG OR TWO FOR THE CROWD.

CREAM OF CILANTRO CHICKEN

CAESARS ATLANTIC CITY
SOUS-CHEF STEVE ORTIZ

Cilantro shines brightly in this dish, adding zip to the creamy sauce that dresses up the grilled chicken breasts. Chef Steve Ortiz says, "I created this recipe at home, and it was such a big hit that I decided to use it for my demo when I came to Caesars to work as a chef. We've been using it ever since."

6 boneless, skinless chicken breast halves

1 bunch cilantro, stemmed

¾ cup heavy cream

1 cup water

1 teaspoon chicken base

3 tablespoons unsalted butter

3 tablespoons all-purpose flour

Salt and freshly ground pepper

SERVES 6

Butterfly the chicken breasts by cutting them in half horizontally almost to the end; open them flat like a book. Heat a grill pan over medium-high heat and oil the pan. Cook the chicken breasts for 5 minutes on each side, then transfer to a plate and keep warm.

In a blender, combine the cilantro, cream, water, and chicken base, blending well; set aside.

In a medium saucepan, melt the butter over medium heat. Stir in the flour and cook, stirring constantly, for 3 minutes; do not brown. Whisk in the cilantro mixture and cook over medium heat, stirring frequently, until the mixture boils and thickens slightly. Season with salt and pepper.

Divide the chicken among plates and serve with the sauce poured over.

TOP 10 FOODS
THAT SHOULD BE IN EVERY FREEZER AND WHY

CAESARS WINDSOR

Although we all prefer to use fresh ingredients, high-quality processed frozen foods as well as food you've prepared and frozen are very helpful. Frozen foods can be highly nutritious and convenient, and they can allow the cook to create new and exciting dishes.

This list is in no particular order as it depends on personal needs and preference. You may have a butcher just around the corner or grow your own herbs year-round.

To begin with, here are a few important points:

+ For processed items, follow the manufacturer's directions for cooking and thawing.

+ Look for individually quick frozen (IQF) foods: Foods that are individually frozen before being packaged make thawing quicker and allow you to use just what you need. You can do this as well. For example, buy fresh chicken breasts in bulk and freeze them on a tray (keep the pieces from touching one another and use parchment paper between the layers). Once frozen, individually wrap the chicken breasts and place them into doubled freezer bags.

+ When processing or repackaging foods, properly label and date them.

+ Thaw frozen food in the refrigerator or under cold running water.

Always keep these foods in your freezer:

1   Meat: Freeze your own chicken breasts, satays, fish, seafood, and steaks, all of which can be thawed quickly in case of unexpected guests.

2   Hors d'oeuvres: Shrimp, meatballs, puff pastry shells, and tart shells for mini quiches.

3   Frozen fruits and berries: These are great for quick desserts, pancakes, or waffle toppings.

4   Vegetables: In most cases, frozen vegetables are picked when perfectly ripe and blanched before freezing. These processes preserve vitamins, color, and texture very effectively. In some cases, fresh vegetables can spend up to a week in transport and are not always better. Take care not to overcook frozen vegetables, as they are already partially cooked due to being blanched.

5   Stocks: Whether you make your own or buy a low-sodium stock, keep it on hand in small quantities, such as frozen into ice cubes. For larger amounts, make sure to use containers that will not burst and leave room for the liquid to expand when frozen. This week's chicken bones from a roasted chicken can be turned into a stock to use in next week's soup.

6   Base sauces: With frozen stock, make extra gravy the next time you have a pot roast. Freeze it and you will have a base for a peppercorn sauce for steak, and so on. A tomato sauce can be turned into a tomato-vegetable sauce, a bolognese, or even a quick tomato soup.

7   Fresh herbs: This is a great way to preserve fresh herbs: Wash, dry, and chop, then freeze covered on a tray, immediately crumble, and store in a bag. They are then ready to use as you would fresh.

8   Shredded potatoes: These are very helpful to have on hand. They can be used for hash browns, potato pancakes, potato-based frittatas, and more.

9   Partially cooked beans: Dried beans too often are avoided because of the cooking time they require. Partially cooking and then freezing them or purchasing them frozen opens up many possibilities for using these great sources of fiber and protein.

10 Breads and doughs: Keep frozen bread dough on hand for pizza, sweet rolls, dinner rolls, and loaves.

MEDITERRANEAN ARTICHOKE CHICKEN

THE RANGE STEAKHOUSE AT HARRAH'S LAUGHLIN
EXECUTIVE SOUS-CHEF JEREMY HUGHES

Of this popular dish, chef Jeremy Hughes remarks, "It was first introduced as a seasonal offering to complement our Mediterranean-themed menu. However, because of the popular demand for the dish, the restaurant has kept it through three menu changes."

3 tablespoons olive oil

1 cup all-purpose flour

Salt and freshly ground white pepper

Four 4-ounce boneless, skinless chicken breast halves

16 white mushrooms, each cut into fourths

4 teaspoons minced garlic

1 tomato, diced

20 artichoke hearts, each cut into fourths

4 teaspoons cracked black pepper

4 teaspoons dried oregano

½ cup fresh lemon juice

1½ cups sweet sherry

¾ cup whipped butter

12 mushroom ravioli

8 ounces feta cheese, crumbled (optional)

SERVES 4

Preheat the oven to 350°F. In a large ovenproof sauté pan or skillet, heat 1 tablespoon of the oil over medium-high heat. Put the flour in a shallow bowl and add salt and white pepper to taste. Coat the chicken in the flour on all sides. Cook the chicken for 2 to 3 minutes on each side. Transfer the pan to the oven and roast for 15 to 20 minutes, or until opaque throughout.

In a medium sauté pan, heat 1 table-spoon of the oil over medium heat and sauté the mushrooms for 1 minute. Add the garlic, tomato, artichokes, black pepper, oregano, and salt and white pepper and sauté for 3 minutes. Add the lemon juice and sherry and simmer for 1 minute. Add the butter, stirring until it is completely melted. Remove from the heat and keep warm.

In a large pot of salted boiling water, cook the ravioli for 5 minutes; drain. Add the ravioli to the vegetable and sherry mixture.

To serve, divide the ravioli among the plates. Spoon some of the vegetables on top of the ravioli, then place a chicken breast on top of each serving. Top with another spoonful of vegetables and some of the pan liquid. Sprinkle the feta cheese on top, if desired.

TOP 10 INGREDIENTS
EVERY KITCHEN SHOULD HAVE AND WHY

HARRAH'S LAKE TAHOE & HARVEYS LAKE TAHOE

1   Unsalted butter: Use unsalted butter to finish a sauce or any dish that's already perfectly seasoned.

2   Extra-virgin and virgin olive oil: Extra-virgin oils are not refined, which means that each one has its own unique character; virgin oils have a little more acidity. I use extra-virgin for vinaigrettes and to drizzle over vegetables. I combine virgin and butter for sautéing.

3   Kosher salt and fleur de sel: Kosher salt has no iodine and has a cleaner taste than regular table salt. Fleur de sel is an unrefined sea salt from France that is also worth having in your pantry.

4   White and black peppercorns, pepper blends, and pepper mills: Pungent, fiery flavor and aroma are the traits that pepper gives so many of the dishes we all love. Many times, this is the ingredient that awakens your taste buds.

5   Good white and red table wines for drinking and cooking: A good rule of thumb where wine and cooking are concerned is if you don't drink it, don't cook with it. Every variety of grape has certain foods that it belongs with.

6   Chicken and beef stock, fresh or from a can: Stock is a base for soups, sauces, and many other preparations. If making your own, cool the stock when finished and put it in ice cube trays to freeze. Seal the frozen cubes in airtight bags for quick pan sauces. Stock made from scratch provides a clean and fresh flavor to food. And the aroma of a stock cooking is as good as it gets.

7   Garlic and shallots: These are the building blocks for many savory recipes. Any haute cuisine recipe for sauce or soup will call for these members of the lily family.

8   A variety of vinegars: Made from wine, fruit juices, and similar acidic liquids, different vinegars have different levels of tartness. Some must-have vinegars include balsamic, Champagne, red and white wine, cider, sherry, and rice vinegar.

9   Herbes de Provence: I use this famous dried herb mixture for roast lamb, chicken, pork, and beef. It's a must in your kitchen, especially when fresh herbs aren't available.

10   Different varieties of rice: I can never get enough risotto, which is made with Arborio or Carnaroli rice. Other kinds of rice to keep on hand include jasmine and basmati.

(Can I sneak in pasta?)

11   A variety of good-quality dried pasta: This is a must for every kitchen. I have orzo, pappardelle, spaghetti, linguine, and conchiglie in my kitchen at home at all times. There are so many to choose from. If you prefer fresh pasta and have the time to make it, go for it.

Always remember, cook with your heart and buy in season.

TOP 10 FOODS
EVERY KITCHEN SHOULD HAVE AND WHY

CAESARS PALACE LAS VEGAS

1   Butter: The best fat, with multiple uses, including searing, emulsion, and more.

2   Heavy cream: The perfect finishing ingredient for such dishes as scrambled eggs, sauces, stews, and so on.

3   Garlic: Chopped, fried, or whole, garlic perfumes all dishes and is very healthy.

4   Shallots or onions: Raw or cooked, these staples will enhance most of the dishes you prepare, including salads, steaks, and fish.

5   Fresh herbs: Always keep some fresh herbs in your refrigerator crisper. Thyme, rosemary, basil, parsley, and others are perfect for all stages of preparation and for final touches and garnishes.

6   Wines: White, red, and sparkling wines are great for cooking, reducing, seasoning, and other uses. Often, wine is a must-have ingredient to create the desired marriage of flavors in a dish.

7   Eggs: When you have eggs in the refrigerator, you always have the makings of a meal. Cook them baked, poached, fried, or sunny side up, or make a cake, French toast—and the list goes on.

8   Cheeses: Cheese, from domestic shredded to fancy artisan ones, is a must-have for gratins, melting, spreading, and so on.

9   Yukon gold potatoes: Potatoes are a cheap, healthy vegetable that can be used to make hot appetizers such as potatoes soufflé, or side dishes like whipped potatoes or potato gratin. And everyone likes these sweet golden potatoes.

10 Tomatoes: A healthy accompaniment to many dishes. Preferably, you should use vine-ripened tomatoes, because they are so sweet and flavorful.

DEEP-FRIED TURKEY

HARRAH'S LOUISIANA DOWNS
EXECUTIVE CHEF J. RYAN GILLESPIE

Deep-fried turkey, which is injected with flavored melted butter before cooking, is moist and delicious. Chef J. Ryan Gillespie adds, "A word of caution: A common problem is that people misjudge the amount of oil needed, not allowing room for the turkey. But even when the oil is at the right level, a partially frozen turkey can also cause hot oil to spew a jet of fire." Use a fresh turkey for this recipe, or thaw a frozen turkey in the refrigerator for about twenty-four hours for every five pounds of turkey.

Note: This dish is best made out of doors, on grass, using the following equipment:

A turkey injection needle

A heavy-duty portable propane burner

A turkey-frying pot or a 40- to 60-quart stockpot

A deep-fat thermometer

A turkey hanger
(which has a hook that is attached deep inside the turkey, through the neck cavity)
or a frying basket
(which comes with a turkey-frying pot and fits inside it)

To figure how much oil to add to the pot: Put the turkey in the pot and add water to come to 3 to 5 inches from the top of the pot. Lift out the turkey and drain it well. Measure the water level in the pot with a ruler, then drain the pot. Dry the pot well. Dry the turkey inside and out as thoroughly as possible. Add oil to the correct level and heat. Keep children and pets away from the pot when it is filled with oil. Let the oil cool completely before draining it from the pot.

1 cup (2 sticks) unsalted butter

2 tablespoons iodized salt
(do not use kosher salt, as it will clog the injector)

2 teaspoons garlic powder

2 teaspoons finely ground white pepper
(do not use black pepper, as it will clog the injector)

2 teaspoons cayenne pepper

½ teaspoon onion powder

One 10- to 14-pound turkey, giblets and excess fat removed

3½ to 5 gallons of peanut oil for deep-frying

SERVES 10 TO 12

In a medium saucepan, melt the butter over low heat. Stir in the seasonings. Pour the mixture into a jar with a lid; close the lid tightly and shake the jar vigorously. Using a turkey injection needle, inject half of the mixture deeply into the two sides of the breast, half of the remaining mixture into the two legs/thighs, and the rest into the two meaty wing sections. Let the turkey sit for 1 hour before deep-frying it.

Fill the pot with oil to the previously measured mark. Heat the oil to 325°F to 350°F. Using the frying basket or the turkey hanger, gradually lower the turkey into the hot oil; it should be completely covered with oil. Cook the turkey for 3½ minutes per pound, 35 to 50 minutes. Carefully remove the turkey from the oil. Insert a meat thermometer into the thickest part of the thigh but not touching bone; the internal temperature should be 165°F to 170°F.

Transfer the turkey to a platter lined with paper towels to drain. Let rest for at least 15 minutes. Transfer to a carving board and carve the turkey.

HARRAH'S LOUISIANA DOWNS'
SIGNATURE RACE IS THE SUPER DERBY.
IT IS TOUTED AS A PREPARATORY RACE
FOR PROSPECTIVE PARTICIPANTS
TO THE BREEDERS' CUP CLASSIC. THE RACE TESTS
THE NATION'S BEST THREE-YEAR-OLD
THOROUGHBREDS AT A DISTANCE OF 1⅛ MILES.
IT IS THE HIGHLIGHT OF HARRAH'S LOUISIANA
DOWNS' DISTINGUISHED STAKES SCHEDULES.

SMOKED TURKEY & WHITE BEAN CASSEROLE

WITH HERBED CRUMB TOPPING

THE SEVEN STARS CLUB AT HARRAH'S RESORT ATLANTIC CITY
CHEF WILLIAM SCAFFIDI

This recipe takes the humble casserole to an entirely new level with a combination of smoky flavors, Cajun seasoning, and Parmesan cheese. Chef William Scaffidi comments, "This hearty casserole is a seasonal favorite with guests at our Seven Stars lounge and bar. Whether served as a side dish or as an entrée, this dish is always well received."

Note: Dried beans must be soaked overnight before cooking.

2 pounds smoked turkey breast or smoked duck breast, finely diced

8 cups chicken stock

¼ cup olive oil, plus 3 tablespoons

2 cups finely chopped onions

1 cup finely chopped celery

½ cup finely chopped bell pepper

2 tablespoons minced garlic

4 teaspoons minced fresh thyme

¼ teaspoon cayenne pepper

1½ teaspoons Cajun seasoning

2 bay leaves

1 pound dried white beans (navy or cannellini), soaked overnight and drained

Salt and freshly ground pepper

1¼ cups Italian bread crumbs

½ cup finely grated Parmesan cheese

2 tablespoons minced fresh flat-leaf parsley leaves

1 tablespoon minced fresh chives

1 tablespoon minced fresh basil

SERVES 6 TO 8

In a medium bowl, combine the diced meat and 2 cups of the chicken stock.

In a large Dutch oven or heavy pot, heat the 3 tablespoons oil over medium heat and sauté the onions, celery, and bell pepper until the vegetables are tender, 4 to 6 minutes. Add the garlic, 2 teaspoons of the thyme, the cayenne pepper, Cajun seasoning, and bay leaves and cook for 1 minute. Add the beans and the remaining 6 cups stock and return to a boil. Reduce the heat to a simmer and cook, partially covered, until the beans are tender but still firm enough to hold their shape, about 1½ hours. The beans should be moist but not soupy. Stir the turkey and stock mixture into the beans and season with salt and pepper. Transfer to a large ovenproof casserole dish.

Preheat the oven to 375°F. In a small bowl, combine the remaining thyme, the bread crumbs, cheese, parsley, chives, and basil. Add the remaining ¼ cup oil and stir with a fork until well blended. Season with salt and pepper. Sprinkle the bread-crumb mixture evenly over the beans. Bake for 25 to 30 minutes, or until the topping is golden brown and the beans are bubbly around the edges.

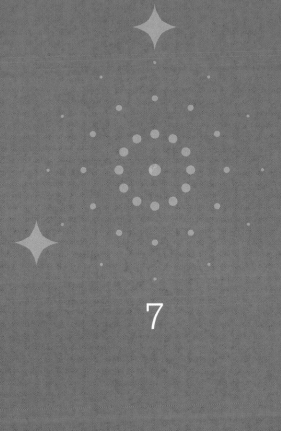

7

PASTA

PENNETTE ALLA VODKA

RAO'S AT CAESARS PALACE LAS VEGAS
CHEF DE CUISINE CARLA PELLEGRINO

Rao's has been a family affair for more than 110 years: Ron Straci and Frank Pellegrino are the powers behind the restaurant today, which began in New York and now is also featured at Caesars Palace in Las Vegas. Here, chef Carla Pellegrino prepares the same kind of simple, honest, Italian food that made the restaurant famous on the East Coast, like this classic pasta dish. The chef explains, "It's possible to find this dish in any Italian region. It's originally from the city of Parma, the ham and Parmesan cheese land. The Parmeggiani (people who were born in Parma) always came up with great recipes to use those two ingredients. This specific one from Rao's is easy, delicious, and memorable when served at any kind of party."

4 cups heavy cream

2 tablespoons unsalted butter

2 tablespoons olive oil

1½ large white onions, finely chopped

8 ounces Italian cooked ham, finely diced

5⅓ cups tomato sauce or blended canned peeled Italian tomatoes

3 tablespoons minced fresh flat-leaf parsley

¾ bottle vodka, preferably Absolut

Salt and freshly ground pepper

2 pounds imported Italian penne pasta, preferably De Cecco

SERVES 8

In a medium, heavy saucepan, bring the cream to a simmer and cook until reduced by half. Set aside.

In a large, heavy sauté pan or skillet, melt the butter with the oil over medium-high heat until the butter foams. Add the onions and sauté for 5 minutes, or until golden. Stir in the ham, reduce the heat to medium-low, and cook for about 15 minutes, stirring occasionally. Stir in the tomato sauce and simmer for 20 minutes. Add the parsley and simmer for 3 minutes. Add the reduced cream. Remove from the heat and stir in the vodka, mixing well. Return to medium-low heat and simmer for 20 minutes, or until thick enough to coat the back of a spoon. Season with salt and pepper. Set aside and keep warm.

Add the penne to a large pot of salted boiling water; stir well, reduce the heat to medium, partially cover the pot, and cook, stirring occasionally, until al dente, about 11 minutes; drain.

Add the cooked penne to the sauce. Simmer for 2 minutes and serve hot.

BLACK PEPPER FETTUCCINE
WITH WILD MUSHROOMS

SAGE ROOM STEAK HOUSE AT HARVEYS LAKE TAHOE
EXECUTIVE CHEF JOE WELLS

The Sage Room Steak House's famous Black Pepper Fettuccine with Wild Mushrooms is the perfect pasta dish on a cold night. Chef Joe Wells comments, "This dish is a little heavier pasta because of the cream sauce, while the peppercorns add spice and warmth, which I enjoy when it is a cold evening outside." It can also be served as an appetizer or a side dish for roasted chicken.

24 ounces black pepper pasta

1 teaspoon olive oil

2 ounces finely chopped pancetta

4 tablespoons whole butter

2 ounces morel mushrooms

2 ounces shiitake mushrooms, stemmed

2 ounces porcini mushrooms, chopped

2 teaspoons minced garlic

2 teaspoons minced shallot

4 artichoke bottoms, sliced

2 tablespoons Madeira wine

1 cup heavy cream

½ cup veal demi-glace

2 teaspoons finely chopped green onions, white part only

2 tablespoons cold unsalted butter

Salt

2 tablespoons crumbled fresh white goat cheese

SERVES 4

In a large pot of salted boiling water, cook the pasta until al dente, 8 to 9 minutes. Drain.

Meanwhile, in a medium sauté pan or skillet over medium heat, heat the oil and sauté the pancetta for 4 to 5 minutes, or until the fat is rendered. Add the 4 tablespoons of butter and the mushrooms and sauté until the mushrooms are tender, 3 to 4 minutes. Add the garlic, shallot, and artichoke bottoms and sauté for 1 minute. Add the wine and stir to scrape up the browned bits from the bottom of the pan. Add the heavy cream, demi-glace, and green onions. Whisk in the 2 tablespoons of unsalted butter, 1 tablespoon at a time. Season with salt.

In a pasta bowl, combine the drained pasta and hot sauce; stir to coat. Serve topped with goat cheese.

HARVEYS LAKE TAHOE WAS OPENED BY HARVEY GROSS IN 1947 AND WAS ACQUIRED BY HARRAH'S ENTERTAINMENT IN 2001.

STEAK & BLUE CHEESE MACARONI

LES ARTISTES STEAKHOUSE AT PARIS LAS VEGAS
ASSISTANT EXECUTIVE CHEF KURTESS MORTENSEN

Guests at Les Artistes enjoy this grown-up version of mac and cheese with its sophisticated combination of steak and blue cheese. Chef Kurtess Mortensen comments, "Beef and blue cheese are a classic pairing in French cuisine, almost as much as macaroni and cheese are for most Americans. We have found that bringing these two together elevates them both to a new level. The fact that the orders keep coming in tells us we are right!" This recipe redefines the concept of comfort food.

MORNAY SAUCE

5 tablespoons unsalted butter

½ cup all-purpose flour

4 cups milk

1 cup shredded Swiss cheese

¼ cup grated Parmesan cheese

Salt and freshly ground pepper

8 ounces elbow macaroni

2 tablespoons unsalted butter

8 ounces top sirloin, cubed

1 cup (5 ounces)
crumbled Roquefort cheese

¼ cup panko
(Japanese bread crumbs)

¼ cup grated Parmesan cheese

Salt and freshly ground pepper

SERVES 4 TO 6

For the sauce: In a large saucepan, melt the butter over medium-low heat. Stir in the flour and cook, stirring constantly, for 2 to 3 minutes. Do not let the mixture brown. Gradually whisk in the milk, continuing to stir as the sauce thickens. Bring to a boil, reduce the heat, and simmer for 4 to 5 minutes. Gradually stir in the cheeses and continue cooking until they are completely melted. Season with salt and pepper. Remove from the heat; set aside and keep warm.

In a large pot of salted boiling water, cook the macaroni until al dente, about 9 minutes. Drain and set aside.

In a large sauté pan or skillet, melt the butter over medium heat; add the sirloin and sauté for 5 minutes, or until medium-rare. Using a slotted spoon, transfer to paper towels to drain.

Preheat the oven to 325°F. In a large bowl, combine the macaroni, beef, and the Mornay sauce; stir well. Put the mixture in a 6-cup baking dish, cover with aluminum foil, and bake for 22 minutes. Remove the foil and top with the Roquefort cheese, panko, and Parmesan cheese. Season with salt and pepper. Return to the oven and bake for 10 minutes, or until golden brown. Remove from the oven and let cool for 5 minutes before serving.

TOP 10 TIPS
FOR HOME COOKS

HARRAH'S CHEROKEE

1   Always play with your food. When creating dishes, think of it as playtime. Are you cooking just to satisfy hunger, or are you trying to create something new?

2   Cook and serve others first, and hopefully a little will be left for you to enjoy. This is the best way to find out if the people you are feeding are enjoying your food. A lot of leftovers means you either cooked too much or they did not like it.

3   Cook like it's your last meal. When creating new dishes, savor the flavors.

4   Some maintain that belching is an option to show appreciation for great food. Use your discretion!

5   A way to a woman's heart is to clean up the kitchen after you have cooked for her. Hey, let's face it, no one likes to clean up after someone else.

6   With your meal, drink the wine you like, not the one "they" tell you to like. Everyone has an opinion of wine. The bottom line is: Who is drinking it?

7   Cook with your heart and soul, and others will follow with knives and forks. If you're a good cook, you'll always have lots of friends.

8   Always cook with passion. If you love to do something, you will always succeed. I cannot stress this enough: Cook with your heart and soul.

9   The best ribs are the ones that leave sauce all over your face. Have you ever seen a two-year-old eat? They have food all over their face, and did you ever notice how happy they look when they're done?

10 The best meals are the ones you eat with the ones you love. Even if the meat loaf is burnt, you are still with the ones you love, so what does it matter?

TOP 10 RULES
FOR HOME COOKS

HORSESHOE TUNICA

1   Start with quality ingredients.

2   Use quality knives.

3   Measure and weigh out ingredients before you start.

4   Have everything handy when cooking.

5   Clean as you go.

6   Enjoy what you are doing.

7   Research ingredients before you use them.

8   Use heavy saucepans to prevent burning or scorching.

9   Taste as you go.

10 Cook with good friends.

MAC & CHEESE

Chef Eric Damidot explains his version of this classic comfort food: "M&C, the most popular, simple-for-anyone dish—you eat it when you are a kid, you eat it after a nightclub 'extravaganza' night, you eat it when you are in a famous steakhouse making a huge business deal . . ." One thing for sure, the mac and cheese that follows is not the kind you ate as a kid.

WHITE CHEDDAR CHEESE SAUCE

½ cup (1 stick) unsalted butter

¼ cup minced garlic

1 bay leaf

2 shallots, minced

3 cups heavy cream

2 cups shredded
white Cheddar cheese

¼ cup grated Parmesan cheese

Salt and freshly ground white pepper

6 ounces pipette pasta

1½ ounces sliced prosciutto, julienned

Toasted bread crumbs for garnish

SERVES 2

For the sauce: In a large, heavy sauté pan or skillet, melt the butter over medium heat and sauté the garlic, bay leaf, and shallots until the shallots are translucent, about 3 minutes. Add the cream and simmer for 10 minutes. Remove from the heat and remove the bay leaf. Stir in the white Cheddar and Parmesan cheeses until melted. Season with salt and pepper. Set aside and keep warm.

In a large pot of salted boiling water, cook the pasta until al dente. Do not overcook. Drain.

Add the drained pasta to the sauce. Add the prosciutto and cook over low heat until slightly thickened. Divide among serving bowls and garnish with the bread crumbs.

RICOTTA RAVIOLI

CASA DI NAPOLI AT SHOWBOAT ATLANTIC CITY
CHEF GEORGEANN LEAMING

The chefs at Casa di Napoli believe that Italian food should be fun, fresh, and uncomplicated. This recipe for cheese ravioli, topped with a creamy tomato, shrimp, and crab sauce, meets that criterion. Chef Georgeann Leaming notes, "This pasta dish is a popular item with our guests. Typically, Italians do not serve cheese with their seafood, but that's the fun thing about cooking—if something tastes good, enjoy it and forget the rules."

1 tablespoon olive oil

8 ounces medium shrimp, shelled and deveined

1 cup diced tomatoes

2 cups marinara sauce

2 cups heavy cream

8 ounces fresh lump crabmeat, picked over for shell

Salt

⅛ teaspoon red pepper flakes

2 tablespoons thinly sliced fresh basil

2 pounds ricotta cheese ravioli

2 tablespoons minced fresh flat-leaf parsley

SERVES 4

In a large sauté pan or skillet, heat the oil over medium-high heat. Add the shrimp and sauté until they curl, about 1½ minutes. Turn the shrimp over and sauté on the other side, about 2 minutes. Reduce the heat to medium and add the tomatoes and marinara. Bring to a simmer, then add the heavy cream. Simmer for 5 minutes, then add the crabmeat, salt to taste, and red pepper flakes. Continue to simmer for another 5 minutes. Add the basil.

Meanwhile, in a large pot of salted boiling water, cook the ravioli until they rise to the surface, 10 to 12 minutes. Drain.

To serve, place the ravioli on a serving platter and pour the sauce over. Lightly toss the ravioli to coat. Garnish with the parsley.

SHOWBOAT CHEFS PURCHASE FRESH PRODUCE FROM THE LOCAL FARMERS' MARKET TO SHOWCASE THEIR RECIPES AND SUPPORT AREA FARMERS.

SIGNATURE LASAGNA

AL DENTE AT BALLY'S LAS VEGAS
CHEF BENOIT CHOBERT

Al Dente prides itself on blending the robust flavors of the Old World with contemporary flair. The secret to this lasagna's success is the ragù napolitano that masterfully blends sausage, beef, and pork for a rich, savory sauce. Chef Benoit Chobert says, "For more than a decade, al Dente has been at the heart of the Las Vegas Italian food scene. Using the best ingredients, we simmer the sauce for many hours, bringing out the boldness of the flavors. This is an everyday challenge, but an exciting one. We hope that you will enjoy this recipe at home and visit us at al Dente in the future."

RAGÙ NAPOLITANO

¼ cup olive oil

8 ounces sweet Italian sausage with fennel, removed from casing

8 ounces ground beef

8 ounces ground pork

1 onion, finely chopped

¾ cup dry red wine

Two 28-ounce cans Italian plum tomatoes with juice, passed through a food mill

Pinch of red pepper flakes

Salt and freshly ground pepper (optional)

2½ pounds lasagna noodles

4 cups fresh whole-milk ricotta cheese

1 teaspoon freshly ground black pepper

1 tablespoon minced fresh flat-leaf parsley

1 teaspoon minced fresh thyme

1 teaspoon dried oregano

1 tablespoon minced fresh basil

1 cup grated Parmesan cheese

1 pound fresh mozzarella cheese, shredded

SERVES 10 TO 12

For the ragù: In a large, heavy saucepan, heat the oil over medium heat and separately sear the sausage, beef, and pork until golden brown, transferring each to a plate with a slotted spoon as it is cooked. Add the onion and stir to scrape up the browned bits from the bottom of the pan. Add the wine, browned meats, tomatoes, and pepper flakes to the pot and bring to a boil. Reduce the heat to a simmer and cook, stirring occasionally and skimming the excess fat when necessary, for 3 hours. Taste and adjust the seasoning, if necessary. Set aside and keep warm.

Preheat the oven to 325°F. In a large pot of salted boiling water, cook the pasta until al dente. Do not overcook. Drain. In a medium bowl, combine the ricotta and the black pepper, parsley, thyme, oregano, and basil. Stir to blend.

Using a 12-by-20-inch lasagna pan, spread ½ cup of the ragù in the bottom of the pan. Top with a layer of lasagna, followed by a layer of ragù, ricotta, Parmesan, and mozzarella. Repeat the process to make 3 to 4 layers. Bake for 45 minutes, or until the top is browned and the lasagna is bubbling at the edges. Remove from the oven and let stand for 10 minutes prior to cutting and serving.

TOP 10 WAYS
TO ADD COLOR TO A PLATE

1   Emulsions: A mixture of two or more ingredients that are normally unblend-able. Culinary emulsions are usually liquids suspended in a fat, such as vinegar and oil in a vinaigrette, or egg yolks and oil in mayonnaise.

2   Reductions: Boiling a liquid (usually stock, wine, or a sauce mixture) rapidly until the volume is reduced by evaporation will thicken the liquid and intensify its color and flavor.

3   Infusions: Flavor and color can be extracted from an ingredient, such as tea leaves, herbs, or fruit, by steeping it in a liquid (usually hot), such as water or even olive oil.

4   Blanching: Plunging food (usually fruits and vegetables) briefly into boiling water, then into cold water to stop the cooking process, firms flesh, loosens skins, and heightens and sets color and flavor.

5   Purées: A purée is any food (usually a fruit or vegetable) that is finely mashed or ground to a smooth, thick consistency, which intensifies the color of the food.

6   Spices and powders: Spices, such as saffron and cumin, and powders, such as wasabi, can be added to foods to give both color and flavor.

7   Searing: Cooking foods over high heat on the stove top, under a broiler or on a grill, or in a very hot oven will give them a browned surface.

8   Caramelizing: Sugar can be cooked until it liquefies and darkens in color from golden to dark brown. The natural sugars in fruits and vegetables will also caramelize when the food is roasted, sautéed, grilled, or broiled.

9   Garnishes: These edible decorations can add color and interest to finished dishes from appetizers to desserts. Garnishes can be placed under, around, or on food, depending on the dish. They vary from simple sprigs of parsley to exotically carved vegetables. Garnishes should not only be appealing to the eye, but should also echo or complement the flavors of the dish.

10 Sauces: A wide variety of thickened, flavored liquids can enhance foods by adding both color and flavor.

RICOTTA GNOCCHI

GRAND BILOXI CASINO, HOTEL & SPA
EXECUTIVE CHEF JASON CARLISLE

These light cheese dumplings are easier to make than potato gnocchi and can be served with any number of sauces. Chef Jason Carlisle comments, "I love gnocchi, but hate potato gnocchi. My fellow chef and brother, Justin Carlisle, gave me this recipe several years ago, and I still use it to this day. It is a very simple all-cheese dumpling with minimal starch."

1 pound whole-milk ricotta

Salt and freshly ground white pepper

Pinch of grated nutmeg

1 large egg

1 cup all-purpose flour

Sauce of choice for serving

SERVES 6 TO 8 AS A FIRST COURSE
OR SIDE DISH

In a large bowl, combine the ricotta, salt and white pepper to taste, nutmeg, and egg. Stir well to mix. Fold in the flour, ⅓ cup at a time, until you can form a ball. Wrap the ball in plastic wrap and refrigerate for at least 30 minutes or up to 24 hours.

Divide the dough into 6 pieces. Roll each piece into a thick log. Cut the logs into teaspoon-size chunks. Roll the chunks into balls and press them onto the back of a fork.

In a large pot of salted boiling water, cook the gnocchi until they rise to the surface, 3 to 4 minutes. Toss with your favorite sauce and serve at once.

CAJUN SEAFOOD PASTA

HARRAH'S NORTH KANSAS CITY
CHEF ROY ASKREN

This hearty pasta dish makes a great main course, and you can also serve it in smaller portions as an appetizer to get your taste buds bubbling for more. It has a bounty of different flavors that is tantalizing to anyone's taste buds. The total combination of different meats, vegetables, and the blending of herbs increases the flavor of the seafood in the dish. And the bacon also adds a new and exciting flavor to this pasta. Chef Roy Askren warns, "Once they taste it, your guests will want more, so make plenty!"

1 pound large sea scallops

Salt and freshly ground pepper

¼ cup olive oil

1½ pounds penne pasta

8 strips bacon, cut into ½-inch pieces

2 ounces andouille sausage, thinly sliced

1 tablespoon finely diced red bell pepper

3 tablespoons mixed finely diced carrot, celery, and onion

1 tablespoon sliced garlic cloves

½ tablespoon minced fresh thyme

6 bay leaves

2½ tablespoons Zatarain's Blackened Seasoning

8 ounces extra-large shrimp, shelled and deveined

2½ cups lobster stock (page 202)

2¼ cups heavy cream

2 finely diced fresh tomatoes

4 ounces fresh lump crabmeat, picked over for shell (optional)

2 tablespoons grated Parmesan cheese

1 tablespoon minced fresh chives

Fried leeks for garnish (optional)

SERVES 6 AS A MAIN COURSE, OR 10 AS A FIRST COURSE

Pat the scallops dry with paper towels and season with salt and pepper. In a large sauté pan or skillet, heat the oil over high heat and sear the scallops until golden, about 4 minutes on each side. Using a slotted spoon, transfer to a plate and keep warm.

In a large pot of salted boiling water, cook the pasta until al dente, about 12 minutes. Drain.

Add the bacon and sausage to the pan used to cook the scallops and cook until lightly browned, about 7 minutes. Add the vegetables, garlic, thyme, bay leaves, seasoning, and shrimp and sauté for 2 or 3 minutes. Remove the shrimp and set aside to keep warm. Add the lobster stock and heavy cream, bring to a simmer, and then add the pasta and tomatoes. Cook to reduce the sauce to about 2 cups. Add the crabmeat, if using, and Parmesan cheese. Toss together and divide among the plates. Divide the scallops and shrimp among the servings, sprinkle with the chives, and the leeks, if you like, and serve at once.

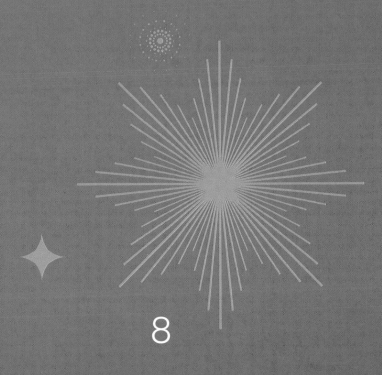

8

FISH + SEAFOOD

TOP 10 TIPS
FOR CHOOSING FISH

HARRAH'S LAUGHLIN

Knowing how to choose fresh fish is a vital skill for a seafood cook. Unless you have caught the fish yourself, you have no way of knowing exactly how fresh it is. But buying fresh fish is easy if you know what to look for.

WHOLE FISH

1. Look for bright, clear eyes: The eyes are the window to a truly fresh fish, for they fade quickly into gray dullness. Dull-eyed fish may be safe to eat, but they are past their prime.

2. Look at the fish: Does it shine? Does it look metallic and clean? Or has it dulled or have discolored patches on it? If so, it is marginal.

3. Smell the fish: A fresh fish should smell like clean water, or a touch briny or even like cucumbers. Under no circumstances should you buy a nasty-smelling fish. Cooking won't improve it.

4. Look at the gills: The gills should be a rich red. When a fish is old, they will be the color of faded brick.

FISH FILLETS

5. Look for vibrant flesh: All fish fade as they age. If a fillet has skin, that skin should look as pristine as the skin on an equally good whole fish (shiny and metallic).

6. Smell them: The smell test is especially important with fillets. They should have no pungent aroma.

7. Is there liquid on the meat? If so, that liquid should be clear, not milky. Milky liquid on a fillet is the first stage of rot.

8. Press the meat with your finger: It should be resilient enough so that your indentation disappears. If your fingerprint remains, move on.

9. If you can, buy your fish at a fish market: These are the places where turnover is so rapid, you can be assured of fresh fish. Make friends with your fish supplier: Find out when a fresh supply comes in and be there to buy that day.

10. When buying live fish, look for "life": When picking live fish, choose one that is swimming around with energy, not just staying in one corner of the tank.

TOP 10 TIPS
FOR PURCHASING SEAFOOD

HARRAH'S LOUISIANA DOWNS

1   Smell the air in the store before you buy anything and notice how busy the seafood department is. You want to find a place that sells a lot of fish, not one that keeps its fish on ice until it starts to get that strong fishy odor.

2   Buy whole fish if you see that the scales are even and attached to moist, glistening skin. If the gills are still attached, skip it if they are brownish or slimy instead of bright red. Also, the eyes should be clear, not cloudy.

3   Select fillets that have an even, appropriate color for that kind of fish (translucent white to deep red, depending on the variety). They should be neatly trimmed, not ragged or torn. You should see no signs of freezer burn, and the flesh should be firm.

4   Reject any smoked fish that feels sticky, has skin and eyes that do not look glossy, or that smells like anything besides smoke.

5   Choose only frozen fish that have no evidence of thawing, freezer burn, or damaged packaging. The flesh should be frozen hard, not mushy or squishy.

6   Buy fresh fish fillets whenever possible. Frozen fish can end up soggy and tasting watery. Check that the fillet is more or less the same thickness throughout. If it is not, the thinner parts will overcook. You can always trim the fillets to remove the thinner sections and cook them separately, starting with the thicker piece first.

7   Look over shellfish carefully. Shells should not be broken, cracked, or damaged in any way. Opened oyster and mussel shells should close when tapped. Lobsters, crabs, and shrimp should feel heavy for their size and not be missing any legs. Live crabs and lobsters should show some signs of movement.

8   When buying mollusks, ask to see shellfish tags. These tags allow you to see when and where the mollusks were harvested.

9   If fish at the store is on sale, ask yourself why and go back through the previous eight steps.

10 Only purchase what you plan on cooking and eating within the next two to three days. Fish will keep better when stored packed in ice in a self-draining container in the refrigerator.

BLUE CORN–CRUSTED RED SNAPPER

WITH WARM TOMATO RELISH

BOBBY FLAY'S MESA GRILL AT CAESARS PALACE LAS VEGAS
CHEF BOBBY FLAY

Famed chef Bobby Flay comments, "This warm, fresh tomato relish is my take on the traditional Mexican recipe, sauce Veracruz. As the tomatoes, olive oil, and capers are also Mediterranean ingredients, the addition of basil and picholine olives is a natural choice. The relish is great with the red snapper or halibut in a crisp blue corn coating." The smoked red pepper sauce, one of the workhorses of the chef's Mesa Grill kitchen, adds a deep color and flavor to this dish and can be used with many others.

WARM TOMATO RELISH

2 tablespoons olive oil

1½ cups halved red cherry or grape tomatoes

2 garlic cloves, minced

2 serrano chiles, thinly sliced

1 cup V8 juice

2 teaspoons honey

½ cup pitted picholine olives

2 tablespoons drained capers

2 tablespoons chopped fresh basil

2 teaspoons chopped fresh oregano

Kosher salt and freshly ground black pepper

BLUE CORN-CRUSTED SNAPPER

1 cup all-purpose flour

3 large eggs

2 tablespoons water

2 cups coarsely crushed blue corn chips

Kosher salt and freshly ground pepper

Four 8-ounce skinless red snapper or halibut fillets

¼ cup canola oil

Smoked Red Pepper Sauce (see recipe facing page)

Fresh oregano leaves, sliced green onion, and microgreens for garnish (optional)

SERVES 4

For the relish: In a medium sauté pan or skillet, heat the oil over high heat. Add the tomatoes, garlic, and chiles and sauté for 1 minute. Add the vegetable juice and honey, bring to a simmer, and cook for 2 to 3 minutes. Add the olives, capers, basil, and oregano and cook for 1 minute more. Season with salt and pepper. Use now, or let cool, cover, and refrigerate for up to 24 hours. Reheat before serving.

For the snapper: Put the flour in a medium, shallow bowl. In another shallow bowl, whisk the eggs with the water. Put the blue corn chips in a third shallow bowl. Season the flour and eggs with salt and pepper.

Season each fillet on both sides with salt and pepper. Dredge one side of each fillet first in the flour, tapping off any excess flour, then in the egg, and finally in the crushed blue corn chips. In a large nonstick sauté pan or skillet, heat the oil over medium-high heat. Put the fish in the pan, coated side down, and cook until a crust forms, 2 to 3 minutes. Flip the fish over and continue cooking for 4 to 5 minutes, or until just opaque throughout.

To serve, spoon some of the relish in each of 4 large shallow bowls. Place the fillets on top, garnish with more of the relish, and drizzle with the Smoked Red Pepper Sauce. Garnish with oregano leaves, green onion, and microgreens, if desired.

✦ ✦ ✦ ✦ ✦ ✦ ✦

Roasting and peeling bell peppers: Brush the peppers with olive oil and season them with salt and pepper. Place on a rimmed baking sheet and roast in a preheated 375°F oven, rotating them until they are charred on all sides, 15 to 17 minutes. Remove from the oven, place in a bowl, and cover with plastic wrap. Let stand for 15 minutes to allow the skin to loosen. Peel and seed. Roasted red peppers can be covered and stored for up to 5 days in the refrigerator.

SMOKED RED PEPPER SAUCE

4 red bell peppers, roasted, peeled, and chopped (see note facing page)

½ small red onion, coarsely chopped

4 cloves roasted garlic (see page 48)

¼ cup red wine vinegar

1 tablespoon honey

1 tablespoon Dijon mustard

1 tablespoon puréed chipotle chiles en adobo

½ cup canola oil

Kosher salt and freshly ground black pepper

In a blender, combine the bell peppers, onion, garlic, vinegar, honey, mustard, and chipotle purée and blend until smooth. With the machine running, gradually add the oil and blend until emulsified. Empty the sauce into a bowl and add salt and pepper. Use now, or cover and refrigerate for up to 24 hours.

MAKES ABOUT 2½ CUPS

PEANUT-CRUSTED TROUT

SYCAMORES ON THE CREEK AT HARRAH'S CHEROKEE
EXECUTIVE CHEF KEITH ANDREASEN

One of the renowned trout-fishing areas in this country is in Cherokee, North Carolina. Chef Keith Andreasen says, "When we opened Sycamores on the Creek, we had to create a great trout dish. We did that with this recipe. Everyone was in agreement that this dish was going to be a favorite of our guests, and it didn't disappoint us. This has turned out to be one of our most popular dishes."

Two 8-ounce skin-on trout fillets

2 tablespoons crushed peanuts

½ cup plus 2 tablespoons canola oil

6 extra-large shrimp, shelled and deveined

1 tablespoon corn kernels

1 tablespoon diced tomato

½ cup baby spinach leaves

½ cup heavy cream

Salt and freshly ground pepper

Mashed potatoes for serving

2 tablespoons minced fresh flat-leaf parsley for garnish

2 lemon wedges for garnish

SERVES 2

Preheat the oven to 350°F. Encrust the flesh-side of the trout with the peanuts. In a large ovenproof sauté pan or skillet, heat the ½ cup oil over medium-high heat and sear the trout, crusted side down, until golden brown, about 4 minutes. Turn the trout over and transfer the pan to the oven. Roast for 5 minutes, or until opaque throughout. Remove from the oven and keep warm.

In a medium sauté pan or skillet, heat the 2 tablespoons oil over high heat. Add the shrimp and cook for 1½ minutes on each side, or until evenly pink. Add the corn, tomato, and spinach and cook until the spinach is lightly wilted. Add the heavy cream and season with salt and pepper. Cook until the sauce has thickened enough to coat the back of a spoon.

To serve, place a scoop of mashed potatoes off-center toward twelve o'clock on a plate. Lean the trout, tail-side up, on the mashed potatoes. Pour the sauce over the trout and place the shrimp on top of the trout. Garnish each plate with parsley and a lemon wedge.

BRONZED FISH
WITH JALAPEÑO TARTAR SAUCE

K-PAUL'S LOUISIANA KITCHEN
CHEF PAUL PRUDHOMME

Chef Prudhomme says: "Bronzing is a wonderful cooking technique for meat or fish—and it's so simple. You roast one side of the meat or fish at a time on a heavy griddle or in a large, heavy aluminum skillet or an electric skillet heated to 350°F. (You can purchase a surface thermometer, or pyrometer, to measure dry temperature of a griddle or aluminum skillet.) If you omit the butter or oil, bronzing produces delicious reduced-fat meat and fish dishes. Just spray the fish or meat surfaces with nonstick cooking spray before seasoning."

Note: Chef Prudhomme's sauces and seasonings are available at www.ChefPaul.com.

JALAPEÑO TARTAR SAUCE

1 cup mayonnaise, preferably Hellman's or Best Foods

1 tablespoon minced green jalapeño chile

2 teaspoons minced red jalapeño chile

½ teaspoon fresh lemon juice

2 tablespoons prepared horseradish sauce

2 tablespoons minced red onion

2 tablespoons minced green bell pepper

¼ cup sweet pickle relish

1 teaspoon minced garlic

2 hard-boiled eggs, shelled and finely diced

1 teaspoon Chef Paul Prudhomme's Vegetable Magic

1 teaspoon Chef Paul Prudhomme's Barbecue Magic

1 teaspoon Chef Paul Prudhomme's Magic Pepper Sauce

Four 4½-ounce fish fillets, each about ½ to ¾ inch thick at thickest part

3 tablespoons unsalted butter, melted, or canola oil

About 4 teaspoons Chef Paul Prudhomme's Seafood Magic

SERVES 4

For the jalapeño tartar sauce:
Combine all the sauce ingredients in a food processor and pulse until well blended. Cover and refrigerate.

Place a nonstick aluminum skillet over medium-high heat until very hot, about 7 minutes. Lightly coat both sides of each fillet with the butter or oil, then sprinkle one side with ½ teaspoon of Seafood Magic. Place the fish in the skillet, seasoned-side down, and sprinkle the top of all the fillets evenly with the remaining seasoning. Cook until the undersides of the fillets are bronzed, about 2½ minutes. Watch as the fish cooks and you'll see a white line coming up the side of each fillet as it turns from translucent to opaque; when the bottom half of the fillet is opaque, the fish is ready to be turned.

Turn the fish and cook about 2½ minutes longer. To test for doneness, simply touch the fish in the center; it should be lightly firm. You also can use a fork to flake the fish at its thickest part—if it flakes easily, it is done. You can turn the fish more than once until cooked to the desired doneness. Do not overcook, as the fish will continue to cook even after you remove it from the heat.

Serve immediately with the jalapeño tartar sauce as a garnish or dipping sauce.

EXECUTIVE CHEF VESA LEPPALA'S

TOP 10 MISTAKES TO AVOID IN THE KITCHEN

HARRAH'S RINCON CASINO & RESORT

1   Using dull knives.

2   Sautéing food in a sauté pan or skillet that is not hot enough, unless you like a boiled dinner.

3   Overloading food in a sauté pan or skillet.

4   Using salt for sugar (except on a margarita).

5   Using a wet rag or kitchen towel to grab a hot pan.

6   Running in the kitchen.

7   Not tasting what you cook or tasting too much of what you cook.

8   Overcooking pasta.

9   Undercooking egg yolks for hollandaise sauce.

10 Invoking the three-second rule. Don't believe in it!

TOP 10 THINGS FOR THE NOVICE CHEF NOT TO DO IN THE KITCHEN

(BASED ON ONE CHEF'S EXPERIENCES)

1   If you burn your hand on a hot pan, do not bend down in agony and then burn your forehead on the stove.

2   When having two people lift a full twenty-gallon, boiling-hot soup pot from the floor onto the steam table, please make sure that the person on one side is not six feet five and the other five feet two.

3   If you answer the wall phone in the kitchen, do not place the handset and cord in or on a mixer while you go looking for the chef, because when you can't find the chef (again) and you return to the mixer and turn it on, this will rip a hole in the wall. The health department does not like holes.

4   Flambéing is not the best way to remove eyebrows, but it may be the fastest.

5   Be careful when ordering sweetbreads for your function as you may receive Mexican pan dulce (sweet rolls) instead. This happens all the time in southern California.

6   When a recipe calls for whole eggs, make sure the shell is removed.

7   Do not taste boiling caramel sauce with your finger (even if it looks good) and especially do not (as a reflex) put the burning finger in your mouth. That's a double whammy.

8   You do not need a huge flatbed truck to go and pick up one horse . . . radish.

9   Don't plate next Wednesday's banquet for 150 people on Wednesday of the current week.

10 Never cook osso buco medium-rare.

Here is one more for good measure:

Never answer your cell phone while standing over a full two-hundred-gallon stock kettle!

SHRIMP STOCK

3 cups shrimp shells

1 gallon water

1 large leek, cut into 1-inch pieces

1 pound carrots, cut into 1-inch pieces

1 pound onions, cut into 1-inch pieces

1 pound celery stalks, cut into 1-inch pieces

1½ tablespoons tomato paste

5 or 6 thyme sprigs

½ bunch flat-leaf parsley sprigs

1 bay leaf

½ teaspoon peppercorns

In a stockpot, combine all the ingredients. Bring to a boil, then reduce the heat to a simmer. Cook for 2 to 3 hours, or until flavorful. Strain. Cover and refrigerate for up to 2 days, or freeze for up to 3 months in a plastic container with a lid.

Lobster Stock: Replace the shrimp shells with lobster shells in the above recipe.

MAKES ABOUT 14 CUPS

RED GROUPER
WITH STEWED TOMATOES, OKRA & CRAWFISH

MAGNOLIA, A DELTA GRILLE AT HORSESHOE TUNICA

The Mississippi Delta, some say, starts in Memphis and ends in New Orleans. This is the area the chefs focus on in the restaurant. Everyone in the South has had stewed tomatoes and okra at some point in their stay there. These foods are homey and local. In this dish, a Cajun/Creole flair is added, making them even better.

CAJUN SEASONING

1 tablespoon paprika

2 teaspoons ground black pepper

1½ teaspoons salt

1 teaspoon garlic powder

1 teaspoon cayenne pepper

½ teaspoon dried oregano

½ teaspoon dried thyme

4 cups shrimp stock
(see recipe facing page)

6 to 8 tomatoes, peeled and quartered

1 to 2 cups fresh or frozen okra

6 ounces cooked and peeled
crawfish tails

Salt and freshly ground pepper

Four 6- to 8-ounce red grouper fillets

3 tablespoons mild-flavored oil or
clarified butter (see page 43)

Minced fresh chives for garnish

SERVES 4

For the seasoning: In a small bowl, combine all the ingredients and stir to blend.

In a medium saucepan, bring the shrimp stock to a simmer. Add the tomatoes and cook for 3 minutes. Add the okra and cook for 2 to 3 minutes. Add the crawfish, salt and pepper to taste, and 1 tablespoon of the Cajun seasoning. Cook for 1 minute. Remove from the heat and keep warm.

Preheat the oven to 500°F. Season the fish with salt, pepper, and Cajun seasoning.

In a large ovenproof sauté pan or skillet, heat the oil or clarified butter over medium-high heat until almost smoking. Add the fish, being careful not to overload the pan, and cook for 1 to 2 minutes on each side, until golden. If cooking in batches, add all the fish to the pan and transfer to the oven for about 5 minutes, or until opaque throughout.

To serve, using a slotted spoon, place some of the tomato mixture in each of 4 large shallow bowls and place the fish on top. Ladle some of the liquid from the tomato mixture into the bowls. Garnish with the chives and serve at once.

BLUESVILLE, HORSESHOE TUNICA'S ENTERTAINMENT VENUE,
IS ONE OF THE BEST IN THE AREA.
GUESTS CAN WATCH HEADLINE ENTERTAINMENT IN AN INTIMATE,
FIFTEEN-HUNDRED-SEAT PERFORMANCE SPACE.
STARS SUCH AS VINCE GILL, CHICAGO, JOE COCKER, FAITH HILL,
ROGER DALTREY, AND RAY CHARLES, TO NAME A FEW,
HAVE PERFORMED ON THE BLUESVILLE STAGE.

PAN-ROASTED HALIBUT
WITH SALSA PROVENÇAL

FIORE AT HARRAH'S RINCON CASINO & RESORT
EXECUTIVE CHEF VESA LEPPALA

Chef Vesa Leppala sums up the appeal of this dish, the most popular seafood offering at Fiore: "It's light, healthy, and full of Mediterranean flavor." The combination of roasted fingerling potatoes, pan-roasted halibut, and a fresh salsa of cherry tomatoes and kalamata olives makes for a satisfying and savory meal.

SALSA PROVENÇAL

⅓ cup extra-virgin olive oil
¼ cup halved cherry tomatoes
¼ cup pitted kalamata olives
1 tablespoon sliced garlic
1 tablespoon minced fresh basil
1 tablespoon capers
Salt

1½ pounds fingerling potatoes
3 tablespoons canola oil
1 tablespoon minced fresh thyme
Salt and freshly ground pepper
2 tablespoons extra-virgin olive oil
Four 8-ounce halibut fillets

SERVES 4

For the salsa: In a medium bowl, combine all the ingredients and stir to blend. Cover and refrigerate for 3 hours.

Preheat the oven to 375°F. In a large bowl, combine the potatoes, canola oil, thyme, and salt and pepper to taste; toss well to coat. Place on a sided baking sheet and roast until tender, about 20 minutes. Remove from the oven, leaving the oven on; set aside and keep warm.

In a large ovenproof sauté pan or skillet, heat the olive oil over medium-high heat until shimmering. Add the halibut and sauté for 3 minutes on each side. Transfer to the oven and roast for 10 minutes, or until the fish is opaque throughout. Transfer to a plate and let stand for 5 minutes. The fish will continue to cook.

To serve, divide the potatoes among the plates, place the halibut on top, and spoon 2 to 3 tablespoons of salsa over each serving of fish. Serve at once.

FIORE WON *WINE SPECTATOR* MAGAZINE'S AWARD OF EXCELLENCE FOR THREE CONSECUTIVE YEARS, 2007, 2008, AND 2009.

LEMON SOLE–WRAPPED ASPARAGUS
WITH ORANGE-CITRUS BEURRE BLANC

SYCAMORES ON THE CREEK AT HARRAH'S CHEROKEE
SOUS-CHEF KEVIN CONRAD

In this beautiful presentation, lemon sole fillets are wrapped around asparagus spears and baked, then served topped with a tangy cloud of beurre blanc. It's a favorite at Sycamores on the Creek and a perfect choice for a special-occasion dinner at home.

Four 6-ounce lemon sole fillets

Salt and freshly ground pepper

20 to 24 asparagus spears, trimmed

1½ tablespoons unsalted butter, melted

2 tablespoons minced shallots

2 tablespoons grated orange zest

½ cup water

BEURRE BLANC

½ cup fresh orange juice

1 tablespoon minced shallot

½ cup (1 stick) cold unsalted butter, cut into 8 pieces

¼ teaspoon salt

Pinch of cayenne pepper

½ teaspoon dry white wine

SERVES 4

Preheat the oven to 450°F. Season the fish with salt and pepper. Lay 5 or 6 asparagus spears across each fillet. Wrap the fish around the asparagus to form a bundle. Using the melted butter, grease a 9-by-13-inch roasting pan and sprinkle the shallots and orange zest in the pan. Add the fish, then the water. Cover the pan with aluminum foil and bake for 20 minutes. Remove from the oven and keep warm.

For the beurre blanc: In a small, heavy saucepan, combine the orange juice and shallot. Bring to a boil over medium-high heat and cook for 4 to 5 minutes, until the shallots are translucent. Reduce the heat to low and whisk in the butter, 1 tablespoon at a time, whisking constantly to make a thick sauce. Remove from the heat and add the remaining ingredients. Drain the juice from the cooked fish into a small, heavy saucepan. Bring to a boil and cook for 2 minutes. Gradually whisk the juice into the beurre blanc.

Serve at once, with the beurre blanc poured over the fish and asparagus.

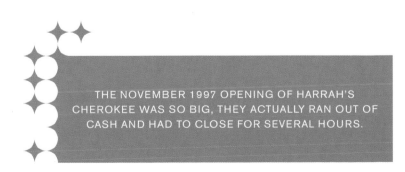

THE NOVEMBER 1997 OPENING OF HARRAH'S CHEROKEE WAS SO BIG, THEY ACTUALLY RAN OUT OF CASH AND HAD TO CLOSE FOR SEVERAL HOURS.

BLACKENED MAHI MAHI
WITH BUTTERNUT SQUASH POLENTA & GRILLED ASPARAGUS

OYSTER BAR AT PENAZZI AT HARRAH'S LAS VEGAS
CHEF BRIAN FAIRHURST

This sophisticated dish from the Oyster Bar at Penazzi can also be a special-occasion feast for the home cook. For family-style serving, spread the butternut squash polenta down the center of a large platter. Place the asparagus on top in a line, then place the blackened mahi mahi on top. Drizzle the sun-dried tomato vinaigrette over the fish.

BUTTERNUT SQUASH POLENTA

2 cups diced butternut squash

3 cups milk

1½ cups quick white grits

1 teaspoon ground nutmeg

3 tablespoons packed brown sugar

Salt and freshly ground pepper

SUN-DRIED TOMATO VINAIGRETTE

1 cup drained oil-packed sun-dried tomatoes

¼ cup pine nuts

½ cup balsamic vinegar

1 cup extra-virgin olive oil

Salt and freshly ground pepper

BLACKENED MAHI MAHI

¼ cup olive oil

Six 5- to 6-ounce mahi mahi fillets

¾ cup blackening spice (page 142)

2 bunches asparagus, trimmed

SERVES 6

For the polenta: In a medium saucepan of salted boiling water, cook the squash until just tender, 8 to 10 minutes. Drain. In another medium saucepan, bring the milk to a boil and gradually stir in the grits. Reduce the heat to low and cook, stirring occasionally, until thickened, about 5 minutes. Stir in the squash, nutmeg, brown sugar, and salt and pepper to taste. Set aside and keep warm.

For the vinaigrette: In a food processor, combine the tomatoes, pine nuts, and balsamic vinegar and purée until smooth. With the machine running, gradually drizzle in the oil until emulsified. Transfer to a bowl and season with salt and pepper. Set aside.

For the mahi mahi: In a large sauté pan or skillet, heat the oil over high heat. Dust one side of each fillet with the blackening spice. Add the fish to the pan, spice side down, and cook for 4 minutes without touching the fish. After 4 minutes, flip the fish and cook on the other side for 3 minutes. Using a slotted metal spatula, transfer the fish to a baking sheet. Add the asparagus to the sauté pan and cook, turning to cook evenly, for 3 minutes, or until crisp-tender.

To serve, spread the polenta in the center of each plate and top with asparagus. Place a fillet on top, drizzle with the vinaigrette, and serve. Or, serve family-style on a large platter, as in the introduction to the recipe.

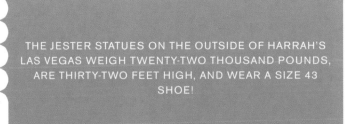

THE JESTER STATUES ON THE OUTSIDE OF HARRAH'S LAS VEGAS WEIGH TWENTY-TWO THOUSAND POUNDS, ARE THIRTY-TWO FEET HIGH, AND WEAR A SIZE 43 SHOE!

PACIFIC SHUTOME SWORDFISH CHOPS

WITH PORT WINE & CHERRY REDUCTION

RESERVE AT BALLY'S ATLANTIC CITY
CHEF BRIAN ANNAPOLEN

Pacific shutome swordfish, generally available from Hawaii, has a much more buttery texture than regular swordfish. Chef Brian Annapolen explains, "I can only describe the flavor as being the way swordfish tasted when I was a kid: rich and meaty, with a slightly gamy note and porklike consistency." The savory braised greens and the sweet port wine and cherries round out the flavor notes of this dish, which is served over creamy risotto.

MARINADE

3 thyme sprigs, chopped

3 oregano sprigs, chopped

3 basil sprigs, chopped

4 garlic cloves, crushed

1 cup olive oil

Four 12-ounce swordfish chops or steaks (see note)

RISOTTO

3 to 4 tablespoons olive oil

3 shallots, minced

2 garlic cloves, minced

2 thyme sprigs

1 cup Arborio rice

½ cup dry white wine

3 to 5 cups chicken stock, simmering

½ cup grated Parmesan cheese

⅓ cup unsalted butter

Salt and freshly ground pepper

✦ ✦ ✦ ✦ ✦ ✦ ✦

Note: Swordfish chops are bone-in, cut from the pectoral fins of the fish. Boneless swordfish steaks can be substituted.

BRAISED GREENS

2 tablespoons olive oil

8 ounces pancetta slices, cut into bite-size pieces

1 red onion, thinly sliced

1 garlic clove, sliced

1 pound mixed braising greens, such as chicory, mustard greens, kale, and collard greens

¼ cup dry white wine

Salt and freshly ground pepper

SAUCE

One 750-ml bottle port wine

1 cup sweet cherry purée (found in specialty foods stores)

2 bay leaves

2 to 3 tablespoons veal demi-glace

4 tablespoons cold unsalted butter, cut into 4 pieces

For the marinade: In a large bowl, combine all the marinade ingredients, mixing well. Add the swordfish chops and refrigerate for 1 to 2 hours.

For the risotto: In a large sauté pan or skillet, heat the oil over medium heat and sauté the shallots, garlic, and thyme for 2 to 3 minutes. Add the rice and stir to coat with the oil. Add the wine and cook, stirring, until almost dry. Add the chicken stock in 3 equal increments, stirring constantly, until al dente, about 25 minutes. Add the cheese and butter, stirring to incorporate. Season with salt and pepper and let stand for 2 minutes before serving.

For the braised greens: Just before the risotto is done, in a large sauté pan or skillet, heat the oil over medium heat and sauté the pancetta until crisp. Add the onion and cook until translucent, about 3 minutes. Using a slotted spoon, transfer the pancetta mixture to a saucer. Reduce the heat to low; add the garlic and sauté until golden brown. Return the pancetta mixture to the pan. Increase the heat to medium and add the greens; sauté until wilted. Stir in the wine and cook until evaporated. Season with salt and pepper. Set aside and keep warm.

For the sauce: Just before cooking the fish, cook the wine in a medium non-reactive saucepan over medium heat to reduce to about 1 cup. Add the cherry purée and bay leaves and cook for 2 or 3 minutes. Add the demi-glace and cook until the mixture is slightly thickened. Gradually whisk in the butter, one piece at a time, to make a thick sauce. Keep warm over tepid water.

Heat a grill pan over medium-high heat and oil the pan. Remove the chops from the marinade and season with salt and pepper. Grill the chops for about 5 minutes on each side, or until opaque throughout.

To serve, divide the risotto among the plates and top with the braised greens. Place a swordfish chop on each serving and drizzle with the sauce.

THE RESERVE AT BALLY'S ATLANTIC CITY IS THE AREA'S HOT SPOT
FOR MODERN SEAFOOD AND HAND-SELECTED STEAK PREPARATIONS.
THE RESTAURANT BOASTS SEASONAL MENUS WITH A STRONG
FOCUS ON LOCAL, FRESH, AND MODERN CUISINE.

PARMESAN-CRUSTED ORANGE ROUGHY

EMBERS AT IMPERIAL PALACE
CHEF MATTHEW HEPPNER

Orange roughy, a fish caught off the shores of New Zealand, is prized for the mild flavor of its flaky white flesh. The crisp, flavorful coating contrasts with the tender fish, which is served topped with a delicate beurre blanc sauce.

BEURRE BLANC

1 cup dry white wine

¼ cup white wine vinegar

2 tablespoons minced shallots

1½ cups heavy cream

4 tablespoons cold unsalted butter, cut into 10 pieces

Kosher salt and white pepper

BREADING

4 large eggs, beaten

¾ cup whole milk

2 cups all-purpose flour

1 teaspoon kosher salt

1 teaspoon freshly ground black pepper

3 cups panko (Japanese bread crumbs)

¾ cup grated Parmigiano-Reggiano cheese

2 tablespoons minced fresh flat-leaf parsley

Four 6-ounce orange roughy fillets

2 tablespoons clarified butter (see page 43)

¼ cup diced red bell pepper for garnish

SERVES 4

For the beurre blanc: In a small, heavy saucepan, combine the wine, vinegar, and shallots. Place over medium heat, bring to a boil, and cook to reduce to ¼ cup. Add the cream and cook to reduce to ¾ cup. Turn the heat to very low and whisk in a piece of butter until melted; repeat to whisk in the remaining butter, 1 piece at a time, to make a thick sauce. Season with salt and white pepper. Strain into a bowl and keep warm over tepid water.

For the breading: In a shallow bowl, whisk the eggs and milk together until blended. In another shallow bowl, combine the flour, salt, and black pepper; stir to blend. In a third shallow bowl, stir the panko, grated cheese, and 1 tablespoon of the parsley (leaving the rest for garnish) together to blend (you will work this together to smash up the larger pieces of panko).

Dredge a fish fillet in the seasoned flour and shake off the excess flour. Next, dip the fillet in the egg mixture to coat evenly and let the excess egg mixture drip off. Finally, coat the fillet in the panko mixture to cover evenly, pressing the crumbs to adhere. Remove any excess breading. Place aside and repeat to coat the remaining fillets.

In a large sauté pan or skillet, heat the clarified butter over medium-high heat until shimmering. Add the fish and cook until firm and golden brown, about 4 minutes on each side.

Serve with the beurre blanc ladled over the top, garnished with the remaining 1 tablespoon of parsley and the bell pepper.

PHILLIPS CLAM BAKE FOR TWO

PHILLIPS SEAFOOD AT THE PIER SHOPS AT CAESARS ATLANTIC CITY
EXECUTIVE CHEF PAUL DREW

In 1956 the Phillips family opened a small carryout restaurant called Phillips Crab House in Ocean City, Maryland. This endeavor grew quickly into a two-story establishment seating fourteen hundred guests. Today, the empire has expanded to include Phillips Seafood at The Pier Shops. All along, the family has held true to a few simple rules: serve the freshest and finest seafood available, provide outstanding service, and create a memorable dining experience, like the following seafood bonanza, for their guests. While the restaurant serves this dish for two people, it can be easily multiplied to serve many more.

Note: Phillips Seafood Seasoning is available at www.phillipsfoods.com.

6 Red Bliss potatoes

2 ears corn, shucked

1 gallon water

2 teaspoons seafood seasoning blend such as Phillips Seafood Seasoning (see note), plus more for sprinkling

4 bay leaves

1 cup dry white wine

3 lemons, 2 halved and 1 cut into 6 wedges

1 teaspoon pickling spice

¼ bunch flat-leaf parsley, stemmed (reserve stems)

Salt and freshly ground pepper

Two 1¼-pound live lobsters

9 extra-large shrimp in the shell

6 littleneck clams, scrubbed

8 Prince Edward Island (P.E.I.) mussels, scrubbed

8 ounces king crab legs

3 romaine or leaf lettuce leaves

¾ cup (1½ sticks) unsalted butter, melted

SERVES 2

Put the potatoes in a medium saucepan of salted cold water; bring to a boil and cook until almost tender, 10 to 12 minutes. Drain and set aside. In a large saucepan of salted boiling water, cook the corn for about 3 minutes, or until almost tender; drain and set aside.

In the bottom of a large (2-gallon) steamer, add the water, the 2 teaspoons seafood seasoning, the bay leaves, wine, the 4 lemon halves, the pickling spice, the reserved parsley stems, and salt and pepper to taste. Cover and bring to a boil. Place the lobsters in the steamer basket, add to the pot, and cover. Cook until the lobster is beginning to turn pink. Add the shrimp, clams, and mussels to the basket, cover, and steam for 5 minutes.

Add hot water to the pot if the level is running low. Add the potatoes, corn, and king crab legs to the steamer basket. Cover, bring to a boil, and cook for about 5 minutes, or until the potatoes are tender and the clams have opened.

To serve, discard any clams or mussels that haven't opened. Arrange the lettuce on a platter. Transfer the lobsters to a cutting board. Split the tail down the back (don't cut all the way through) and, with the back of your knife, crack the claws. Transfer the shrimp, clams, mussels, crab legs, corn, and potatoes to the serving plate. Place the lobsters on top. Sprinkle some of the Phillips Seafood Seasoning over the steamed seafood. Garnish with the parsley leaves and lemon wedges. Pour the melted butter into a small bowl and serve on the side.

BARBECUED SHRIMP

MAGNOLIA BUFFET AT HARRAH'S NEW ORLEANS
CHEF HOYCE OATIS

A simple dish straight from the heart of New Orleans. Chef Hoyce Oatis says, "This recipe represents the unique style of Cajun and Creole cuisine, which is noted for its spices and seasonings. One of the authentic ways of eating this dish is to dip small portions of French bread into the sauce, which many consider to be the best part of this dish. It can be served as a main course or appetizer."

½ cup canola oil

1 small onion, diced

6 garlic cloves

1 bay leaf

1 teaspoon minced fresh thyme

1 teaspoon minced fresh rosemary

1 teaspoon minced fresh oregano

1 teaspoon sweet paprika

1 teaspoon minced fresh flat-leaf
parsley

1 pound 16/20 shrimp with shells and
heads

¼ cup brandy

¼ cup dry white wine

½ cup water

½ cup (1 stick) unsalted butter at room
temperature

SERVES 4

In a large sauté pan or skillet, heat the oil over medium-high heat until shimmering. Add the onion and sauté until lightly browned, about 5 minutes. Add the garlic cloves and sauté until golden, about 2 minutes. Add the herbs and spices and sauté for 1 minute. Add the shrimp and sauté for 2 minutes.

Turn off the heat and pour in the brandy. Standing back from the stove, light the brandy with a long match or long-handled lighter. Using caution, shake the pan until the flames subside. Add the wine and return to medium heat. Cook for 1 minute and then add the water.

To finish, add the butter and stir until melted. Serve divided among shallow bowls.

POKER WAS INVENTED IN
NEW ORLEANS ON CANAL STREET
IN THE EIGHTEENTH CENTURY.

SEARED SCALLOPS, ASPARAGUS & CRABMEAT
WITH HOLLANDAISE SAUCE & POTATO CAKES

VOGA AT FLAMINGO LAS VEGAS
EXECUTIVE CHEF CHRISTOPHE DOUMERGUE

This fusion of Old World culinary technique and New World culinary flair is a fitting dish for Voga, a mixture of city chic and Neapolitan gusto. Chef Christophe Doumergue comments, "This dish is our best portrayal of what Voga is all about."

YUKON POTATO CAKES

2 cups chopped peeled Yukon gold potatoes

2 tablespoons heavy cream

1 teaspoon minced garlic

1 teaspoon unsalted butter

Salt and freshly ground pepper

1 tablespoon all-purpose flour

1 egg beaten with 1 teaspoon water

1 cup dried bread crumbs

1 tablespoon olive oil

1 cup asparagus tips

8 sea scallops

Salt and freshly ground pepper

¼ cup extra-virgin olive oil, plus more for drizzling

4 ounces fresh lump crabmeat, picked over for shell

Hollandaise Sauce
(see recipe facing page)

SERVES 2

For the potato cakes: Add the potatoes to a small saucepan of salted cold water; bring to a boil and cook for 30 minutes, or until tender. Drain. Add the cream, garlic, butter, and salt and pepper to taste. Using a whisk or an electric mixer, beat until smooth. Spread the mixture into a ½-inch-thick round on a baking sheet. Refrigerate for 1 hour, or until firm. Cut into cakes with a 2-inch round biscuit cutter.

Put the flour, egg mixture, and bread crumbs in three separate shallow bowls. Season the flour with salt and pepper. Coat each potato cake first in the flour, then the egg mixture, then the crumbs.

In a large sauté pan or skillet, heat the oil over medium heat and fry the potato cakes until golden brown, about 2 minutes on each side. Transfer to a low oven to keep warm.

In a medium saucepan of salted boiling water, cook the asparagus tips for 4 minutes, or until crisp-tender. Drain. Set aside and keep warm.

Season the scallops with salt and pepper. In a large sauté pan or skillet, heat the ¼ cup oil over medium-high heat until shimmering and sauté the sea scallops for 3 minutes on each side, or until opaque throughout. Transfer to a plate and keep warm.

To serve, preheat the broiler. Divide the asparagus, potato cakes, and scallops between 2 ovenproof plates. Top each scallop with the crabmeat and then the Hollandaise Sauce. Place under the broiler about 3 inches from the heat source until lightly browned, about 2 minutes. Remove from the broiler, drizzle with extra-virgin olive oil, and serve at once.

VOGA, MEANING "FASHION" IN ITALIAN, OPENED IN JANUARY 2008 AND WAS VOTED ONE OF THE BEST NEW RESTAURANTS IN LAS VEGAS.

HOLLANDAISE SAUCE

1 cup clarified butter (see page 43)
3 large egg yolks
2 tablespoons fresh lemon juice
2 pinches salt
Cayenne pepper or Tabasco sauce

In a small saucepan, heat the butter until hot. In a blender, combine the egg yolks, lemon juice, and salt and blend at high speed for 2 minutes. With the machine running, gradually add the butter in a very thin stream to make a thick sauce. Stir in the cayenne to taste. Keep warm over tepid water.

MAKES 1 CUP

SEAFOOD RISOTTO

MOSAIC AT HARRAH'S JOLIET
CHEF MATTHEW E. SECKO

Chef Matthew E. Secko explains the romantic history behind his seafood risotto: "This is a great dish to prepare and serve to someone you want to impress to make an everlasting first impression. I first served this dish when asked to make a special meal for someone, who fell in love with it. And to this day, almost three years later, that person talks about how amazing it was. It is a well-balanced dish that is very bold and flavorful, but will not leave you feeling weighed down and uncomfortable. All the flavors complement each other, and the lemon and lime zest provide a very refreshing citrus taste to accent the seafood as well as the risotto. Enjoy, and I hope that your luck with this dish is as good as mine."

6 cups chicken stock

1 cup (2 sticks) unsalted butter

1 cup Arborio rice

1 teaspoon Boursin cheese

Salt and freshly ground pepper

1 teaspoon minced garlic

1 teaspoon minced shallot

6 sea scallops

6 large shrimp, shelled and deveined

1 lobster tail, halved lengthwise

Grated zest of ½ lemon

Grated zest of ½ lime

½ cup citron vodka

Asparagus tips, basil sprigs, and microgreens for garnish (optional)

SERVES 2

In a large saucepan, bring the chicken stock to a low simmer. In a large sauté pan or skillet, melt 4 tablespoons of the butter over medium heat, add the rice, and stir until opaque, 2 to 3 minutes. Stir in just enough stock to cover the rice and cook, stirring constantly, until almost all the stock is absorbed. Repeat this process until the rice is al dente, about 25 minutes. Stir in the Boursin and season with salt and pepper.

Halfway through cooking the risotto, melt 4 more tablespoons of the butter over medium heat in a large sauté pan or skillet. Add the garlic and shallot and sauté for 3 minutes. Add the scallops and sauté until golden brown on the bottom, about 1½ minutes. Turn the scallops over and add the shrimp. Sauté until the shrimp curl. Season with salt and pepper. Add the lobster and lemon and lime zests. Turn off the heat and add the vodka. Return to medium heat and stir to scrape up the browned bits on the bottom of the pan. Cook until the liquid is reduced to about ¼ cup. Add the remaining ½ cup butter, remove from the heat, and swirl the pan to combine all the ingredients.

To serve, mound the risotto in the center of a large serving plate and space the scallops around the outside of the risotto. Place the shrimp in between the scallops and place the lobster on top of the risotto. Pour the sauce over the scallops and shrimp. Garnish with asparagus tips, basil sprigs, and microgreens, if desired.

CELEBRITY CHEF RICK BAYLESS WAS ON HAND FOR THE GRAND OPENING OF MOSAIC IN 2006.

CRAB & EGGPLANT LASAGNA

CASA DI NAPOLI AT SHOWBOAT ATLANTIC CITY
CHEF GEORGEANN LEAMING

In this no-pasta lasagna, eggplant slices are marinated in herb oil, then coated in flour and fried until golden brown. Sandwiched with a creamy crabmeat filling and topped with a crumb crust flavored with sun-dried tomatoes, the slices are baked to yield a dish that combines textures, flavors, and colors. Serve with a glass of wine and a green salad for a satisfying, luxurious meal.

HERB OIL

1 cup olive oil

¼ cup fresh whole basil leaves

¼ cup fresh flat-leaf parsley leaves, chopped

1 teaspoon fresh lemon juice

1 teaspoon kosher salt

½ teaspoon freshly ground pepper

Eight ¼-inch-thick globe eggplant slices

SUN-DRIED TOMATO CRUST

2 cups fresh bread crumbs

½ cup julienned oil-packed sun-dried tomatoes

2 tablespoons minced fresh basil

1 teaspoon kosher salt

½ teaspoon freshly ground pepper

CRAB FILLING

1 pound fresh lump crabmeat, picked over for shell

1 tablespoon finely diced red bell pepper

1 tablespoon finely diced onion

1 teaspoon Dijon mustard

1 cup mayonnaise

½ cup fresh bread crumbs

Olive oil for sautéing

All-purpose flour for dredging

Balsamic glaze (see notes)

SERVES 4

For the herb oil: Combine all the ingredients in a blender and purée until smooth.

Pour half of the herb oil into a large baking dish and add the eggplant slices. Let stand at room temperature for 15 minutes, turning the slices halfway through. Remove from the marinade and shake off the excess.

For the crust: Combine the ingredients in a food processor and pulse until finely ground. Set aside.

For the filling: In a large bowl, combine the ingredients; stir to blend and set aside.

Preheat the oven to 400°F. In a large sauté pan or skillet, heat ¼ inch oil over medium-high heat until shimmering. Dredge 2 eggplant slices in the flour, shaking off the excess. Add to the pan and sauté until golden brown, about 5 minutes on each side. Using a slotted metal spatula, transfer to paper towels to drain. Repeat with the remaining slices. Put 4 eggplant slices on a baking sheet and spread each slice with one-fourth of the crab filling. Top with the remaining eggplant slices. Spread about ¼ cup of the sun-dried tomato mixture on each top slice. Bake for 15 to 20 minutes, or until the crusts are browned and the filling is hot.

To serve, place the lasagnas on a platter and drizzle with some of the remaining herb oil and the balsamic glaze.

✦✦✦✦✦✦✦

Balsamic glaze: In a small, heavy saucepan, bring 1 cup balsamic vinegar to a simmer over medium heat and cook until reduced to a syrup. Remove from the heat, let cool, and transfer to a squeeze bottle.

Note: Balsamic glaze is also available in specialty foods markets.

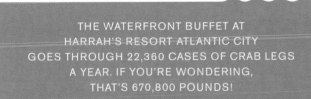

THE WATERFRONT BUFFET AT
HARRAH'S RESORT ATLANTIC CITY
GOES THROUGH 22,360 CASES OF CRAB LEGS
A YEAR. IF YOU'RE WONDERING,
THAT'S 670,800 POUNDS!

LOBSTER MAC CASSEROLE

JACK BINION'S STEAKHOUSE AT HORSESHOE SOUTHERN INDIANA
EXECUTIVE SOUS-CHEF JOSHUA MIRAGLIOTTA

Lobster Mac Casserole was created especially for Jack Binion's Steakhouse guests who love seafood. Chef Joshua Miragliotta comments, "This dish combines succulent lobster, shell pasta, a creamy, bubbling white Cheddar béchamel scented with white truffle oil, and a topping of toasted bread crumbs. It is one of our most popular dishes."

CHEDDAR BÉCHAMEL SAUCE

2 tablespoons unsalted butter

2 tablespoons all-purpose flour

3 cups heavy cream

3 cups half-and-half

4 bay leaves

1 yellow onion, cut into fourths

Pinch of ground nutmeg

2½ cups shredded
white Cheddar cheese

2 teaspoons kosher salt

2 teaspoons freshly ground
white pepper

2¼ pounds shell pasta

4 tablespoons unsalted butter, melted

1¼ pounds uncooked lobster meat, cut
into 1-inch cubes

1½ cups panko
(Japanese bread crumbs)

1½ cups clarified butter
(see page 43)

1½ cups shredded Gruyère cheese

White truffle oil for drizzling

SERVES 6

For the sauce: In a small saucepan, melt the butter over low heat and whisk in the flour; stir constantly for 2 to 3 minutes; do not let brown. Remove from the heat and set aside.

In a medium saucepan, combine the heavy cream and half-and-half. Add the bay leaves, onion, and nutmeg. Bring the mixture to a simmer over medium-low heat and cook for 10 minutes. Strain, discarding the solids, and return the cream mixture to the pan. Return to a simmer over medium-low heat. Gently whisk in the white Cheddar cheese, 1 cup at a time, until melted. Cook, whisking constantly, for a few minutes until thickened slightly; remove from the heat as necessary to keep from scorching. Whisk in the butter and flour mixture and cook, whisking, for several minutes. Whisk in the salt and pepper. Remove from the heat and let cool.

Preheat the oven to 400°F. In a large pot of salted boiling water, cook the pasta until al dente, 10 to 12 minutes; drain and set aside.

In a medium sauté pan or skillet, heat the butter over medium heat and sauté the lobster meat for 2 or 3 minutes. Add the béchamel and cook for about 2 minutes, stirring constantly. Stir in the pasta.

In a small bowl, combine the bread crumbs and clarified butter and stir to moisten evenly. Butter six 8-ounce casserole dishes or ramekins. Fill each prepared dish with the pasta mixture. Top each serving with ¼ cup Gruyère and ¼ cup bread crumbs. Place on a baking sheet and bake for 7 to 8 minutes, or until the bread crumbs are golden brown and the cheese has completely melted. Remove from the oven and drizzle each serving with white truffle oil.

SINCE OPENING IN 2004,
THE BUFFET AT HARRAH'S LOUISIANA DOWNS
HAS FED 1.5 MILLION PEOPLE.
IT SERVES MORE THAN 1,800 POUNDS
OF CATFISH AND 1,000 POUNDS OF
PEEL AND EAT SHRIMP EVERY WEEK.

GRILLED SHRIMP SKEWERS

EAT UP! BUFFET AT HARRAH'S ST. LOUIS
EXECUTIVE CHEF RAY LEUNG

This light dish of skewered shrimp and cherry tomatoes is quick and easy to prepare, but will dazzle any palate. The orange-Champagne vinaigrette adds a zesty flavor and a touch of glamour to the shrimp, and the rosemary-stalk skewers add their own pungent taste and make for a beautiful presentation. Chef Ray Leung promises that this dish will be sure to "impress at your next barbecue."

2 tablespoons Champagne vinegar

2 tablespoons grated orange zest

1 cup fresh orange juice

1 tablespoon olive oil

1 tablespoon Italian dressing mix

20 large shrimp, shelled and deveined

Twenty 5-inch rosemary stalks

20 cherry tomatoes

SERVES 4

Prepare a medium fire in a charcoal grill or preheat a gas grill to 350°F. In a medium bowl, combine the vinegar, orange zest and juice, oil, and Italian dressing mix. Whisk to blend. Add the shrimp and toss to coat. Set aside.

Strip off all the leaves from the rosemary stalks except the top few. Skewer 1 shrimp and 1 cherry tomato on each rosemary skewer. Wrap the leafy end of each rosemary skewer in a 2-inch aluminum foil square to prevent burning during grilling. Grill for about 2 minutes per side, or until the shrimp turn pink. Remove the foil from the ends of the skewers and serve.

P.E.I. MUSSELS IN MAGNERS CIDER

TRINITY PUB & CARVERY AT THE PIER SHOPS AT CAESARS ATLANTIC CITY
CHEF BRIAN PERRY

This mussel dish was designed to showcase the seafood side of Trinity Pub & Carvery's Irish menu. Chef Brian Perry comments on one of the dish's standout ingredients: "We use Magners Irish Cider not only because of the Irish theme but because it matches really well with seafood like mussels."

2 tablespoons canola oil

½ cup minced shallots

½ cup minced garlic

½ cup diced plum tomatoes

2 pounds Prince Edward Island (P.E.I.) mussels, scrubbed

½ cup dry white wine

¾ cup Magners Irish Cider

2 teaspoons minced fresh thyme

2 teaspoons minced fresh tarragon

2 teaspoons minced fresh flat-leaf parsley

Salt and freshly ground pepper

2 tablespoons cold butter

4 thick slices grilled crusty white bread

¼ cup sliced green onions, including some green parts

SERVES 2

In a large sauté pan or skillet, heat the oil over medium-high heat. Add the shallots and garlic and sauté until the shallots are translucent, about 2 minutes. Add the tomatoes and sauté for 30 seconds. Add the mussels, tossing them in the pan. Add the wine. Cook to reduce the wine by one-half, then add the cider and herbs and season with salt and pepper. Toss the mussels, then cover and cook for 1½ minutes, or until the mussels have opened. Turn off the heat and add the butter, swirling the pan until it is incorporated. Discard any mussels that have not opened.

To serve, divide the mussels and broth between two bowls. Cut the grilled bread in half lengthwise and arrange it with the points touching in the center of the bowl. Garnish with the green onions.

9

BREAKFAST BUFFET

BOURSIN CHEESE, LOBSTER & COGNAC OMELET

STERLING BRUNCH AT BALLY'S STEAKHOUSE AT BALLY'S LAS VEGAS
CHEF ERIC PISTON

Start your day in luxury with this Sterling Brunch signature omelet. A mixture of rich ingredients makes it perfect for that special breakfast or brunch. Chef Eric Piston says, "Flavor-wise, the lobster meat and Cognac work very well together, and the Boursin cheese adds a smoothness to the omelet as well as a very light garlic flavor." Even if you're planning to serve more than one person, make one omelet at a time; once you have all your ingredients in place, each one takes just a few minutes.

2 large eggs

1 tablespoon clarified butter
(see page 43)

1 teaspoon finely chopped onion

1 ounce cooked lobster meat, chopped

2 tablespoons Cognac

1 tablespoon Boursin cheese

2 tablespoons shredded
white Cheddar cheese

SERVES 1

In a small bowl, whisk the eggs until blended. In a nonstick 6-inch pan, heat the clarified butter over medium heat and sauté the onion until golden, about 5 minutes. Add the lobster and Cognac and cook for 30 seconds. Add the eggs and let set for a few seconds, then cook for 1 minute, pushing in the sides to let the uncooked egg flow under. Sprinkle with the cheeses and fold the omelet in half. Cook for 1 more minute and serve.

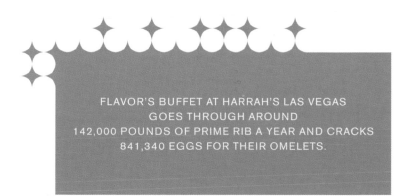

FLAVOR'S BUFFET AT HARRAH'S LAS VEGAS
GOES THROUGH AROUND
142,000 POUNDS OF PRIME RIB A YEAR AND CRACKS
841,340 EGGS FOR THEIR OMELETS.

HOLLANDAISE SAUCE

2 large egg yolks

2 cups unsalted butter, melted

Juice of 2 lemons

Pinch of cayenne pepper

Salt and freshly ground pepper

Put the egg yolks in a stainless-steel bowl and set the bowl over a saucepan filled with 2 inches of simmering water. Cook, whisking constantly, until thick enough that you can see the bottom of the bowl when the whisk makes a path through the mixture. Gradually whisk in the butter, beginning with a few drops and progressing to a very thin stream as the mixture thickens. Season with the lemon juice, cayenne, and salt and pepper. Keep warm over tepid water if necessary.

MAKES 2 CUPS

POACHED EGGS
WITH BACON-POTATO HASH & HOLLANDAISE SAUCE

HARRAH'S CHESTER CASINO & RACETRACK
EXECUTIVE CHEF SEAN KINOSHITA

Chef Sean Kinoshita explains how he created this brunch specialty: "One of my all time-favorite brunch dishes is the classic eggs Benedict. For this recipe, I added more of my favorite foods, like bacon, potatoes, and biscuits. With this recipe, you get my version of the best of all breakfast items."

CORNMEAL–BROWN BUTTER BISCUITS

5 tablespoons unsalted butter

1¼ cups all-purpose flour

¼ cup cornmeal

2 tablespoons sugar

2 teaspoons baking powder

¼ teaspoon salt

½ cup heavy cream

2 teaspoons vanilla extract

2 large egg yolks, beaten

BACON-POTATO HASH

1 cup chopped bacon

1 onion, diced

1 red bell pepper, seeded, deveined, and diced

1 green bell pepper, seeded, deveined, and diced

Canola oil for deep-frying

2 russet potatoes, peeled and diced

⅓ cup chicken stock

4 tablespoons butter

Salt and freshly ground pepper

3 tablespoons minced fresh flat-leaf parsley

1 tablespoon salt

1 tablespoon white vinegar

4 large eggs

Hollandaise Sauce
(see recipe facing page)

SERVES 4

For the biscuits: Preheat the oven to 375°F. In a small, heavy saucepan, cook the butter over medium-low heat until browned, about 5 minutes. Pour into a small bowl and freeze for 1 hour until hard.

In a large bowl, combine the flour, cornmeal, sugar, baking powder, and salt. Stir with a whisk to blend. Cube the hard butter and add. Using a pastry cutter, cut in the butter until the mixture resembles coarse meal. Using a fork, mix in the cream, vanilla, and egg yolks. Turn the dough out onto a floured work surface. Lightly knead. Roll out to a ½-inch thickness. Using a 2-inch round biscuit cutter, cut out 8 biscuits. Place on a small baking sheet and refrigerate until firm, about 1 hour. Transfer the pan to the oven and bake the biscuits for 15 minutes, or until golden brown. Remove from the oven and transfer the biscuits to wire racks.

For the hash: In a medium sauté pan or skillet, cook the bacon over medium heat until crisp, about 3 minutes. Using a slotted spoon, transfer to paper towels to drain. In another medium sauté pan or skillet, heat the bacon fat over medium heat and cook the onion and bell peppers separately until tender. Transfer the vegetables to a pie pan and add the bacon.

In a Dutch oven or heavy casserole, heat 2 inches of the oil to 350°F on a deep-frying thermometer and cook the potatoes in two batches until golden, about 6 minutes; using a slotted spoon, transfer to a bowl. Return all the ingredients including the chicken stock and butter to one of the sauté pans or skillets and heat through over low heat. Season with salt and pepper. Add the parsley and toss just before serving.

Meanwhile, poach the eggs: In a large sauté pan, bring 2 inches of water to a bare simmer. Add the salt and white vinegar. Crack the eggs, one at a time, into a saucer and slide into the water. Cook until the egg whites are firm but the yolks are soft, 4 to 5 minutes. Using a slotted metal spatula, transfer to a plate.

To serve, place 2 biscuits on each plate and top with ¼ cup hash, then a poached egg. Pour some of the Hollandaise Sauce over each serving.

BACON & CREAM CHEESE FRITTATA
WITH ROASTED RED PEPPER HOLLANDAISE

THE RIVERCREST AT HARRAH'S METROPOLIS
EXECUTIVE CHEF JON M. KELL

In this brunch buffet staple from The Rivercrest at Harrah's Metropolis, smoky bacon and mellow cream cheese are complemented by the robust flavor of a hollandaise flavored with roasted red peppers. A versatile dish, the frittata can be served either hot or at room temperature, making it perfect for a buffet or picnic.

4 russet potatoes, peeled and shredded

½ cup (1 stick) unsalted butter, melted

1 pound bacon, cooked, drained, and crumbled

1 pound cream cheese, cubed

12 large eggs

6 egg whites (save yolks for hollandaise, below)

¼ teaspoon salt

¼ teaspoon freshly ground pepper

ROASTED RED PEPPER HOLLANDAISE

6 large egg yolks (reserved from above)

2 teaspoons water

½ teaspoon sugar

¾ cup (1½ sticks) cold unsalted butter, cut into 24 pieces

1 teaspoon kosher salt

4 teaspoons fresh lemon juice

¼ teaspoon cayenne pepper

One 10.6-ounce can roasted red peppers, drained and finely chopped

1 bunch asparagus, trimmed and steamed for 2 to 3 minutes

SERVES 6

Preheat the oven to 350°F. Coat a large baking dish with nonstick cooking spray. Spread the potatoes evenly in the dish. Pour the butter over the potatoes as evenly as possible. Bake for 20 minutes, or until lightly browned. Sprinkle the bacon crumbles and cream cheese cubes evenly over the potatoes. Set aside, leaving the oven on.

In a large bowl, whisk the eggs and egg whites until blended, then whisk in the salt and pepper. Pour the egg mixture over the potatoes in the baking dish. Return to the oven and cook for 20 to 30 minutes, or until the eggs are firm. Remove from the oven and keep warm.

For the hollandaise: In a medium stainless-steel bowl, combine the egg yolks and water and whisk until the mixture lightens in color, 1 to 2 minutes. Add the sugar and whisk for another 30 seconds. Set the bowl over a saucepan with 2 inches of barely simmering water and whisk constantly for 3 to 5 minutes, or until a path is drawn in the mixture when you pull your whisk through. Remove the bowl from the pan and gradually whisk in the butter, 1 piece at a time, until all the butter is incorporated. Put the bowl back over the simmering water occasionally if necessary so that it will be warm enough to melt the butter. Add the salt, lemon juice, and cayenne pepper. Fold in the peppers. Keep warm over tepid water or in a thermos.

To serve, cut the frittata into squares and serve on a pool of hollandaise. Garnish with the asparagus.

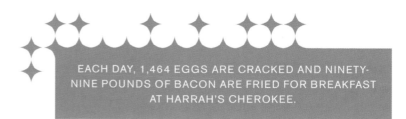

EACH DAY, 1,464 EGGS ARE CRACKED AND NINETY-NINE POUNDS OF BACON ARE FRIED FOR BREAKFAST AT HARRAH'S CHEROKEE.

HAZELNUT PANCAKES

HARRAH'S JOLIET
EXECUTIVE CHEF SCOTT D. LECOMPTE

Impress your family by making a great American breakfast with a twist. Serve these pancakes, fragrant with hazelnuts, as a special treat on Saturday morning with some chocolate chips, pure maple syrup, whipped butter, and whipped cream.

¾ cup all-purpose flour

¼ cup hazelnut flour (found in specialty foods stores)

½ teaspoon baking powder

¼ teaspoon baking soda

Pinch of salt

⅞ cup milk

1 teaspoon maple syrup

3 large eggs

1½ teaspoons vanilla extract

1 teaspoon honey

¾ cup (1½ sticks) unsalted butter, melted

Toppings of choice for serving

SERVES 4

In a large bowl, combine the dry ingredients and stir with a whisk to blend. In a medium bowl, whisk together the milk, maple syrup, eggs, vanilla, and honey until smooth. Add to the dry ingredients and stir to blend. Fold in the butter just until blended.

Heat a lightly oiled griddle or skillet over medium-high heat. Pour the batter onto the griddle, using about 1 tablespoon for small pancakes or ¼ cup for larger ones. Cook for 2 to 3 minutes, or until bubbles have stopped coming to the surface; turn and cook on the second side until golden brown. Serve at once, with your favorite toppings.

COCONUT CRÊPES

WITH CARAMELIZED CINNAMON APPLES, CHOCOLATE WHIPPED CREAM & CARAMEL SAUCE

HARRAH'S CHESTER CASINO & RACETRACK
EXECUTIVE CHEF SEAN KINOSHITA

This might just be the most delicious dish you will ever have in the morning. Coconut, whipped cream, chocolate, and caramel! Together they will make an awesome start to your day.

COCONUT CRÊPES

2 cups all-purpose flour

4 large eggs, beaten

1 cup well-stirred or shaken canned coconut milk

1 cup water

½ teaspoon salt

¼ cup melted unsalted butter

Canola oil for brushing

CARAMELIZED CINNAMON APPLES

2 cups sugar

Pinch of salt

¼ teaspoon ground cinnamon

½ cup (1 stick) unsalted butter

8 Fuji apples, peeled, cored, and each cut into 8 wedges

CHOCOLATE WHIPPED CREAM

½ cup heavy cream

1 tablespoon sugar

⅛ teaspoon sifted unsweetened cocoa powder

Caramel Sauce (see recipe facing page)

4 mint sprigs

SERVES 4

For the crêpes: In a large bowl, whisk together the flour and eggs. Gradually whisk in the coconut milk and water. Add the salt and butter, beating until smooth. Heat a 6-inch crêpe pan or skillet over medium-high heat and brush with oil. Pour a scant ¼ cup batter into the pan and tilt the pan with a circular motion so that the batter coats the surface evenly. Cook for about 1 minute, or until the bottom is light brown. Loosen with a spatula, and then turn and cook the other side. Place the crêpe on a plate and cover to keep warm. Repeat to cook the remaining batter, stacking the finished crêpes as you go.

For the apples: In a large bowl, mix together the sugar, salt, and cinnamon. In a large nonstick sauté pan or skillet, melt the butter over medium heat. Toss the apples in the cinnamon sugar mixture and add to the pan. Sauté until tender, about 5 minutes. Remove from the heat and keep warm.

For the whipped cream: In a medium bowl, combine all the ingredients. Using an electric mixer, beat the cream until stiff peaks form.

Preheat the oven to 350°F. Place a crêpe on a work surface and place ⅓ cup of the apples in the center. Fold the crêpe over the filling like an envelope. Place, seam-side down, on a baking sheet. Repeat to use the remaining crêpes and apples, making 12 filled crêpes. Place in the oven until heated through, about 7 minutes.

To serve, place 3 crêpes on each plate. Place a dollop of chocolate whipped cream on top of each serving and drizzle with Caramel Sauce. Top with a mint sprig and serve at once.

CARAMEL SAUCE

1 cup sugar

¼ cup water

½ cup heavy cream

4 tablespoons unsalted butter, melted

In a large, heavy saucepan, combine the sugar and water and cook over medium heat, tilting the pan occasionally but not stirring, until the mixture turns a deep amber. Brush the sides of the pan with a wet pastry brush if sugar crystals form. Remove from the heat and carefully whisk in the cream; take care, as it will spatter. Whisk in the butter. Serve warm.

MAKES 2 CUPS

FLAVOR'S BUFFET LEMON SQUARES

FLAVOR'S BUFFET & THE RANGE STEAKHOUSE AT HARRAH'S LAS VEGAS
EXECUTIVE PASTRY CHEF AMY BYRO

Everybody loves lemon squares, including the guests at Flavor's Buffet. Chef Amy Byro explains just how popular this dessert is: "On average, we go through about five hundred each day in the Flavor's Buffet. They are light and creamy, and not too tart, making them very addictive! They are so easy to make, and many of our guests tell us they remind them of home. We have even shipped them all over the United States. Often requested specifically by our Seven Stars guests, these lemon squares are a must-try!" While they are popular throughout the day, these lemon squares are a particular hit with the brunch crowd.

CRUST

1 cup (2 sticks) unsalted butter at room temperature

½ cup sifted confectioners' sugar

2 cups all-purpose flour

1 cup chopped pecans (optional)

Pinch of salt

FILLING

4 large eggs

2 cups granulated sugar

¼ cup all-purpose flour

1 teaspoon lemon extract

⅓ cup fresh lemon juice

Confectioners' sugar for dusting

MAKES 24 SQUARES

For the crust: Preheat the oven to 350°F. Lightly spray a 9-by-13-inch baking pan with nonstick cooking spray. In a large bowl, combine all the ingredients and stir to blend well. Pat the mixture evenly into the bottom of the prepared pan. Bake for 15 to 18 minutes, or until set and lightly golden. Transfer to a wire rack and let cool in the pan, leaving the oven on.

For the filling: In a large bowl, combine all the ingredients and stir well to blend. Spread over the cooled crust. Return to the oven and bake for 15 minutes, or until the filling is set, rotating the pan halfway through the cooking time to bake evenly.

Transfer the pan to a wire rack and let cool completely. Dust with confectioners' sugar. Cut into 24 squares.

CHEF ROY ASKREN'S

TOP 10 TIPS FOR CREATING AN UNFORGETTABLE SEVEN STARS BUFFET AT HOME

HARRAH'S NORTH KANSAS CITY

1   To create a dramatic raised centerpiece for your buffet, find a sturdy container, place it upside down in the center of the buffet table, and cover it with a decorative tablecloth. Place a vase filled with seasonal flowers on top of it.

2   Always use the freshest, most vibrant produce, herbs, and extra-virgin or virgin olive oil for all of your cooking.

3   When creating your menu, think of color coordination and eye appeal. We all know that people eat with their eyes first.

4   Timing is a key to quality and freshness. Do not make your buffet food too far in advance. The longer it stands before your guests arrive, the more the quality and freshness will diminish.

5   Look for interesting decorations for your buffet, including fresh flowers. If you can find them, ivy runners are nice to use.

6   Use a small backlight behind your centerpiece to show how beautiful the piece is on your buffet.

7   Use different sizes of elevation on your buffet table to break up an otherwise flat look. Start from the centerpiece and work your way toward each end of the table.

8   For displaying foods, use different sizes of dishes, platters, soup cups, bowls, and so on, and mix and match patterns for an artistic effect.

9   Use only edible decorations for your buffet dishes, such as tomato roses, lemon roses, radish flowers, and carrot cups. There are numerous books that will show you how to create these decorations. Here are two of my favorite books on the subject: *Food Art: Garnishing Made Easy* by John Gargone, and *Garnishing: A Feast for Your Eyes* by Francis T. Lynch. These books will be your secret weapon to impress your guests.

10 When choosing seafood, poultry, beef, pork, or lamb, ask your butcher to give you the freshest available. The meats should be free of any discoloration.

10

VIP
LUNCHEON

ARTISANAL CHEESE PLATTER

NERO'S AT CAESARS PALACE LAS VEGAS
EXECUTIVE CHEF ERIC DAMIDOT

Everyone loves cheese, especially when accompanied with a good bottle of wine. Chef Eric Damidot's beautiful cheese platter will add an elegant touch to your next dinner party. Choose the specific cheeses listed below, or your own favorite selection, varying the textures and flavors. Serve this as a first course, as for the VIP luncheon, or preceding, or in place of dessert for a dinner party.

RED WINE PEAR PURÉE

1 pear, peeled, cored, and quartered

1 cup dry red wine

1 wedge blue Benedictin cheese

1 square Old Chatham Hudson Valley Camembert cheese

1 wedge Tourmalet cheese

1 wedge tomme de Savoie cheese

1 disk cabecou feuille cheese

HERBED APPLES

1½ tablespoons unsalted butter

1 rosemary sprig

2 Fuji apples, peeled, cored, and quartered

1 wedge guava paste

Fig Chutney (recipe follows)

2 handfuls mâche, dressed with a vinaigrette, for garnish

Baguette slices for serving

SERVES 4

For the pear purée: In a medium bowl, combine the pear and red wine. Cover and refrigerate for 48 hours. Pour off the wine and save for another use. Purée the pear in a blender or food processor until smooth.

Take the cheeses from the refrigerator at least 30 minutes before serving, removing any wrappings. Place on a large serving plate.

For the apples: In a small sauté pan or skillet, combine the butter and rosemary. Melt the butter over medium heat and cook until lightly browned. Add the apples and toss several times to coat well in the butter. Remove from the heat when you can insert the tip of a small paring knife inside each apple and the center feels tender.

Serve the pear purée, apples, guava paste, and Fig Chutney in small spoonfuls on the same plate as the cheese. Garnish the plate with the dressed mâche. Serve with slices of baguette.

FIG CHUTNEY

½ cup port wine

1½ cups dry red wine

3 star anise pods

2 tablespoons sugar

1 pound Black Mission figs, stemmed and quartered

1½ tablespoons fresh lemon juice

In a heavy, medium nonreactive saucepan, combine the port wine, red wine, star anise, sugar, and figs. Bring to a boil; reduce the heat to a simmer and cook until thickened, about 1½ hours. Remove from the heat and stir in the lemon juice. Use now, or spoon into sterilized jars, close tightly, and refrigerate for up to 2 weeks.

MAKES ABOUT 2 CUPS

THE BAND BARENAKED LADIES, WHILE PERFORMING IN TOWN, ALSO PLAYED SEVERAL HANDS OF BLACKJACK IN THE WHISKEY PIT AT HORSEHOE COUNCIL BLUFFS.

ROAST BEEF
WITH CREAMY HORSERADISH & BLUE CHEESE SPREAD

SEVEN SISTERS LOUNGE AT HARRAH'S CHEROKEE
CHEF RANDY PHILLIPS

Don't wait for a party! Fix these tasty little morsels any time you want to indulge yourself with a Seven Stars snack. The classic flavor duo of roast beef and horseradish harmonizes well with blue cheese. Add a little depth and balance with some red onion and capers, and you have an appetizer that is a hit with any crowd.

CREAMY HORSERADISH & BLUE CHEESE SPREAD

½ cup whipped cream cheese at room temperature

⅓ cup crumbled Danish blue cheese

¼ cup sour cream

1 tablespoon mayonnaise

2 teaspoons prepared horseradish sauce

1 tablespoon minced onion

1 tablespoon Italian seasoning

Dash of hot pepper sauce

4 slices peppered bacon, cooked until crisp and crumbled

2 loaves cocktail pumpernickel bread (32 slices)

32 slices deli roast beef (2 pounds)

½ cup diced red onion

One 3½-ounce jar small capers, drained

MAKES 32 APPETIZERS

For the spread: In a food processor, combine the cream cheese, blue cheese, sour cream, mayonnaise, horseradish, onion, Italian seasoning, and pepper sauce. Pulse the mixture until it is very smooth. Add the bacon and pulse until just blended. Transfer to a bowl, cover, and refrigerate until the flavors are well integrated, for at least 1 hour or overnight.

Preheat the oven to 325°F. On a baking sheet, arrange the bread slices. Bake in the preheated oven for 10 minutes, or until lightly toasted, turning the slices over halfway through. Remove from the oven and transfer to wire racks.

Pat the roast beef dry with paper towels. Fold each slice of beef into a triangle and place one on each slice of toast. Top with a small amount of the spread. Garnish with a few pieces of the red onion and several capers.

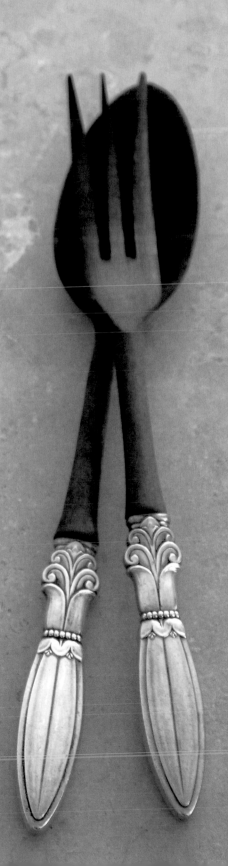

CHEF WILLIAM DWORZAN'S

TOP 10 TIPS FOR PREPARING
A MULTICOURSE MEAL

HARRAH'S NORTH KANSAS CITY

1   Write out your menu and have it in front of you when you are cooking and preparing.

2   Have all your food preparation done way in advance so you don't have to stop and prep anything. That way, the actual cooking will go more smoothly and you will have more time to enjoy your company.

3   Prepare any cold dishes, such as salads or desserts, earlier in the day.

4   Know how long each dish takes to cook so you can time them properly. Make a schedule of when to start each dish.

5   Make sure to preheat the oven at least 30 minutes before baking or roasting.

6   Allow enough time for meats to rest before carving.

7   Keep foods warm in a low oven if needed.

8   Set your table with all the silverware and glassware needed for the meal.

9   Pick out your food vessels and serving utensils in advance and have them handy for serving the finished dishes.

10 If serving meat, be sure to ask your guests how well done they would like it.

SMOKED SCALLOPS
WITH CUCUMBER–RED PEPPER SALSA

DIAMOND LOUNGE AT HARRAH'S RENO
CHEF STEPHEN TUCKER

The deep flavors of smoke and balsamic vinegar in this dish are balanced by the fresh salsa. Chef Stephen Tucker suggests, "If you'd like to serve this dish as a salad, simply chop the scallops and add them to the salsa. Also, remember to smoke the scallops lightly—don't overcook them."

SMOKED SCALLOPS

20 sea scallops

2 tablespoons Old Bay Seasoning

¼ cup dry white wine

CUCUMBER–RED PEPPER SALSA

2 cucumbers, peeled, seeded, and finely diced

1 red bell pepper, roasted, peeled, and finely diced (see page 196)

1 green onion, chopped (including some green parts)

2 tablespoons fresh lemon juice

2 tablespoons chopped fresh cilantro

1 tablespoon chile-garlic paste

Kosher salt and freshly ground white pepper

PEPPERED TOAST POINTS

10 slices firm sandwich bread, such as pullman bread, crusts removed

4 tablespoons unsalted butter, melted

½ cup grated Parmesan cheese

Ground black pepper

Balsamic Reduction (recipe follows)

MAKES 40 APPETIZERS

For the smoked scallops: Heat a smoker to 300°F following the manufacturer's instructions. Or, use a wok to smoke the scallops (see page 146). In a large bowl, toss the scallops with the Old Bay Seasoning and wine to coat. Place the scallops in a small baking pan in a single layer. Put the scallops in the smoker and smoke until just cooked through, 10 to 15 minutes. They will be opaque and firm with a slight give to the touch. Remove the scallops from the smoker and let cool in the pan.

For the salsa: In a medium bowl, combine all the ingredients and stir to blend.

For the toast points: Preheat the oven to 350°F. Brush the bread with the butter. Sprinkle the cheese evenly over the bread. Dust the cheese with the pepper. Place on a baking sheet and bake until the cheese is melted and golden brown, about 10 minutes. Remove from the oven and transfer to a cutting board. Cut each slice of bread into 4 triangles. Transfer to wire racks to cool.

To serve, place 1 tablespoon salsa on each toast point. Cut the scallops in half horizontally. Place a halved scallop on the salsa on each toast point. Drizzle the scallops with the Balsamic Reduction.

BALSAMIC REDUCTION

1 cup balsamic vinegar

1 cup dry white wine

¼ cup sugar

Salt and freshly ground white pepper

In a small, heavy saucepan, combine the balsamic vinegar and wine and heat to a simmer. Cook to reduce to 1 cup. Add the sugar and cook until thickened to a syrup. Season with salt and pepper. Use now, or pour into a bottle, seal, and refrigerate for up to 1 month.

MAKES ABOUT 1 CUP

CHEF ROLF'S
VIP FINGER SANDWICHES

BALLY'S ATLANTIC CITY
FOOD SERVICE DIRECTOR ROLF J. WEITHOFER

No cocktail party is complete without classic finger sandwiches. Chef Rolf J. Weithofer creates these signature appetizers by layering two types of bread with smoked salmon, cucumbers, Swiss cheese, ham, and more. Served in a checkerboard pattern on a beautiful silver tray, these appetizers will make your guests feel like very important people indeed at your gathering.

6 slices white sandwich bread

6 slices whole-wheat sandwich bread

4 tablespoons whipped cream cheese

1 English cucumber, cut into thin diagonal slices

4 slices smoked salmon

2 tablespoons mustard mixed with 2 tablespoons mayonnaise

8 slices Swiss cheese

8 slices ham

16 pitted olives or cherry tomatoes for garnish (optional)

MAKES 16 APPETIZERS

Lay a slice of white bread and a slice of wheat bread on a work surface. Spread each with 1 tablespoon of the cream cheese, an overlapping layer of cucumber slices, then a slice of salmon. Top the white bread with a slice of wheat bread and the wheat bread with a slice of white. Spread each slice with 1 tablespoon of the mustard mixture. Top each with 2 thin slices of cheese and 2 thin slices of ham. Top each with the same kind of bread used for the first layer. Using a large knife, cut the crusts off the bread and cut each sandwich into 4 crosswise pieces. Repeat to make 8 more finger sandwiches. Pierce an olive or cherry tomato, if using, with a food pick and insert it in the center of each sandwich to hold it together. Arrange the sandwiches in a checkerboard pattern on a tray and serve immediately, or cover and chill until needed.

✦✦✦✦✦✦✦✦✦✦

ESCARGOTS PROVENÇAL

LE PROVENÇAL AT PARIS LAS VEGAS
CHEF ROBERT DERWINSKI

Le Provençal at Paris Las Vegas proudly serves traditional French-Italian cuisine, including this Provence-style dish. Chef Robert Derwinski sautés escargots with shallots, garlic, artichokes, and white wine to craft an unforgettable appetizer. Chef Robert explains, "The salty escargots and sweet artichokes complement each other well, while the white wine butter sauce helps bring it all together."

Eight or twelve ¼-inch-thick diagonal baguette slices

¼ cup olive oil, plus extra for brushing

Salt and freshly ground pepper

12 ounces canned escargots, rinsed and drained

2 tablespoons julienned shallot

2 teaspoons minced garlic

1 cup quartered artichoke hearts

½ cup dry white wine

1 cup (2 sticks) cold unsalted butter, cut into 8 pieces

½ cup diced peeled tomatoes

¼ bunch flat-leaf parsley, stemmed and minced

SERVES 4 TO 6 AS AN APPETIZER

Preheat the oven to 350°F. Brush the bread with olive oil on one side and season with salt and pepper. Place on a baking sheet and toast for about 5 minutes, or until beginning to brown. Remove from the oven and transfer the toasts to wire racks.

In a medium sauté pan or skillet, heat the ¼ cup olive oil over medium heat. Add the escargots and sauté for 1 minute. Add the shallot and garlic and sauté until the shallot is translucent, about 3 minutes. Add the artichokes and sauté for 30 seconds. Add the wine and cook to reduce by half. Reduce the heat to low and stir in the butter, 1 piece at a time, until all the butter is incorporated. Add the tomatoes and parsley and season with salt and pepper.

To serve, divide among serving bowls and top each bowl with 2 toasts.

LOBSTER & CRAB TARTS

BANQUET KITCHEN AT HARRAH'S LAKE TAHOE & HARVEYS LAKE TAHOE
CHEF RICK MARICLE

Created for New Year's Eve dinner at Harrah's Lake Tahoe and Harveys Lake Tahoe several years ago, this appetizer is perfect for any festive occasion. Chef Rick Maricle suggests, "A variation to the dish would be to substitute the shellfish with wild mushrooms sautéed in butter and flamed with brandy, and add chopped fresh chives for garnish."

2 slices bacon, minced

¼ cup finely chopped onion

¼ cup finely diced cooked lobster

¼ cup fresh lump crabmeat, picked over for shell and flaked

3 large eggs, beaten

⅔ cup heavy cream

1 cup grated Parmesan cheese

Kosher salt and freshly ground white pepper

Four 4-inch tart shells, partially baked

SERVES 4 AS AN APPETIZER

Preheat the oven to 350°F. In a medium skillet over medium-high heat, sauté the bacon and onion until the bacon is crisp, about 5 minutes. Using a slotted spoon, transfer to paper towels to drain.

In a medium bowl, combine the lobster and crabmeat; stir in the bacon and onion. In another medium bowl, combine the eggs, cream, cheese, and salt and pepper to taste. Whisk to blend well.

Evenly divide the lobster mixture among the tart shells. Fill each tart shell to the rim with the egg mixture. Place the tarts on a baking sheet. Bake for 15 to 20 minutes, or until the custard is set (a toothpick inserted in the center will come out clean). Remove from the oven and let cool slightly on wire racks. Serve warm.

HARRAH'S LAKE TAHOE'S SOUTH SHORE ROOM CELEBRATED ITS FIFTIETH ANNIVERSARY IN 2009. IT OPENED IN DECEMBER 1959 IN ADVANCE OF THE 1960 WINTER OLYMPIC GAMES AT LAKE TAHOE. SOME OF THE MANY STARS WHO HAVE PERFORMED AT THE SOUTH SHORE ROOM INCLUDE BILL COSBY, DON RICKLES, JIMMY DURANTE, RED SKELTON, DEAN MARTIN, FRANK SINATRA, LIZA MINNELLI, JUDY GARLAND, AND SAMMY DAVIS JR.

DUCK WITH PORCINI MUSHROOMS

PENAZZI AT HARRAH'S LAS VEGAS
CHEF GEORGE ALBERTO TAPIA

The recipe for this traditional Tuscan appetizer was brought to Penazzi from Italy by chef George Alberto Tapia. It soon became as popular at the restaurant as it is in its home region.

8 thin slices prosciutto

4 Muscovy duck breast halves, cut into 8 pieces

Salt and freshly ground pepper

2 tablespoons olive oil

2 tablespoons unsalted butter

1 tablespoon minced shallot

½ teaspoon minced garlic

2 ounces porcini mushrooms, sliced

2 tablespoons brandy

Pinch of minced fresh rosemary

1 teaspoon truffle oil

1 cup chicken stock

SERVES 4 AS AN APPETIZER,
OR 1 TO 2 AS A MAIN COURSE

Wrap a slice of prosciutto around each piece of duck and season with salt and pepper. In a large sauté pan or skillet, heat the oil over medium heat and sear the packets until lightly browned, about 2 minutes on each side. Transfer to a plate and keep warm in a low oven.

In the same pan, melt the butter over medium heat and sauté the shallot, garlic, and mushrooms for 2 minutes. Remove from the heat and add the brandy, stirring to scrape up the browned bits from the bottom of the pan. Return to medium heat and add the rosemary, truffle oil, and chicken stock. Cook to reduce the liquid for about 5 minutes.

To serve, place the duck packets on a platter and pour the pan sauce over them. Serve immediately with a seasonal salad of choice.

THE ORIGINAL HARRAH'S LAS VEGAS, BUILT IN 1973, HAD A FAÇADE WITH A STEAMBOAT MOTIF AND WAS NAMED THE HOLIDAY CASINO. IT WAS RENAMED HARRAH'S LAS VEGAS IN 1992.

PISTACHIO-ENCRUSTED LOIN OF LAMB

WITH MINT-INFUSED RICE & PORT WINE REDUCTION

HARRAH'S AK-CHIN
CHEF JAMES SHEWMAKE

Lamb has a natural affinity for both pistachios and mint, and here a loin is rolled in a mixture of the bright green nuts and served with a mint-flavored pilaf. This is a simple but elegant dish that really warms the heart and soul. Great for all seasons, this dish has wonderful diversity; it is sweet and savory and really hits your palate with unique flavor combinations.

MINT-INFUSED RICE

3 tablespoons unsalted butter

¼ cup diced celery

¼ cup diced onion

2 garlic cloves, minced

Salt and freshly ground pepper

2 cups lamb stock or chicken stock

1 cup long-grain rice

Leaves from 4 mint sprigs, chopped

PORT WINE REDUCTION

1½ cups tawny port wine

1 to 2 tablespoons unsalted butter

PISTACHIO-ENCRUSTED LOIN OF LAMB

½ cup pistachios (see note)

2 tablespoons olive oil

One 8- to 10-ounce lamb loin, trimmed of fat and silver skin

¼ teaspoon salt

½ teaspoon freshly ground pepper

SERVES 2 AS A MAIN COURSE

For the rice: In a large, heavy saucepan, melt the butter over medium heat. Add the celery, onion, and garlic. Sauté for 2 to 3 minutes, until the onion is translucent, then season with salt and pepper. Add the lamb stock and bring to a boil. Add the rice and mint, and then return to a boil. Cover and reduce the heat to a simmer. Simmer for 15 to 20 minutes, or until the rice is tender. Remove from the heat and fluff with a fork. Cover and keep warm.

For the port wine reduction: In a heavy, small saucepan, bring the port wine to a boil over high heat. Reduce to a simmer and cook until reduced to ½ cup. Remove from the heat and whisk in the butter. Set aside and keep warm.

For the lamb: Preheat the oven to 350°F. In a food processor, chop the pistachios until coarsely ground. In an ovenproof medium sauté pan or skillet, heat the oil over medium heat. Season the lamb with the salt and pepper and roll it in the pistachios. Sear the lamb on all sides until golden brown, about 1 minute per side. Transfer the pan to the oven and roast the lamb for 10 minutes for medium-rare. Remove from the oven, transfer the lamb to a cutting board, and tent with aluminum foil for about 5 minutes.

To serve, cut the lamb into medallions. Portion the rice in the center of each plate, place the lamb on the rice, and spoon ¼ cup of the port wine reduction over each serving.

++++++++++

Skinning pistachios: If your pistachios still have their brown skin, blanch them in boiling water for 2 minutes, then drain, wrap in a towel, and rub to remove the skins. Put them in a colander and shake well to remove any leftover skins.

MAHI MAHI & GRILLED SHRIMP
WITH BLACK BEANS & MANGO

SEVEN STARS LOUNGE AT HORSESHOE HAMMOND
CHEF CHRIS BASIL

Mahi mahi, also called dolphinfish, is found in warm waters around the world. For this Seven Stars favorite, chef Chris Basil pairs it with grilled shrimp. Black beans, mango, and a vanilla-flavored sauce add their tropical flavors. Chef Chris advises, "I like serving this dish in either the spring or summertime. It works best with a Pinot Grigio."

SHRIMP

¼ teaspoon minced garlic

½ teaspoon red pepper flakes

¼ teaspoon ground ginger

¼ cup canola oil

8 extra-large shrimp, shelled and deveined

BLACK BEANS AND MANGO

2 cups cooked black beans, drained (and rinsed, if canned)

1 mango, peeled, cut from pit, and cut into ⅜-inch dice

½ cup ⅜-inch-diced sweet white onions, such as Vidalia or Walla Walla

VANILLA SAUCE

½ cup sugar

⅓ cup distilled white vinegar

1 vanilla bean, split lengthwise, or 1 teaspoon vanilla extract

1 tablespoon finely chopped onion

½ teaspoon dry mustard

1¼ cups canola oil

Fresh lemon juice as needed

Salt and freshly ground pepper

MAHI MAHI

Eight 4-ounce mahi mahi steaks

Salt and freshly ground pepper

½ cup macadamia nuts, finely ground in a food processor

1 cup clarified butter (see page 43)

For the shrimp: In a medium bowl, combine the garlic, red pepper flakes, and ginger. Stir in the oil. Add the shrimp and stir to coat.

Cover and refrigerate for 2 hours, stirring the shrimp every 30 minutes. Remove from the refrigerator 30 minutes before cooking. Heat a medium sauté pan or skillet over medium heat and sauté the shrimp for 1 minute on each side. Remove from the heat and empty onto a plate.

For the black beans and mango: In a large bowl, combine all the ingredients, gently tossing together. Set aside.

For the vanilla sauce: In a blender, combine the sugar and vinegar. Scrape the seeds from the vanilla bean into the blender (reserve the pod for another use) or add the vanilla extract. Add the onion and mustard. With the machine running, gradually add the oil in a thin stream. Add the lemon juice if the sauce is too thick. Stir in salt and pepper to taste.

For the mahi mahi: Preheat the oven to 400°F. Season the fish with salt and pepper, then dredge in the macadamia nuts. In a large ovenproof sauté pan or skillet, heat the clarified butter over medium-high heat and sauté the fish for 2 minutes on each side. Remove from the heat, add the shrimp to the pan, and transfer the pan to the oven. Roast for 5 minutes, or until the mahi mahi is opaque throughout. Remove from the oven.

To serve, overlap 2 pieces of fish on each plate. Spoon some of the black bean mixture in the center and divide the shrimp on each side of the plate. Drizzle the fish with the vanilla sauce.

SERVES 4 AS A MAIN COURSE

MAO PAO TOFU

Chef Thierry Mai-Thanh says this traditional dish, an Ah Sin favorite, is supposedly named after the woman who created it. In this dish, tofu takes on the spirited flavors of stir-fried jalapeños, garlic, green onions, chile paste, and hoisin sauce. To serve this to your favorite vegetarians, replace the chicken broth with vegetable stock.

1½ pounds soft tofu, cut into 1-inch cubes

¼ cup canola oil

2 jalapeño chiles, seeded and sliced

3 tablespoons minced garlic

1 cup canned straw mushrooms, drained and halved

¼ cup finely chopped green onion, including some green parts

1 teaspoon sambal oelek chile paste, or more to taste

2 cups chicken broth

2 tablespoons soy sauce

½ cup hoisin sauce

Steamed jasmine rice for serving

SERVES 4 TO 6 AS A MAIN COURSE

Pat the tofu dry with paper towels and set aside. In a wok, heat the oil over medium-high heat and stir-fry the jalapeños, garlic, mushrooms, green onions, and chile paste for 40 seconds. Add the chicken broth and cook to reduce to ½ cup. Add the soy sauce and bring to a boil. Add the hoisin sauce and cook to reduce to a demi-glace consistency. Add the tofu, gently tossing so as not to break it up, and cook until it absorbs the flavor from the sauce, about 1 minute. Remove from the heat. Serve over rice in deep bowls.

CRAB-STUFFED SALMON FILLETS

HARRAH'S NORTH KANSAS CITY
SOUS-CHEF JERRY ROXAS

After enjoying this sumptuous dish at Harrah's North Kansas City, guests often ask chef Jerry Roxas, "How can I cook this at home?" Here is the recipe for a dish to impress and honor your guests with.

Six 8-ounce salmon fillets, skin and pin bones removed

Salt and freshly ground pepper

CRABMEAT STUFFING

8 cups panko (Japanese bread crumbs)

1 pound fresh lump crabmeat, picked over for shell, or canned crabmeat, drained

2 garlic cloves, minced

½ teaspoon dry mustard

1 tablespoon Worcestershire sauce

2 large eggs, beaten

¾ cup finely diced red bell pepper

¼ cup olive oil

6 lemon slices

GARNISH

1 cup finely diced fresh pineapple

1 cup finely diced English cucumber

¼ cup finely diced red bell pepper

¼ cup minced fresh cilantro

1½ tablespoons minced fresh thyme

1½ tablespoons minced fresh basil

SERVES 6 AS A MAIN COURSE

Preheat the oven to 400°F. With a sharp knife, cut a pocket in the side of each fillet. Be careful to not cut through the fillets. Season the fillets with salt and pepper.

For the stuffing: In a large bowl, combine all the ingredients. Stir to blend. Spoon ⅓ cup of the stuffing into the pocket in each fillet.

In a large ovenproof sauté pan or skillet, heat the olive oil over medium-high heat and cook the salmon for 4 minutes on each side to achieve a golden brown color on the fish. Put the lemon slices on top of the salmon. Transfer the pan to the oven and roast the salmon for 6 to 7 minutes, or until still slightly translucent in the center. Remove from the oven and keep warm.

For the garnish: In a medium bowl, combine the pineapple, cucumber, bell pepper, and cilantro. Stir to blend. Portion the mixture on top of each fillet and sprinkle with the thyme and basil. Serve at once.

HARRAH'S WAS FIRST LISTED ON THE AMERICAN STOCK EXCHANGE IN 1972.

EXECUTIVE CHEF RAY LEUNG'S

TOP 10 ALCOHOLIC BEVERAGES
EVERY HOME BAR SHOULD HAVE

HARRAH'S ST. LOUIS

1   Jack Daniel's whiskey

2   Kahlúa

3   Baileys Irish Cream

4   Stoli (Stolichnaya) vodka (Russian
    vodka), chilled

5   Malibu rum, chilled

6   VSOP (Very Superior Old Pale)
    Cognac, chilled

7   Otokoyama sake, chilled

8   Nigori sake, chilled

9   Don Julio tequila, chilled

10 Negra Modelo
    (Mexican dark beer), chilled

CRÈME BRÛLÉE IN TUILE CUPS

GRAND BILOXI CASINO, HOTEL & SPA
EXECUTIVE CHEF JASON CARLISLE

A fabulous meal deserves an extraordinary dessert. Chef Jason Carlisle comments, "I love using this recipe at home, for dinner parties and special occasions. It takes guests by surprise, as the entire dish is edible. The crème brûlée with its thin caramel crust sits in a thin cookie cup called a tuile cup. It takes a little time and a disciplined hand, but the outcome is unforgettable."

TUILE CUPS

1 cup (2 sticks) unsalted butter, melted and cooled

2 cups confectioners' sugar, sifted

1⅓ cups all-purpose flour, sifted

12 large egg whites

CRÈME BRÛLÉE CUSTARD

2 cups heavy cream

½ vanilla bean, split lengthwise

12 large egg yolks

½ cup plus 2 tablespoons granulated sugar

6 tablespoons granulated sugar

Fresh berries, whipped cream, and mint sprigs for garnish

SERVES 6

For the tuile cups: Preheat the oven to 400°F. Put the butter in the bowl of a stand mixer fitted with the paddle attachment and gradually beat in the confectioners' sugar on low speed until smooth. Add the flour in the same fashion and beat until smooth. Add the egg whites, one at a time, beating just until smooth so as not to incorporate air in the mixture. Strain the mixture through a fine-mesh sieve into a bowl. Let rest for 30 minutes.

Spray a nonstick baking sheet with nonstick cooking spray. Pour a tablespoonful of batter on the prepared pan. In a circular motion, spread the batter to form a very thin round about 6 inches in diameter.

Place a custard cup upside down on the counter near the oven. You will use this to shape the tuile. Have a pot holder and a metal spatula ready. Bake the tuile for 5 minutes, or until browned around the edges and lightly colored in the center. Remove from the oven. Using the metal spatula, immediately transfer the tuile to the custard cup, centering it so that it drapes down to form a scalloped cup. Let cool, then carefully transfer the delicate cup to a work surface. Repeat to make a total of 6 cups.

For the custard: In a heavy, medium saucepan, combine the cream and vanilla bean. Cook over medium-low heat until bubbles form around the edges of the pan. In a large bowl, whisk the egg yolks and sugar together until smooth. Gradually whisk ½ cup of the hot cream into the egg mixture. Return to the saucepan, turn the heat to low, and cook, whisking constantly, until the custard is very thick. Remove from the heat and strain through a fine-mesh sieve into a bowl, pushing the last part through with the back of a large spoon; let cool. Cover and refrigerate for at least 30 minutes or up to 2 days.

To assemble, just before serving place about ½ teaspoon custard in the center of a dessert plate. Place a tuile cup on top of the custard; this will keep the cup from sliding on the plate. Fill the cup three-fourths full with custard. Repeat with the remaining cups and custard.

In a small, heavy saucepan, cook the 6 tablespoons sugar over medium-low heat; do not stir, just move the pan in a circular motion. The sugar will begin to liquefy and caramelize. When the color is a dark amber, remove from the heat and bring the pan to the work surface, holding it over a custard-filled cup. Dip a fork into the caramel and drizzle it over the custard to cover it in a thin layer. Repeat to top the remaining custards. Garnish each plate with berries, whipped cream, and mint. Serve at once.

CHOCOLATE-COCONUT CAKE

PAYARD PÂTISSERIE & BISTRO AT CAESARS PALACE LAS VEGAS
CHEF FRANÇOIS PAYARD

Celebrated pastry chef François Payard tells this story: "A chef visiting my kitchen happened to see our recipe for this cake, and his immediate response was, 'There is something missing here!' But there is not. I had been experimenting with variations of sponge cake and devised this one, which is like a macaroon layer. A serving of this cake is like popping a coconut macaroon into your mouth. It is so simple that you may not believe how delicious it is until you actually try it. I suggest serving it with vanilla ice cream or chocolate sorbet." For a shimmery effect, edible gold leaf can be used as a garnish.

COCONUT SPONGE CAKE

4 large eggs

1½ cups sugar

3⅔ cups unsweetened shredded dried coconut

GANACHE

10½ ounces bittersweet chocolate, finely chopped

3½ ounces milk chocolate, finely chopped

1⅔ cups heavy cream

1 cup unsweetened shredded dried coconut, toasted (see note)

MAKES ONE 5-BY-10-INCH CAKE; SERVES 6 TO 8

For the cake: Preheat the oven to 350°F. Spray a 12½-by-17½-inch jelly roll pan with nonstick cooking spray. Line the bottom of the pan with parchment paper.

Fill a medium saucepan one-third full with water and bring to a simmer. Whisk together the eggs and sugar until blended. Place the bowl over the pan of simmering water and whisk constantly until the egg mixture is warm to the touch. Transfer the bowl to a stand mixer and beat on high speed until it has tripled in volume, about 5 minutes. Using a rubber spatula, fold in the coconut just until blended. Pour the batter onto the prepared pan and spread it evenly in the pan with a rubber spatula.

Bake the cake for 20 to 25 minutes, or until the top is a light golden brown and a toothpick inserted in the center comes out clean. Remove from the oven and let cool in the pan on a wire rack for 15 minutes. Run a small sharp knife around the sides of the pan to loosen the cake. Place a wire rack over the cake and invert. Carefully peel off the parchment paper (the cake is extremely delicate). Let cool completely.

For the ganache: In a large bowl, combine the bittersweet and milk chocolates. In a medium saucepan, bring the cream to a boil. Immediately pour the hot cream over the chocolate and whisk until the chocolate is completely melted and smooth. Cover with plastic wrap, pressing it directly onto the surface of the ganache. Let cool, then refrigerate until firm enough to pipe, about 4 hours.

To assemble, trim off any uneven edges of the cake and cut it crosswise into three equal rectangles, each measuring about 5 by 10 inches. Place one of the rectangles on a serving platter. Using a small metal offset spatula, spread a generous layer of the ganache over the top of the cake layer. Cover with another cake layer and spread a layer of the ganache over it. Top with the third cake layer and spread a layer of the ganache over the top and sides of the cake. Sprinkle the toasted coconut over the tops and sides of the cake. If not serving immediately, refrigerate the cake. The cake can be made up to 1 day ahead. Bring to room temperature before serving.

✦ ✦ ✦ ✦ ✦ ✦ ✦ ✦ ✦

Toasting coconut: Spread the coconut on a sided baking sheet and toast in a preheated 350°F oven until golden, 6 to 10 minutes, shaking the pan 2 or 3 times as the coconut toasts. Empty onto a plate and let cool completely.

1 Let time work for you, not against you: This means allowing adequate time to plan for the party or event you are throwing. Give yourself time to shop for supplies, create any party favors, organize activities, and clean your house.

2 Choose food wisely: If you aren't a real whiz in the kitchen, pick easy, make-ahead recipes. Even if you are a French-trained chef, it's still a good idea to select dishes that can be prepped ahead of time. That way, all you're doing the day of your event is putting on the finishing touches, not creating something from start to finish.

3 Set the mood: People's moods are very affected by their environment. Choose appropriate lighting (low light for a cocktail party, ample lighting for a kids' party with arts and crafts, etc.). Use music to help you set the mood as well.

4 Have an emergency supply of foods: Keep snacks in the pantry that you can serve to guests in case you run low on food or burn one of your dishes. Also, keep plenty of beverages on hand in case you run low.

5 The glass should always be at least half full: Keep an eye on guests' beverages. Offer to fill them up before they are completely drained. That will keep people from having to leave conversations or activities they might be enjoying.

6 Introduce your guests: A good host or hostess makes sure guests are introduced with a tip on what they have in common for a conversation starter. Happy guests make for a successful party.

7 Choose your attitude: If you're having a bad day, don't let that affect your guests. Put your happy face on and enjoy the evening. If you're laughing, talking to people, and having a good time, chances are greater your guests will be, too.

8 Do your homework: Know who your guests are and think about what you can do to help them feel comfortable. For example, if many of your guests are elderly, have enough places for them to sit.

9 Establish a "last call": Determine the hour when no more alcoholic drinks are served and coffee and tea become the beverages of choice. Remember, though, that coffee and tea do not make you sober.

10 Make sure your guests get home safely: Find out who needs a ride, a taxi, or a designated driver.

TOP 10 GIFTS
FOR YOUR HOST OR HOSTESS

HARRAH'S RENO

1   A set of crystal wineglasses or Champagne glasses

2   A crystal bowl

3   Signed cookbooks by celebrity chefs: Have cookbooks autographed and personally inscribed at book signings, or by sending the book to the author in care of their publisher

4   A knife set, such as one by J.A. Henckels or Wüsthof

5   Bottled sauces and seasonings

6   Gift cards from kitchenware stores

7   Gift baskets filled with foods and/or kitchen utensils: For example, imported Italian pasta, pasta sauces, wooden spoons or other kitchen utensils, assorted nuts and dried fruits

8   Chocolate truffles or cookies

9   A gift certificate for a local wine and/or food tasting at a local winery

10 A great bottle of Napa Valley wine

11

DESSERTS

BERRY NAPOLEON

ANDREOTTI AT HARRAH'S RENO
EXECUTIVE PASTRY CHEF CATHY HAYNES

At Andreotti, guests are entertained by both the northern Italian food and the singing restaurateur Pier Perotti, who performs operatic arias while musician Corky Bennett accompanies him. Serve this favorite Andreotti dessert for your next dinner party, and play some Pavarotti in the background, unless, of course, you have an opera singer at your beck and call.

6 thawed frozen filo pastry sheets

4 tablespoons unsalted butter, melted

Granulated sugar for sprinkling

2 cups heavy cream

¼ cup confectioners' sugar, sifted

2 tablespoons Grand Marnier

2 cups mixed fresh berries

SERVES 6

Preheat the oven to 350°F. Keeping the filo covered with a cloth, transfer one sheet to a work surface and brush with butter. Top with a second sheet, brush with butter, and repeat until all sheets have been stacked and brushed. Sprinkle the top lightly with granulated sugar. Place the stack with a long side toward you. Using a large knife, cut the stack into thirds lengthwise and into sixths crosswise to make 18 pieces. Bake for 12 to 15 minutes, or until golden. Remove from the oven and place the pan on a wire rack to cool.

In a medium bowl, beat the cream until soft peaks form. Fold in the confectioners' sugar and Grand Marnier until blended.

To assemble the dessert, place 1 piece of filo on a dessert plate and top with a dollop of cream, then some berries. Repeat with 1 more layer of filo, then cream and berries. Top with another layer of filo. Repeat to use the remaining filo, cream, and berries, making a total of 6 desserts. Garnish the plates with additional berries and serve.

SAMMY'S SHOWROOM WAS NAMED FOR LEGENDARY PERFORMER SAMMY DAVIS, JR., WHO STARTED HIS CAREER AT HARRAH'S RENO.

EXECUTIVE PASTRY CHEF CHRISTINE BAIRD'S

TOP 10 TIPS FOR
SERVING UNFORGETTABLE DESSERTS

HARRAH'S LAKE TAHOE

1   Plan your dessert in relation to the main course. For example, if your menu features a robust dish, the dessert should be a lighter one, such as a delicate mousse.

2   Offering a sampler plate with a variety of textures and tastes will help the most discriminating palates enjoy the end of the meal.

3   Having a "theme" for your dinner will help you choose the last course. For instance, a fall dinner that features harvest-type vegetables and venison might end with a dessert using figs or apples.

4   Always remember: "The eyes eat first!" The best-tasting dessert will lose appeal if it is not presented well.

5   Revamping classical desserts by using unexpected ingredients and interesting presentations can turn a simple meal into a lasting memory.

6   Turn the day upside down, for a change: For example, serve a breakfast waffle topped with ice cream and an exciting sauce for dessert.

7   Use the best ingredients available to make unforgettable finales to your meals.

8   Healthy choices that look rich and inviting can greatly contribute to a wonderful dining experience.

9   A meal should be a harmonious blend of ingredients, and the dessert should complement the courses that precede it.

10 Most of all, keep it simple; don't overdo the different kinds of ingredients and garnishes for your dessert. The last course should be a beautiful end to a memorable occasion.

PAULA DEEN'S GOOEY BUTTER CAKE

PAULA DEEN BUFFET AT HARRAH'S TUNICA
PAULA DEEN & EXECUTIVE SOUS-CHEF TAMMY WILLIAMS-HANSEN

When butter, vanilla, and a culinary superstar join forces, you have a Southern dessert that is a favorite at the Paula Deen Buffet. Chef Tammy Williams-Hansen explains, "Paula's Gooey Butter Cake is a melt-in-your-mouth Southern treat that can be enhanced with many flavors. One of Paula's favorite variations is the Elvis-inspired cake, which is made with peanut butter and banana and is a perfect ending to any great meal." To transform this cake into Paula Deen's Elvis Presley Gooey Butter Cake, incorporate ½ cup peanut butter and 1 puréed banana into the filling.

CAKE

One 18¼-ounce package yellow cake mix

1 large egg

½ cup (1 stick) unsalted butter, melted

FILLING

One 8-ounce package cream cheese at room temperature

2 large eggs

1 teaspoon vanilla extract

½ cup (1 stick) unsalted butter, melted

One 16-ounce box confectioners' sugar, sifted

Ice cream for serving (optional)

MAKES ONE 9-BY-13-INCH CAKE; SERVES 15 TO 20

For the cake: Preheat the oven to 350°F. Lightly grease a 9-by-13-inch baking pan.

In the bowl of an electric mixer, combine the cake mix, egg, and butter. Mix well. Pat the mixture evenly into the bottom of the prepared pan.

For the filling: In a large bowl, beat the cream cheese until smooth. Add the eggs, vanilla, and butter and beat until blended. Gradually beat in the confectioners' sugar until blended.

Spread the filling evenly over the cake and bake for 40 to 50 minutes, or until the edges are set but a toothpick inserted in the center comes out wet. Remove from the oven and let cool in the pan on a wire rack. Let the cake set for 1 hour after coming out of the oven. To serve, cut into squares and top with ice cream, if desired.

PAULA IS THE "QUEEN OF BUTTER,"
SO IT'S NO SURPRISE THAT THE PAULA DEEN BUFFET
USES TWO HUNDRED POUNDS OF BUTTER EVERY DAY.

PECAN PRALINE CHEESECAKE

FRESH MARKET BUFFET AT HARRAH'S NORTH KANSAS CITY
CHEF ANTHONY GALATE

A match made in culinary heaven: crunchy pecans and brown sugar blended with velvety cream cheese, eggs, and vanilla. Chef Anthony Galate comments, "This recipe is such a particular favorite of our Seven Stars guests that it has become a signature item at Harrah's North Kansas City. Guests also order this cheesecake to take home for the holidays to their families to enjoy."

1 cup sweetened condensed milk

½ cup finely chopped pecans

¼ cup packed brown sugar

¼ cup unsalted butter, melted

¾ cup graham cracker crumbs

16 ounces cream cheese at room temperature

3 large eggs, beaten

2 tablespoons vanilla extract

PECAN PRALINE TOPPING

⅓ cup heavy cream

⅓ cup packed brown sugar

⅓ cup chopped pecans

MAKES ONE 9-INCH CAKE;
SERVES 10 TO 12

Preheat the oven to 300°F. In a medium saucepan, combine the condensed milk, pecans, brown sugar, and butter, mixing well. Cook over medium-low heat, stirring frequently, for about 5 minutes, or until slightly thickened. Remove from the heat and let cool to room temperature.

Press the graham cracker crumbs firmly into the bottom of a 9-inch springform pan.

In a large bowl, beat the cream cheese until fluffy. Gradually stir the cooled pecan mixture into the cream cheese until blended. Stir in the eggs and vanilla, mixing well to blend. Pour the filling into the crust. Bake for 55 to 60 minutes, or until the center is set.

For the topping: In a medium saucepan, combine the heavy cream and brown sugar. Bring to a simmer over medium-low heat and cook, stirring constantly, for 5 to 10 minutes, until the mixture thickens slightly. Remove from the heat and let cool to room temperature. Stir in the pecans.

Remove the cheesecake from the oven and let cool for 10 minutes on a wire rack. Run a dinner knife around the inside of the pan to loosen the cheesecake. Lift off the sides of the pan. Let cool completely. Top the cheesecake evenly with the topping.

FRIDAY'S PEANUT BUTTER MOUSSE CUPS

FRIDAY'S STATION STEAK & SEAFOOD GRILL AT HARRAH'S LAKE TAHOE
EXECUTIVE PASTRY CHEF CHRISTINE BAIRD

This irresistible dessert was developed by chef Christine Baird especially for Friday's and is available by special request at the restaurant. The chocolate cups can also be used to serve fresh berries, chocolate mousse, strawberries Romanoff, strawberry Bavarian cream, and many other delectable fillers.

Note: You will need 4 small balloons to make the cups.

8 ounces semisweet chocolate, chopped

½ cup cream cheese at room temperature

2 tablespoons sugar

½ cup smooth peanut butter

1 tablespoon unsalted butter at room temperature

½ teaspoon pure vanilla extract

1¼ cups heavy cream

CHOCOLATE GANACHE

4 ounces semisweet chocolate, chopped

½ cup heavy cream

1½ teaspoons light or dark corn syrup

Whipped cream for garnish

SERVES 4

In a medium stainless-steel bowl set over a saucepan with 2 inches of barely simmering water, melt the chocolate and stir until smooth. Remove from the heat and let cool to room temperature.

Meanwhile, inflate 4 small balloons to a diameter of about 3 inches, stretching the top until smooth and tying the end of each balloon securely into a knot. Line a baking sheet with parchment paper or waxed paper.

Dip a balloon halfway into the chocolate to coat. Shake it gently to let the excess chocolate drip off. Transfer the balloon to the prepared pan and hold it in place upside down for a few moments until it can stand on its own. Repeat to coat a total of 4 balloons. With the remaining chocolate, make handles for the bowls, if you like, by piping them from a small parchment paper cone.

In the large bowl of an electric mixer, combine the cream cheese and sugar. Beat on low speed to blend. Add the peanut butter and butter, beating on medium speed until light and fluffy. Stop the mixer and scrape down the sides and bottom of the bowl, as well as the paddle or beaters. Add the vanilla and mix to blend.

In a medium bowl, whisk ¼ cup of the cream until soft peaks form. Gently fold it into the peanut butter mixture, making sure there are no white streaks in the mix. Cover and refrigerate the filling for at least 4 hours or up to 24 hours.

In a deep bowl, whisk the remaining 1 cup cream until soft peaks form. With the whisk, stir the peanut butter mousse until smooth. Fold in one-third of the whipped cream at a time.

Remove the balloons from the chocolate cups by piercing them with a small knife. Remove all balloon residue from the chocolate, then fill each cup with peanut butter mousse. Refrigerate while preparing the ganache.

For the ganache: Put the chocolate in a medium bowl. In a small, heavy saucepan, combine the cream and corn syrup. Bring to a boil over medium heat and immediately pour over the chocolate, stirring until melted and smooth. Let cool to room temperature; take care that it is not warm.

To serve, top the peanut butter cups with the cooled ganache. Garnish each serving with a dollop of whipped cream.

PROSECCO GELÉE

CAESARS ATLANTIC CITY
EXECUTIVE CHEF KEITH MITCHELL

A perfect warm-weather treat: vanilla-flavored sparkling-wine gelatin, molded in martini glasses and served with fresh peaches and cream. Serve this grown-up gelatin dessert after a cookout for the perfect end to a summer day. Chef Keith Mitchell suggests this variation: "Use a sparkling rosé or a still red wine in place of the Prosecco, and fresh berries in place of the peaches."

1¼ cups water
1 package unflavored gelatin
1 cup sugar
1 vanilla bean, split lengthwise
2½ cups Prosecco or other sparkling wine
3 peaches, peeled, pitted, and sliced
Sweetened whipped cream for garnish

SERVES 6

Put ¼ cup of the water in a small bowl and sprinkle the gelatin over; let stand until softened. Put the sugar in a small bowl. Scrape the seeds from the vanilla bean into the sugar and stir to blend.

In a large saucepan, combine the remaining 1 cup water and the vanilla-sugar mixture. Cook over medium heat until simmering. Stir in the gelatin mixture until dissolved. Add the wine and stir gently. Divide the liquid among 6 extra-large martini glasses. Place on a baking sheet and refrigerate until set, about 2 hours.

To serve, divide the peach slices among the glasses and top with dollops of whipped cream.

✦✦✦✦✦✦✦✦✦✦✦

PASSION FRUIT CRÈME BRÛLÉE

RED PEARL AT BALLY'S ATLANTIC CITY
EXECUTIVE PASTRY CHEF MICHAEL D'ANGELO

Everyone loves the play of textures in crème brûlée: rich, smooth custard with a crackling caramelized sugar topping. Here, chef Michael D'Angelo dresses up the classic by adding the sweet tropical flavor of passion fruit.

3 cups heavy cream
½ vanilla bean, split lengthwise
10 large egg yolks
⅓ cup sugar, plus 6 tablespoons for topping
½ cup passion fruit purée (not juice)
Florentine cookie sticks with sliced almonds or other cookies for garnish

SERVES 6

Preheat the oven to 325°F. In a large, heavy saucepan, combine the cream and vanilla bean. Cook over medium-low heat until bubbles form around the edges of the pan. In a large bowl, whisk together the egg yolks and the ⅓ cup sugar. Remove the vanilla pods from the hot cream and gradually whisk the cream into the egg mixture. Stir in the passion fruit purée.

Divide the mixture among 6 shallow ramekins. Place them in a baking pan and add water to the pan to come halfway up the sides of the ramekins. Bake for 35 to 40 minutes, or until the center is set. Remove from the oven and the water bath. Let cool for 30 minutes, then refrigerate for at least 2 hours or up to 24 hours.

To serve, evenly sprinkle 1 tablespoon sugar over the surface of each custard. Caramelize with a torch, or place under a preheated broiler for about 2 minutes, or until the sugar melts to a golden brown caramel on top. Remove from the oven and let cool for at least 10 minutes. Garnish with cookies of your choice.

OREO COOKIE MACAROONS

VOGA AT FLAMINGO LAS VEGAS
EXECUTIVE PASTRY CHEF OLIVIER CARLOS

Chef Olivier Carlos explains the inspiration behind these cunning treats: "Everyone likes Oreos! My grandmother used to give me Oreo cookies so I could dunk them in a glass of milk. My childhood came into play when I created this recipe. The outcome was a reinvention of the famous Oreo with a hint of French flair that brought it all to perfection. The taste will surprise you and make you wonder what else you can do with an Oreo cookie." Here, the all-American cookies are combined with French macaroons and brownies for a sophisticated treat.

FRENCH MACAROONS

2 cups blanched almonds

2 cups granulated sugar

4 large egg whites, lightly beaten

1 teaspoon vanilla extract

2 tablespoons crushed Oreo cookies

¼ cup confectioners' sugar

EASY SAUCEPAN BROWNIES

6 tablespoons unsalted butter

2 ounces unsweetened dark chocolate

½ teaspoon vanilla extract

1 cup granulated sugar

2 large eggs

¾ cup all-purpose flour

¼ teaspoon baking powder

¼ teaspoon salt

½ cup chopped pecans or walnuts

OREO COOKIE SANDWICH MOUSSE

2 teaspoons unflavored gelatin

2½ tablespoons water

⅓ stick unsalted butter at room temperature

½ cup cream cheese at room temperature

1 drop vanilla extract

½ tablespoon granulated sugar

1½ tablespoons sour cream

1 cup heavy cream

⅓ cup chopped Oreo cookies

½ cup semisweet chocolate, chopped

MAKES 10 COOKIES

For the macaroons: Preheat the oven to 400°F. Line a baking sheet with parchment paper.

In a food processor, combine the almonds, sugar, egg whites, and vanilla extract and pulse to a very coarse paste. Turn the food processor on high speed and blend the paste for 2 minutes, or until it is very smooth and thick. Add the Oreo pieces and continue to blend at high speed until well incorporated. Spoon the batter into a pastry bag fitted with a wide plain tip and pipe the batter into uniform 1-inch mounds on the prepared pan. Let rest, uncovered, for 15 minutes. Bake the macaroons for 12 minutes, or until slightly golden brown. Remove from the oven and transfer the macaroons from the pan to a wire rack. Let cool to room temperature. Dust with the confectioners' sugar before serving.

For the brownies: Preheat the oven to 325°F. Grease and flour a 12-inch square baking pan; knock out the excess flour. In a large, heavy saucepan, melt the butter and dark chocolate over low heat, stirring constantly until smooth. Remove from the heat and let cool. With a whisk, beat in the vanilla and sugar. Whisk in the eggs, one at a time, beating well after each addition.

In a small bowl, combine the flour, baking powder, and salt. Stir with a whisk to blend. Stir the flour mixture into the chocolate mixture. Stir in the nuts, blending well. Spoon the mixture into the prepared pan and spread evenly.

Bake for about 25 minutes, or until a toothpick comes out clean when inserted. Remove from the oven and transfer the pan to a wire rack. Let cool completely. Unmold the cake onto a cutting board. Using a 2-inch biscuit cutter, cut the brownies into 10 rounds.

For the sandwich mousse: In a small bowl, sprinkle the gelatin over the water and let stand for 5 minutes to soften. In a large bowl, cream the butter, cream cheese, vanilla, and granulated sugar together until light and fluffy, stopping once or twice to scrape down the sides and bottom of the bowl. Melt the gelatin in a microwave for 10 seconds and then mix with the sour cream. Stir the sour cream mixture into the cream cheese mixture. Whip the heavy cream to soft peaks, then fold it into the previous mixture. Fold in the Oreo pieces until just incorporated.

To assemble, pipe sandwich mousse on top of half of the macaroons. Place another macaroon on top of each to form a sandwich. Refrigerate for about 2 hours to set the mousse.

In a double boiler over barely simmering water, melt the chocolate. Remove from the heat and stir until smooth. Dip the sandwiched macaroons vertically halfway into the chocolate to coat. Place a macaroon sandwich on top of each brownie. Refrigerate for 30 minutes to set the chocolate.

TOP 10 TIPS FOR HOSTING A SEVEN STARS DINNER PARTY AT HOME

With a little creativity and the tips below, anyone can throw a Seven Stars–inspired dinner party.

1   Fun: The ultimate rule for any dinner or event is to make sure everyone has a good time and enjoys themselves.

Always remember, your guests come first. They should be enthralled by the entertainment (even if it is not live but rather a playlist you created), impressed by the decorations, absolutely captivated by the other guests (always invite an interesting group of people with many different interests and professions), and, of course, your guests should enjoy every bite of the food you serve.

2   Expenses: It's not essential to spend a lot of money on your dinner, but the ingredients should be the best available and the setting should be comfortable and memorable for your guests.

3   Day of the week: Choose a day that will work for all the guests you want to attend. A cocktail party or fund-raising dinner may work well during the week when people can attend after work, but larger gala-type dinners and relaxing dinner parties with friends should be reserved for Friday and Saturday nights when no one has to get up early the next day.

4   Time: The starting time for your dinner is just as important as what day you choose. The best time to start is usually between 6 and 8 P.M.—early enough for after-work cocktails on weeknights, and not so early that guests will feel rushed on weekends.

5   Weather: The season and local weather forecast will help you decide if your dinner should be indoors or out-doors. The goal is to make sure your guests are com-fortable, and not too hot or too cold. If you are planning an outdoor dinner, make sure you have back-up plans in case Mother Nature decides to throw you a curveball.

6   Décor: Place settings and centerpieces can enchant your guests and give them an experience they'll never forget. Draw your inspiration for décor from nature, specific occasions, and your own imagination.

7   Music: The right music will always enhance your dining event. Know your guests, and play music they will enjoy and appreciate; also make sure the music suits the occasion.

8   Help: If you can, hire someone to assist you with your event, either in the kitchen or serving. This will give you more time to enjoy yourself with your guests.

9   Menu: Give your menu great thought and attention, use the freshest products you can find, and make sure the food for your event is the best it can possibly be.

10   Plan, plan, plan: To ensure the best results for your event, you need to think ahead. Make the guest list and shopping lists for food, drinks, and decorations; sched-ule when you will clean the house and decorate it for the event; decide when and how to send out invitations; create a music playlist; plan your wardrobe; and make a schedule of when to start and finish each dish on the menu so that all the food can be served at the right time.

CHOCOLATE FUN-DO

VOGA AT FLAMINGO LAS VEGAS
EXECUTIVE PASTRY CHEF OLIVIER CARLOS

Chocolate Fun-Do takes chocolate fondue to a new level: In place of fruit, mini cheesecakes in a variety of flavors are dipped into warm chocolate sauce. Chef Olivier Carlos comments, "This dish was created to give you and your guests the feeling of being at a party right in your own backyard." Serve this dish as a fun ending to any dinner party.

CHEESECAKES

Four 8-ounce packages cream cheese at room temperature

1 cup sugar

⅓ cup unsalted butter, melted

1 teaspoon vanilla extract

4 large eggs

½ cup mango purée

½ cup raspberry purée

3 ounces bittersweet chocolate, melted

2 tablespoons coffee powder

1 tablespoon pistachio paste (found in specialty foods stores)

HOT CHOCOLATE SAUCE

6 tablespoons unsalted butter

1 cup water

1¼ cups heavy cream

3½ tablespoons honey

14 ounces bittersweet chocolate, chopped

3½ tablespoons dark rum

SERVES 8

For the cheesecakes: Preheat the oven to 300°F. Oil two 12-cup muffin pans. In an electric mixer, beat the cream cheese, sugar, butter, and vanilla on medium speed until the mixture is well blended. Add the eggs, one at a time, mixing on low speed after each addition just until blended.

Divide the batter equally among 5 small bowls. Add the mango purée to one bowl, the raspberry purée to a second bowl, the chocolate to a third, the coffee powder to a fourth, and the pistachio paste to the fifth bowl. Stir each to blend. Divide among the prepared muffin cups and bake until set, 30 minutes. Remove from the oven and let cool completely. Unmold onto a baking sheet and refrigerate for 1 hour.

For the chocolate sauce: In a heavy, medium saucepan, melt the butter over medium-low heat. Add the water, cream, and honey, and bring to a simmer over medium-high heat. Put the chocolate in a medium bowl and pour the hot cream over. Let stand for 1 minute, then stir until smooth. Stir in the rum.

To serve, cut the cheesecakes in half. Pour the chocolate sauce into a fondue bowl or other heavy bowl. Using fondue forks, dip the cheesecake pieces into the sauce.

NUMBER OF CUPCAKES SOLD ANNUALLY
IN THE EAT UP! BUFFET AT HARRAH'S ST. LOUIS:

BOSTON CREAM • 21,000

CUPCAKE OF THE MONTH • 3,000

GERMAN CHOCOLATE • 22,500

CARROT • 22,000

OREO • 17,000

TOTAL • 85,500

COCONUT PANNA COTTA
WITH RUM-FLAMED BERRIES

THE POOL AT HARRAH'S RESORT ATLANTIC CITY
EXECUTIVE CHEF EDWARD DAGGERS, ATLANTIC CITY COUNTRY CLUB

The exquisite Italian gelled dessert is given a tropical accent here with coconut milk and rum in place of the usual milk and cream. The rum-flamed berries provide just the right finishing touch. Chef Edward Daggers suggests, "This panna cotta works well as a dessert or a side dish with fruit or salad, or it could be served with a fruit purée." At The Pool at Harrah's, it's sometimes served with a tropical fruit salad.

PANNA COTTA

2 cups well-shaken canned coconut milk

1½ cups sugar

2 envelopes unflavored gelatin

1 cup whole milk

½ cup dark rum

1 teaspoon vanilla extract

RUM-FLAMED BERRIES

3 tablespoons unsalted butter

2 cups mixed fresh strawberries, blackberries, and raspberries

1 tablespoon brown sugar

¼ cup dark rum

2 tablespoons coconut, toasted (optional; see page 261)

4 to 6 mint sprigs (optional)

SERVES 4 TO 6

For the panna cotta: In a large, heavy saucepan, combine the coconut milk and sugar. Bring to a low simmer over medium heat.

In a medium saucepan, sprinkle the gelatin into the whole milk and bring to a low simmer over medium heat. Stir in the rum. Add this mixture to the coconut milk mixture, return to a simmer, and cook for 5 minutes. Remove from the heat and pour into a serving bowl or glass. Stir in the vanilla. Let cool for 20 minutes, then cover and refrigerate until set, about 4 hours.

For the berries: In a medium sauté pan or skillet, melt 2 tablespoons of the butter over medium heat until foaming. Add the berries and brown sugar and sauté for 1 minute. Turn off the heat and add the rum, stirring well. Standing back from the stove, light the rum with a long match or long-handled lighter. Using caution, shake the pan until the flames subside. Return to medium heat and cook to reduce for 2 minutes. Stir in the remaining 1 tablespoon butter.

To serve, spoon the panna cotta into bowls and top with the berries. Garnish with the coconut and mint sprigs, if desired.

POLISTINA'S AT HARRAH'S RESORT ATLANTIC CITY
REPORTS TIRAMISÙ AS THE MOST
POPULAR DESSERT ON THE MENU.

TIRAMISÙ

JACK BINION'S STEAK HOUSE AT HORSESHOE HAMMOND
ASSISTANT PASTRY CHEF MARY THERESE PRIESOL

In chef Mary Therese Priesol's version of this famous Italian sweet, ladyfingers are dipped in a mixture of espresso and Kahlúa instead of Marsala, and the mascarpone cream is flavored with rum. Chef Mary Therese says, "This layered Italian dessert is a classic and has been for many years here at the Horseshoe. The creamy texture, with the slight taste of rum, combined with the espresso and Kahlúa–soaked cookies is a timeless dessert that is sure to leave a lasting impression on your dining experience."

MASCARPONE CREAM

4 cups heavy cream

5 large egg yolks

¾ cup sugar

1 pound mascarpone cheese at room temperature

⅓ cup light rum

4 cups cold brewed espresso

½ cup Kahlúa

70 to 90 ladyfingers

4 ounces bittersweet chocolate, cut into shavings

Unsweetened cocoa powder for dusting

SERVES 8

For the mascarpone cream: In a large bowl, whip the cream to stiff peaks. In another large bowl, combine the egg yolks, sugar, and mascarpone cheese and beat until light in color. Add the rum to the mascarpone mixture and beat until combined. Fold the whipped cream into the mascarpone mixture until blended.

In a shallow bowl, combine the espresso and Kahlúa. Line an 8-by-10-inch baking pan with plastic wrap, allowing extra plastic wrap to hang over two sides of the pan. Dip 2 or 3 ladyfingers in the espresso mixture and place in the bottom of the prepared pan, making sure all the ladyfingers are pointing in the same direction. Repeat to line the entire bottom of the pan in one layer.

Spread half of the mascarpone cream evenly on top of the soaked ladyfingers. Make another layer of ladyfingers on top of the cream, soaking 2 or 3 at a time and pointing them in the same direction as the bottom layer. In the same fashion, make a third layer, placing the ladyfingers at right angles to the ones in the second layer. Add the remaining mascarpone cream and smooth the top. Sprinkle with the chocolate shavings. Cover in plastic wrap and refrigerate for 12 hours.

Remove from the refrigerator 30 minutes before serving. Unmold by lifting the two sides of the plastic wrap to remove the dessert. Remove the plastic wrap. Cut the tiramisù into slices and serve on dessert plates; dust edges of plates with cocoa powder.

+++++++++++

VARIATION

To prepare tiramisùs as in the photo, use eight 2½-inch-wide by 3-inch-tall ring molds. Line the outside of each ring mold with plastic wrap to come halfway up the sides. Dip the ladyfingers into the espresso mixture and line the bottom of each mold with one layer, breaking them as needed to make them fit. Spread about ¼ cup mascarpone mixture evenly on top of the ladyfingers. Repeat to make three layers of cookies and mascarpone mixture in each mold. Freeze for 4 hours. To unmold, dip a plastic-wrapped mold into a bowl of hot water for about 5 seconds; remove immediately. Remove the plastic wrap and let the tiramisù slide out of the mold onto a plate. Beat about 2 cups heavy cream until soft peaks form. Pipe a little whipped cream on the flat side of a ladyfinger and press it vertically against the side of the tiramisù. Repeat to line the desserts. Omit the chocolate shavings and finish with sifted cocoa.

DESSERTS

280   281

SEVEN SISTERS LOUNGE ORANGE CAKE

SEVEN SISTERS LOUNGE AT HARRAH'S CHEROKEE
EXECUTIVE CHEF KEITH ANDREASEN

Vibrant in both color and taste, this orange cake is welcome year-round, but especially in winter when oranges are at their peak of flavor. Chef Keith Andreasen notes, "This cake is great with many dishes."

CAKE

1½ cups cake flour

¾ cup granulated sugar

1½ teaspoons baking powder

½ teaspoon salt

¼ teaspoon cream of tartar

¼ cup water

¼ cup canola oil

3 large eggs, separated

3 tablespoons fresh orange juice

½ teaspoon grated lemon zest

ORANGE CREAM CHEESE FROSTING

1½ cups (12 ounces) cream cheese at room temperature

1 teaspoon grated orange zest

2 tablespoons plus 2 teaspoons fresh orange juice

¾ cup sifted confectioners' sugar

3 drops yellow food coloring

3 drops red food coloring

2 oranges, segmented (see page 51)

MAKES ONE 10-INCH CAKE;
SERVES 6 TO 8

For the cake: Preheat the oven to 350°F. In a large bowl, sift together the flour, sugar, baking powder, salt, and cream of tartar. Make a well in the center of the dry ingredients. Add the water, oil, egg yolks, orange juice, and lemon zest. Beat until smooth. In a large bowl, beat the egg whites until soft peaks form. Gradually fold the egg whites into the cake batter with a rubber spatula until blended. Pour the batter into an ungreased 10-by-2-inch round cake pan and smooth the top. Bake for 25 to 30 minutes or until golden and a toothpick inserted in the center comes out clean.

Remove the cake from the oven and let cool completely in the pan on a wire rack. To unmold, run a knife around the edges of the pan and invert on a plate. With a long serrated knife, cut the cake into 2 horizontal layers.

For the frosting: In a large bowl, beat the cream cheese until fluffy. Add the orange zest and juice. Gradually blend in the confectioners' sugar until well blended. Add the yellow and red food coloring and blend well. Put ½ cup of the frosting in a separate bowl. Reserve 6 to 8 orange segments and drain them in a colander. Coarsely chop the remaining orange segments and stir them into the ½ cup frosting. Spread this filling on one layer of the cake. Top with the second layer of cake and frost the top and sides with the remaining frosting.

To serve, garnish each portion with an orange segment.

EIFFEL TOWER RASPBERRY SOUFFLÉS

EIFFEL TOWER RESTAURANT AT PARIS LAS VEGAS
CHEF JEAN JOHO

Chef Jean Joho says: "The Eiffel Tower Restaurant is famous for its soufflés, and we serve thousands of them every year. We always have at least ten different flavors at the restaurant, depending on the season. Guests love watching these being made at the dessert station in the kitchen." Although this recipe is for raspberry soufflés, perfect for spring and summer, it can be varied to reflect the season or your whim, such as pumpkin in the fall or mandarin orange in the winter, or chocolate, Grand Marnier, and pistachio any time of the year.

Note: The soufflé base needs to be refrigerated at least 4 hours or overnight before cooking.

SOUFFLÉ BASE

4 cups whole milk

2 large eggs

18 large egg yolks

3 tablespoons plus 1 teaspoon sugar

1½ cups all-purpose flour

6 tablespoons cornstarch

3½ tablespoons cold unsalted butter, cut into cubes

8 large egg whites

2 tablespoons sugar

½ teaspoon cream of tartar

¼ cup puréed fresh or frozen raspberries

¼ cup Chambord liqueur

Confectioners' sugar for dusting

Vanilla sauce for serving (recipe follows)

MAKES 6 INDIVIDUAL SOUFFLÉS

For the soufflé base: In a medium saucepan, bring the milk to a boil over high heat, then turn off the heat. In a large bowl, combine the eggs, egg yolks, and sugar and whisk until blended. Combine the flour and cornstarch in a small bowl. Stir with a small whisk to blend. Add two-thirds of the flour mixture to the egg mixture and whisk to blend. Whisk in 1 cup of the hot milk. Add the remaining flour mixture and whisk until smooth (the mixture should be fairly liquid). Bring the remaining milk to a boil again and add it to the egg mixture all at once, whisking constantly until smooth. Immediately whisk in the butter until fully incorporated. The mixture should have the consistency of heavy cream. Let cool. Cover and refrigerate for at least 4 hours or, preferably, overnight (the base will perform better after it has rested for a day).

Preheat the oven to 375°F. Butter and sugar six 4½-ounce ramekins, tapping each to remove the excess sugar. In a large bowl, beat the egg whites until frothy. Gradually beat in the sugar and cream of tartar and continue beating until soft peaks form.

Stir the raspberry purée and liqueur into the soufflé base. Add about one-fourth of the beaten whites to the soufflé base and stir to combine. Fold in the remaining whites with a rubber spatula until just incorporated. Divide the batter among the ramekins. Place the ramekins in a baking pan, then place the baking pan in the oven and carefully pour boiling water into the pan to reach halfway up the sides of the ramekins. Bake for 20 minutes, or until puffed and golden brown.

Immediately transfer each ramekin to a serving plate, dust with confectioners' sugar, and serve with the vanilla sauce on the side. Each guest should crack open the top of his or her soufflé with a spoon, then pour about 2 tablespoons of the sauce into the soufflé.

Vanilla Sauce: In a small saucepan, combine 1 cup milk and ½ vanilla bean, split lengthwise, and cook over medium heat until bubbles form around the edges of the pan. Remove from the heat and remove the vanilla bean. Whisk 3 egg yolks and 3 tablespoons sugar together in a small bowl. Gradually whisk ¼ cup of the hot milk into the egg yolks, then whisk in the remaining milk. Return to the pan and cook over medium-low heat, stirring constantly, until the mixture coats the back of the spoon. Makes about 1 cup.

VARIATIONS

Pumpkin Soufflés: Replace the raspberry purée and the liqueur with ¼ cup pumpkin purée and ½ cup Southern Comfort.

✦✦✦✦✦✦✦✦✦✦✦

Mandarin Orange Soufflés: Replace the raspberry purée with mandarin purée (found in specialty foods stores or online) and the liqueur with ¼ cup mandarin liqueur or mandarin vodka.

✦✦✦✦✦✦✦✦✦✦✦

Chocolate Soufflés: Replace the raspberry purée with ¼ cup shaved dark chocolate and the liqueur with ¼ cup coffee liqueur.

✦✦✦✦✦✦✦✦✦✦✦

Grand Marnier Soufflés: Delete the raspberry purée and replace the liqueur with ¼ cup Grand Marnier.

✦✦✦✦✦✦✦✦✦✦✦

Pistachio Soufflés: Replace the raspberry purée with ¼ cup pistachio paste (found in specialty foods stores or online) and the liqueur with ¼ cup amaretto liqueur.

12

HIGH
ROLLERS'
BAR

ABSINTHE SAZERAC

BESH STEAK AT HARRAH'S NEW ORLEANS
CHEF JOHN BESH

Now that absinthe is once again legal in the United States, Besh Steak has restored the classic New Orleans Sazerac to its original recipe by using Absinthe Superior for the rinse instead of an anise-flavored liquor substitute.

Absinthe Superior, preferably Versinthe, for rinsing

Ice cubes

3 ounces rye whiskey, such as Old Overholt

Splash of Peychaud's bitters

Splash of simple syrup (recipe follows)

1 lemon twist

Rinse a rocks glass with the absinthe. In a cocktail shaker filled with ice, combine the whiskey, bitters, and simple syrup. Shake vigorously and strain into the rinsed glass. Garnish with the lemon twist.

Simple Syrup: Combine 1 cup sugar and 1 cup water in a small, heavy saucepan and bring to a boil over low heat, stirring to dissolve the sugar. Boil for 1 minute, then remove from the heat and let cool completely. Store in a tightly covered glass container in the refrigerator indefinitely. Makes about 1⅓ cups.

SERVES 1

BESH STEAK BOASTS AN ORIGINAL "BLUE DOG" PAINTING BY GEORGE RODRIGUE.

GERMAN CHOCOLATE CAKE

VIP LOUNGES & HIGH LIMIT BAR AT HARRAH'S LAKE TAHOE & HARVEYS LAKE TAHOE
BEVERAGE MANAGER CHARLOTTE ROGERS

German chocolate cake in a glass: coconut rum, crème de cacao, and hazelnut liqueur. Serve this drink in place of dessert and win the hearts of your guests.

¾ ounce Malibu coconut rum

¾ ounce white crème de cacao

¼ ounce Frangelico liqueur

Splash of half-and-half

Ice cubes

Sweetened whipped cream, unsweetened cocoa powder, and 1 maraschino cherry for garnish

In a cocktail shaker, combine the rum, crème de cacao, Frangelico, and half-and-half. Shake well and strain over ice cubes in a chilled hurricane glass. Garnish with whipped cream, dust with cocoa, and top with the cherry.

SERVES 1

HIGH ROLLERS' BAR

SEX IN THE BIGGEST LITTLE CITY

SAPPHIRE AT HARRAH'S RENO
ASSISTANT BEVERAGE MANAGER MICHAEL BAYS

The Reno ("Biggest Little City in the World") version of *Sex and the City's* Cosmo adds peach schnapps and pineapple juice to make a refreshing cocktail. It's also Sapphire's best-selling drink out of the long list on their menu.

Peach sugar for rimming glass (found at liquor stores)

Ice cubes

1 ounce Absolut vodka

1 ounce peach schnapps

1 ounce cranberry juice

1 ounce pineapple juice

Pour some peach sugar on a saucer. Wet the rim of a Cosmo glass and dip it in the sugar to coat. In a cocktail shaker filled with ice, combine the vodka, schnapps, and two juices. Shake well and strain into the prepared glass.

SERVES 1

THE STEAKHOUSE AT HARRAH'S RESORT ATLANTIC CITY WON THE 2009 *WINE SPECTATOR* AWARD OF EXCELLENCE FOR HAVING ONE OF THE BEST WINE LISTS IN THE COUNTRY.

OASIS TROPICAL TREAT

HARRAH'S AK-CHIN
BEVERAGE SUPERVISOR JOSEPH CARUSO

You can't go wrong when pineapple juice meets refreshing melon, citrus, and coconut flavors. Ak-Chin's beverage supervisor Joseph Caruso says, "Escaping to paradise never tasted so good, or was so easy!"

Ice cubes

½ ounce Absolut Citron vodka

1 ounce Malibu rum

½ ounce melon liqueur

3 ounces pineapple juice

Splash of sweet and sour mix

Splash of Sierra Mist soft drink

1 maraschino cherry for garnish

Fill a 9-ounce cocktail glass with ice. Pour the vodka, rum, liqueur, juice, sweet and sour, and soft drink over the ice. Stir, and garnish with the cherry.

SERVES 1

HIGH ROLLERS' BAR

MINT JULEP

THE RANGE STEAKHOUSE AT HARRAH'S METROPOLIS
EXECUTIVE CHEF JON M. KELL

Fresh mint and bourbon in a traditional silver tumbler make this cocktail a favorite all year-round. Use an ultra-premium small-batch bourbon to put this drink over the top. Chef Jon M. Kell suggests, "To begin your search for that unforgettable bourbon, check out www.smallbatch.com."

8 fresh mint leaves, plus 1 sprig

1½ tablespoons simple syrup (see page 289)

1½ ounces bourbon

¼ teaspoon Angostura bitters

Shaved ice

SERVES 1

In a blender, combine the mint leaves, simple syrup, bourbon, and bitters and blend on high speed until the mint is puréed. Strain into a silver tumbler or other decorative glass packed with shaved ice. Garnish with the mint sprig.

PARROTHEAD-CHEF MARGARITA

HARRAH'S CHEROKEE
EXECUTIVE CHEF KEITH ANDREASEN

Chef Keith Andreasen named his version of the Margarita after himself: "I'm a huge Jimmy Buffett fan, or what is known as a 'parrothead.' Whenever there's a Buffett concert going on, you can count on me being there with several blenders of these margaritas. And if I'm having a cookout at my house, everyone looks forward to these margaritas being served."

Salt for rimming the glasses

One 6-ounce can frozen limeade, preferably Minute Maid

2 tablespoons fresh lemon juice

¼ cup sugar

6 ounces Margaritaville tequila (white or gold, depending on your preference)

2 ounces Grand Marnier liqueur

6 ounces water

¾ cup ice cubes

4 orange wedges for garnish

SERVES 4

Pour some salt into a saucer, moisten the rim of a margarita glass, and dip it in the salt to coat. In a blender, combine the limeade, lemon juice, sugar, tequila, Grand Marnier, and water, blending until smooth. Add the ice and blend. Pour into a pitcher and add more ice and water, if desired. Serve with the salt-rimmed glasses, garnished with the orange wedges.

HIGH ROLLERS' BAR

TOP 10 TIPS
FOR PAIRING WINE AND FOOD

1   Match the weight of the dish with the body of the wine. White wine is usually best with fish and white meat while red wine works with red meat. Achieving balance is the main goal.

2   Salty and fatty foods require wines that are high in acidity, such as Chablis, Pinot Grigio, Chianti, and Sauvignon Blanc (my personal favorite is Staete Landt Sauvignon Blanc, from New Zealand.)

3   Foods served with tomato sauces require red wines that are high in acidity, such as Chianti and Barbera.

4   Duck or goose will taste less fatty with younger, tannic wines. Rare meats are also best served with younger, tannic wines.

5   Well-done meats are best served with more mature, less tannic wines.

6   Spicy foods are best served with wines that are low in acidity. For example, Gewürztraminer or sweet Riesling wines are perfect with Asian cuisine. However, if the food is very spicy, go with beer.

7   The dessert wine should always be sweeter than the dessert, otherwise it will taste tart.

8   For dinners with multiple courses, serve light wines before heavier wines, dry wines before sweet, and young wines before old.

9   Never serve white wines too cold or red wines too warm. Use the Fifteen-Minute Rule: Take whites from the fridge 15 minutes before serving. And, unless your reds are in a cellar, refrigerate them for 15 minutes before serving.

10 Champagne, the most versatile wine, can be served with every course.

Bonus tip
Regional wines match best with regional foods.

TOP 10 TIPS
FOR PAIRING BEER AND FOOD

It may seem odd for a sommelier to compile a list of beer matches, but there are times when only beer will satisfy. Every beer has its perfect moment, and that is the essence of refreshment, isn't it?

1   A savory starter: Some sharp, acidic cheeses are meant to be served with more acidic beers, such as Belgian Gueuze. These beers are elegance, complexity, and finesse in a bottle.

2   Shellfish: Since Victorian times, the English have enjoyed a Guinness with a plate of oysters. A dry porter or stout can work with a variety of shellfish, such as mussels, clams, scallops, and other crustaceans.

3   Smoked food: Not surprisingly, beers malted over an open flame pair well with the smoked foods and preserved meats found on a charcuterie platter. Try a Rauchbier, a Stone beer, or a smoked porter.

4   Fish: Serve a fine Pilsner or a clean, golden lager. Their fresh palates don't overwhelm the delicate flavor of fish.

5   White meats: Red beers are a perfect partner for lighter meats, whatever the cooking method. Some red beers have a spicy sweetness that can stand up to roasted fowl or pancetta-laced pasta.

6   Beef: Something with a bolder profile is needed in this match. As in Old World/New World wines, there are two distinct styles of pale ale. From the United Kingdom, you'll find Burton-style ales with a light maltiness and a hint of cedar. These are satisfying when accompanying steak and frites. The ales from North America are somewhat more assertive and lively, often displaying an orange-fruit edge.

7   Pizza: Go for something with a nutty, yeasty aroma. It's a symbiotic relationship if ever there was one. North American red ales and Vienna lagers come to mind.

8   Fruity desserts: Fruit beers work well with those fruit-based desserts. Think of a raspberry lambic paired with glazed raspberry flan. Heaven.

9   Chocolate and coffee: Here, pull out all the stops and look for a big, rich, not-too-dry stout. Nothing else will mirror the powerful flavors of bittersweet chocolate quite so harmoniously. Some stouts actually have chocolate and espresso added as flavorings.

10   Digestifs: Beer can work here as well. Try a double bock, Abbey-style dark ale, or barley wine. These tend to start out very dense and creamy, evolving into an almost Armagnac-like pruniness and finishing somewhat dry. All have a propensity toward 8 percent and higher alcohol.

CUCUMBER-MINT SPLASH

THE STEAKHOUSE AT HARRAH'S RESORT ATLANTIC CITY
BEVERAGE OPERATIONS MANAGER JOSEPH CRILLEY

Muddled mint, minced cucumber, and vodka create a cool cocktail for warm days.

Sugar for rimming

4 fresh mint leaves

One ½-inch-thick slice peeled cucumber, finely chopped

Ice cubes

1½ ounces vodka

Club soda as needed

SERVES 1

Pour sugar into a saucer. Moisten the rim of a 12-ounce glass and dip in the sugar to coat the rim. Muddle the mint leaves in the glass. Add the cucumber. Fill the glass with ice. Add the vodka and top off the glass with club soda. Stir and serve.

THE STEAKHOUSE AT HARRAH'S RESORT IS ALSO HOME TO THE BLUEPOINT RAW BAR, VOTED BEST SEAFOOD BAR IN ATLANTIC CITY IN 2008 BY *CASINO PLAYER* MAGAZINE.

JEWEL OF THE DESERT

HARRAH'S AK-CHIN
BEVERAGE SUPERVISOR JOSEPH CARUSO

Enjoying this bright blue drink is like finding fresh water in the desert. It's just the cocktail to sip while relaxing by the pool.

Ice cubes

1 ounce Malibu rum

1 ounce blue curaçao

4 ounces sweet and sour mix

Splash of Sierra Mist soft drink

1 lime wedge for garnish

SERVES 1

Fill a 9-ounce cocktail glass with ice. Pour the ingredients over, stir, and garnish with the lime wedge.

HIGH ROLLERS' BAR

GOODNIGHT KISS MARTINI

TOBY KEITH'S I LOVE THIS BAR & GRILL AT HARRAH'S LAS VEGAS
TOBY KEITH & ENTERTAINMENT FLAIR BARTENDER ROB VERGARA

Finish off a great evening in style with this delectable combination of citrus vodka, vanilla vodka, and Cointreau. But be warned—this drink is so good, you may feel like having more than one Goodnight Kiss.

Sugar
Ice cubes
1 ounce citrus vodka
½ ounce vanilla vodka
1 splash Cointreau liqueur
2 ounces sweet and sour mix
Dash of sugar
Juice of ½ lemon
Lemon twist, cinnamon stick, and maraschino cherry for garnish

Pour some sugar onto a saucer. Moisten the rim of a martini glass and dip it in the sugar to coat the rim. In a cocktail shaker filled with ice, combine the vodkas, Cointreau, sweet and sour, sugar, and lemon juice. Shake well and strain into the sugar-rimmed glass. Garnish with the lemon twist and cinnamon stick.

SERVES 1

CARNAVAL COURT, AN OUTDOOR BAR AT HARRAH'S LAS VEGAS, EMPLOYS MORE CHAMPION FLAIR BARTENDERS THAN ANY PLACE ON THE LAS VEGAS STRIP, AND IT HAS NO DRESS CODE!

INVISIBLE HOMBRE

BAJA BLUE RESTAURANT & CANTINA AT HARRAH'S LAUGHLIN
BEVERAGE MANAGER DEBORAH ORAM

Take your party guests south of the border with the lemon-lime delight of this simple-to-make drink. Baja Blue's beverage manager Deborah Oram says, "The Invisible Hombre has really surprised our guests with the fresh twist it offers."

Ice cubes
1½ ounces José Cuervo white tequila
½ ounce fresh lime juice
½ ounce fresh lemon juice
Splash of tonic water

SERVES 1

Fill a cocktail shaker with ice and add the tequila and two juices. Shake well and strain into a rocks glass. Add the tonic.

GULF COAST BLOODY MARY

GRAND BILOXI CASINO, HOTEL & SPA
EXECUTIVE CHEF JASON CARLISLE

A perfect drink for the Gulf Coast: a spicy Bloody Mary garnished with an array of favorite regional foods. Chef Jason Carlisle comments, "This drink is more like a lagniappe than a beverage, but either way you take it, it is phenomenal!" The recipe makes a pitcherful for your next brunch or backyard cookout.

1½ cups tomato juice

¾ cup vodka

1½ tablespoons fresh lemon juice

1½ tablespoons fresh lime juice

1 tablespoon prepared horseradish sauce

1½ teaspoons Worcestershire sauce

2 teaspoons hot sauce

1 teaspoon Old Bay Seasoning

½ teaspoon salt

½ teaspoon freshly ground black pepper

¼ teaspoon cayenne pepper

GARNISH

24 crawfish tails

2 to 3 shakes Tabasco sauce per drink

12 pitted green olives

6 pickled or cooked green beans

6 pickled or fresh okra pods

6 extra-large shrimp, shelled, deveined, and steamed

12 cooked blue crab claws

SERVES 6

In a pitcher, combine all the ingredients except the garnish, stirring to combine. Refrigerate until well-chilled, about 1 hour.

For the garnish: In a small bowl, combine the crawfish tails and Tabasco. Toss to coat. Wearing rubber gloves, stuff 2 crawfish tails into each green olive. Pour the drink into rock glasses filled with ice. Divide the garnish evenly among the glasses and serve.

HARRAHCANE

MASQUERADE AT HARRAH'S NEW ORLEANS
BEVERAGE SUPERVISOR RICKIE DEANO

Southern Comfort, coconut rum, fruit juices, and grenadine join forces to create this potent drink, which can be served on the rocks or frozen. Harrahcane warning: You may want more than one.

1¼ ounces Southern Comfort whiskey

1¼ ounces Cruzan coconut rum

2 ounces orange juice

2 ounces pineapple juice

1 ounce fruit punch

Dash of grenadine

Ice cubes

In a cocktail shaker, combine the whiskey, rum, juices, punch, and grenadine. Shake well and pour over ice in a Collins glass.

Frozen Harrahcane: Combine all the ingredients in a blender and blend until frozen.

SERVES 1

CLOUD NINE

VOODOO LOUNGE AT HARRAH'S NORTH KANSAS CITY
MANAGER AARON LUND

VooDoo Lounge manager Aaron Lund comments, "Our players enjoy having a perfect meal and have been known to drink their desserts from time to time." The versatile Cloud Nine can be served either hot or cold. This version of the classic drink adds nocello, a walnut liqueur, to give flavor and depth to an already smooth libation.

½ ounce Frangelico liqueur

3 ounces Skyy vodka

½ ounce nocello liqueur

1 ounce chocolate syrup

4 cups cold brewed coffee

1 cup milk

10 ice cubes

2 tablespoons sugar

Whipped cream for garnish

In a blender, combine all the ingredients except the garnish. Blend until the ice cubes are crushed. Pour into a tall, footed coffee mug and top with a generous portion of whipped cream.

VARIATION

To serve the Cloud Nine hot, use hot coffee and steamed milk; delete the ice and the blender. Combine the hot coffee and milk in the coffee mug with all the other ingredients except the garnish; stir to blend, then top with the whipped cream.

SERVES 4

THE VOODOO LOUNGE HAS HOSTED PERFORMERS
INCLUDING JAMES BROWN,
THE BLACK CROWES, AND WAYNE NEWTON
IN AN INTIMATE CONCERT VENUE
WITH STATE-OF-THE-ART SOUND AND LIGHTING.

RASPBERRY LEMONADE

CARNAVAL COURT BAR & GRILL AT HARRAH'S LAS VEGAS
ENTERTAINMENT FLAIR BARTENDER JOSHUA A. NEMEROW

Bartender Joshua A. Nemerow explains the origin of this popular drink: "I was inspired to make this drink while I was backpacking in Canada. I was on a trail that was surrounded by fresh raspberries, which I collected in a bag to snack on later down the trail. While setting up camp, I was drinking lemonade and snacking on the raspberries, which made me think that this would be a great combination to explore with liquor when I returned to my real job as a bartender in Las Vegas. Once I returned home, I played around with the combination of flavors and ended up creating the Raspberry Lemonade. I think it is perfect for quenching your thirst on a hot summer day, while daydreaming of your next vacation."

Ice cubes

1½ ounces Bacardi Limón rum

½ ounce Chambord liqueur

3 ounces sweet and sour mix

Juice of ½ lime

Fresh raspberries for garnish

1 lime wedge for garnish

SERVES 1

Fill a cocktail shaker with ice and add all the ingredients except the raspberries and lime wedge. Shake well and strain into a Collins glass with ice cubes. Garnish with the raspberries and lime wedge.

TAHOE WABO
LAKE TAHOE'S TRADEMARK MARGARITA

SAMMY HAGAR'S THE CABO WABO CANTINA AT HARVEYS LAKE TAHOE
RESTAURANT MANAGER KEVIN MCGIRK

Harveys Lake Tahoe reimagines the classic margarita, Tahoe-style, using legendary rocker Sammy Hagar's signature Cabo Wabo blanco tequila.

Ice cubes

1½ ounces Cabo Wabo blanco tequila

½ ounce Triple Sec

Sweet and sour mix

Splash of Chambord liqueur

1 lime wedge for garnish

SERVES 1

Fill a 12- to 14-ounce margarita glass or a 12-ounce double rocks glass with ice and add the tequila and Triple Sec. Fill the remainder of the glass with the sweet and sour mix and stir to mix. Add the Chambord and garnish with the lime wedge. Serve with a straw.

HIGH ROLLERS' BAR

TOP 10 TIPS FOR CHOOSING THE RIGHT MUSIC FOR YOUR DINING EVENT

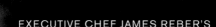

HORSESHOE COUNCIL BLUFFS

1. Cocktail party: More than just about any other event, a cocktail party naturally lends itself to background music. For perfect cocktail-party music, try one of Michael Bublé's albums, such as *Call Me Irresponsible, Come Fly with Me*, or *It's Time*.

2. Romantic candlelight dinner: To put the finishing touch on your next romantic evening, I recommend anything by Frank Sinatra. The album *Sinatra: Nothing But the Best* is a good place to start.

3. Wine dinner: For music on the soft side, I would go with pieces by Norah Jones, such as "Come Away With Me" and "Not Too Late."

4. BBQ cookout: Enjoy Jimmy Buffett's music while hanging out at the beach, around the pool, or if you just want to chill. "Cheeseburger in Paradise," "Margaritaville," "Come Monday," and "It's Five O'Clock Somewhere" will never go out of style.

5. Italian dinner: Are you ordering pizza tonight? Why not kick it up a bit? Add a red and white checkered tablecloth, candles, a straw-wrapped bottle of Chianti, and a musical selection that includes "O Sole Mio," "That's Amore," "Volare," and "Santa Lucia." It'll make pizza or pasta night at your house something special.

6. Latin dinner: Arturo Sandoval & The Latin Train's energetic beats will get you grooving at your Latin-themed dinner with songs like "Be-Bop," "La Guarapachanga," and "The Latin Trane."

7. Louisiana Cajun dinner: Gumbo, jambalaya, dirty rice, beignets, corn bread and biscuits, and shrimp, crab, and crawfish boil all call out for The Jambalaya Trio's *Jazz Brunch at the Pizza on the Park*, with songs like "Way Down Yonder in New Orleans," "Rose Room," and "Poor Butterfly," or the Jambalaya Cajun Band's *C'est Fun*, with "C'est Fun (It's Fun)," "Jig Cadien (The Cajun Jig)," and "Oh, Ma Belle (Oh, My Belle)."

8. Fiesta dinner party: What would a fiesta be without a mariachi band? Originating in Mexico, a mariachi band is usually made up of a spirited grouping of violins, trumpets, a Spanish guitar, a vihuela (a high-pitched five-string guitar), and a guitarrón (a small-scaled acoustic bass). To add an authentic flair to your fiesta, play some selections from Plácido Domingo's *100 Years of Mariachi*. If that isn't setting the right mood, change it up with the classic sounds of Los Lobos, Ritchie Valens, or Los Lonely Boys.

9. Luau: The music you choose for your Hawaiian luau can be either traditional Hawaiian music or fun beach party music. I also suggest choosing some selections from the man who is synonymous with Hawaiian music, Don Ho. Start with Don Ho's *Hawaii's Greatest Hits*, *Hawaiian Favorites*, and *A Night in Hawaii with Don Ho*. For beach party music, you can never go wrong with anything by the Beach Boys, including *Sounds of Summer: The Very Best of the Beach Boys*, *Summer Love Songs*, and *Good Vibrations: Thirty Years of the Beach Boys* box set.

10. Chinese New Year dinner: Chinese New Year music is played on Chinese drums and other traditional instruments. Musical selections for your celebration might include pieces from Heart of the Dragon Ensemble's *Chinese New Years Music*, including "Celebration," "Lion Dance," and "New Year Is Coming."

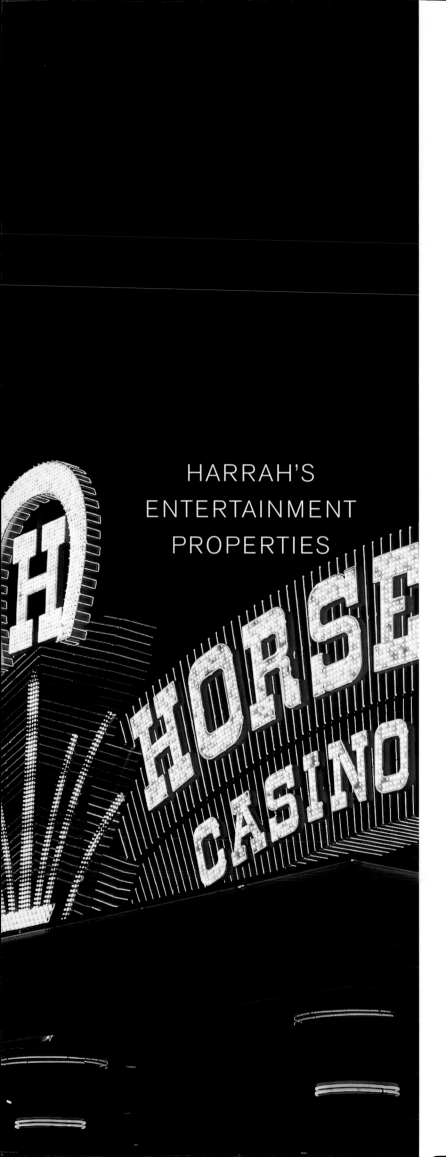

HARRAH'S
ENTERTAINMENT
PROPERTIES

Bally's Atlantic City
Park Place and the Boardwalk
Atlantic City, NJ 08401
609-340-2000
www.ballysac.com

Bally's Las Vegas
3645 Las Vegas Boulevard South
Las Vegas, NV 89109
877-603-4390
www.ballyslasvegas.com

Caesars Atlantic City
2100 Pacific Avenue
Atlantic City, NJ 08401
609-348-4411
www.caesarsac.com

Caesars Palace Las Vegas
3570 Las Vegas Boulevard South
Las Vegas, NV 89109
866-227-5938
www.caesarspalace.com

Caesars Windsor
377 Riverside Drive East
Windsor, Ontario
N9A 7H7 Canada
800-991-7777
www.caesarswindsor.com

Flamingo Las Vegas
3555 Las Vegas Boulevard South
Las Vegas, NV 89109
888-902-9929
www.flamingolasvegas.com

Grand Biloxi Casino, Hotel & Spa
280 Beach Boulevard
Biloxi, MS 39530
800-WIN-2-WIN
www.grandbiloxi.com

Harrah's Ak-Chin
15406 Maricopa Road
Maricopa, AZ 85239
480-802-5000
www.harrahsakchin.com

Harrah's Cherokee
777 Casino Drive
Cherokee, NC 28719
828-497-7777
www.harrahscherokee.com

Harrah's Chester Casino & Racetrack
777 Harrah's Boulevard
Chester, PA 19013
800-480-8020
www.harrahschester.com

Harrah's Council Bluffs
1 Harrah's Boulevard
Council Bluffs, IA 51501
712-329-6000
www.harrahscouncilbluffs.com

Harrah's Joliet
151 North Joliet Street
Joliet, IL 60432
800-HARRAHS
www.harrahsjoliet.com

Harrah's Lake Tahoe
15 Highway 50
Stateline, NV 89449
800-HARRAHS
775-588-6611
www.harrahslaketahoe.com

Harrah's Las Vegas
3475 Las Vegas Boulevard South
Las Vegas, NV 89109
800-214-9110
www.harrahslasvegas.com

Harrah's Laughlin
2900 South Casino Drive
Laughlin, NV 89029
702-298-4600
www.harrahslaughlin.com

Harrah's Louisiana Downs
8000 East Texas Street
Bossier City, LA 71111
800-HARRAHS
318-742-5555
www.harrahslouisianadowns.com

Harrah's Metropolis
100 East Front Street
Metropolis, IL 62960
800-929-5905
www.harrahsmetropolis.com

Harrah's New Orleans
8 Canal Street
New Orleans, LA 70130
800-847-5299
www.harrahsneworleans.com

Harrah's North Kansas City
One Riverboat Drive
North Kansas City, MO 64116
816-472-7777
www.harrahsnkc.com

Harrah's Reno
219 North Center Street
Reno, NV 89501
775-786-3232
www.harrahsreno.com

Harrah's Resort Atlantic City
777 Harrah's Boulevard
Atlantic City, NJ 08401
609-441-5000
www.harrahsresort.com

Harrah's Rincon Casino & Resort
777 Harrah's Rincon Way
Valley Center, CA 92082
877-777-2457
www.harrahsrincon.com

Harrah's St. Louis
777 Casino Center Drive
Maryland Heights, MO 63043
314-770-8100
www.harrahsstlouis.com

Harrah's Tunica
13615 Old Highway 61 North
Robinsonville, MS 38664
800-WIN-4WIN
www.harrahstunica.com

Harveys Lake Tahoe
18 Highway 50
Stateline, NV 89449
800-HARVEYS
www.harveys.com

Horseshoe Bossier City
711 Horseshoe Boulevard
Bossier City, LA 71111
800-895-0711
www.horseshoebossiercity.com

Horseshoe Council Bluffs
2701 23rd Avenue
Council Bluffs, IA 51501
712-323-2500
www.horseshoecouncilbluffs.com

Horseshoe Hammond
777 Casino Center Drive
Hammond, IN 46320
866-711-SHOE (7463)
www.chicagohorseshoe.com

Horseshoe Southern Indiana
11999 Casino Center Drive SE
Elizabeth, IN 47117
866-676-SHOE (7463)
www.horseshoe-indiana.com

Horseshoe Tunica
1021 Casino Center Drive
Robinsonville, MS 38664
800-303-7463
www.horseshoetunica.com

Imperial Palace Las Vegas
3535 Las Vegas Boulevard South
Las Vegas, NV 89109
800-351-7400
www.imperialpalace.com

Paris Las Vegas
3655 Las Vegas Boulevard South
Las Vegas, NV 89109
877-796-2096 (Reservations)
877-603-4386 (Hotel Main)
www.parislasvegas.com

Rio All-Suite Hotel & Casino
3700 West Flamingo Road
Las Vegas, NV 89103
866-746-7671
www.riolasvegas.com

Showboat Atlantic City
801 Boardwalk
Atlantic City, NJ 08401
800-621-0200
www.showboatac.com

Tunica Roadhouse Casino & Hotel
1107 Casino Center Drive
Tunica, MS 38676
800-391-3777
www.tunicaroadhouse.com

INDEX

INDEX

INDEX

REGISTERED TRADEMARKS

DESTINATION PHOTO INDEX

TABLE OF EQUIVALENTS

The exact equivalents in the following tables have been rounded for convenience.

LIQUID/DRY MEASURES

U.S.		METRIC
¼ teaspoon		1.25 milliliters
½ teaspoon		2.5 milliliters
1 teaspoon		5 milliliters
1 tablespoon	(3 teaspoons)	15 milliliters
1 fluid ounce	(2 tablespoons)	30 milliliters
¼ cup		60 milliliters
⅓ cup		80 milliliters
½ cup		120 milliliters
1 cup		240 milliliters
1 pint	(2 cups)	480 milliliters
1 quart	(4 cups, 32 ounces)	960 milliliters
1 gallon	(4 quarts)	3.84 liters
1 ounce (by weight)		28 grams
1 pound		454 grams
2.2 pounds		1 kilogram

LENGTH

U.S.	METRIC
⅛ inch	3 millimeters
¼ inch	6 millimeters
½ inch	12 millimeters
1 inch	2.5 centimeters

OVEN TEMPERATURE

FAHRENHEIT	CELSIUS	GAS
250	120	½
275	140	1
300	150	2
325	160	3
350	180	4
375	190	5
400	200	6
425	220	7
450	230	8
475	240	9
500	260	10

ACKNOWLEDGMENTS

Countless people have lent their extraordinary talents and expertise to *The Seven Stars Cookbook*, many more than I could ever thank. This book would not have been possible without each and every one of you.

Many thanks to each of the Harrah's Entertainment executive chefs and their inspired teams of chefs and kitchen and restaurant staff, who contributed recipes, Top 10 lists, and valuable advice to this book. It is a tribute to your creativity, hard work, and amazing culinary skills.

My gratitude to David Norton, Matt Bowers, Kathy Hickman, and Mindy Rabinowitz, who were driving forces behind this project at Harrah's Entertainment. A special thanks in particular to Mindy, who spent endless hours helping to manage this project, secure recipes, fact-check, organize logistics, and make sure this book was the best it could be. I owe her a debt of gratitude that can never be repaid in this lifetime. Thanks also to the food and beverage executive teams, the property marketing teams, and the dozens of other employees at each Harrah's Entertainment property who contributed their time and talents to this project. We also appreciate Harrah's Entertainment's restaurant partners for providing recipes from their outstanding restaurants.

A big thank-you to Gary W. Loveman, CEO of Harrah's Entertainment, Inc., for his support of this project and for writing the preface. He knows well what the art of entertaining truly means and entails.

A million thanks to Paula Deen for writing such a thoughtful and entertaining foreword.

It has been a great pleasure for me and Harrah's Entertainment to work with Chronicle Books on this project. Special thanks to the amazing team they assembled to make sure this cookbook made it into your hands, including Michael Ashby, Mikayla Butchart, Ken DellaPenta, Pamela Geismar, David Hawk, Catherine Huchting, Ben Kasman, Bill LeBlond, Laurel Leigh, Carolyn Miller, Peter Perez, and Beth Weber.

I owe an enormous debt of gratitude to our photographer extraordinaire, Frankie Frankeny, and her masterful team, including her assistant, Molly Johnstone, and one of the world's most talented food stylists, Alison Richman, who all helped bring this book to life in vivid color. It was such a pleasure to work with them. And, many thanks to Public, San Francisco, for creating beautiful layouts showcasing the recipes.

Finally, thank you to literary agent Steve Troha, who understood and supported the vision for this undertaking from the very beginning.